Canadian Poetry
Index to Criticisms
(1970-1979)

Poésie Canadienne
Index de critiques
(1970-1979)

By

Phyllis Platnick

Copyright © 1985 Canadian Library Association
All rights reserved.
ISBN 0-88802-194-1

Canadian Cataloguing in Publication Data

Platnick, Phyllis
   Canadian poetry : index to criticisms,
1970-1979 = Poésie canadienne : index de
critiques, 1970-1979

Text in English and French.
ISBN 0-88802-194-1

1. Canadian poetry (English)--History and
criticism--Indexes. 2. Canadian poetry
(French)--History and criticism--Indexes.
I. Canadian Library Association II. Title.
III. Title: Poésie canadienne.

PS8155.P43 1985   016.811   C85-090120-0E
PR9190.5.P43 1985

Printed and bound in Canada

Dedicated to the memories of my husband
David Platnick and my parents Clara and
Michael Sandler who saw me through the
pains of this work but did not live to
see its completion.

TABLE OF CONTENTS

page

Preface vii

Collections analyzed for essays on Canadian poetry xi

Sources and authorities xv

Abbreviations of periodical titles xvii

Other abbreviations used xxi

Periodicals used in the Index xxiii

Index to criticisms of Canadian poetry 1

PREFACE

Working in a reference department of a Canadian college in the early nineteen-seventies was a frustrating job. This was particularly true at Glendon College of York University, a bilingual college specializing in Canadian studies. The dearth of reference tools available to students taking Canadian courses was appalling. This was most evident when searching for articles in Canadian literature, as there were some excellent tools for English and American literatures. Palmer and Dyson's American drama criticism and English novel explication as well as Gerstenberg and Hendrick's The American novel were particularly useful indexes. Their format is simple and logical; they are quick to use and have satisfactory coverage of a limited field.

In the field of Canadian literature, a beginning has been made by Clara Thomas' Our nature our voices, Frank Davey's From there to here, and Reginald Hamel's Dictionnaire pratique des auteurs québécois. They are, however, highly selective of the authors and material covered. Even more selective are Michael Gnarowski's A concise bibliography of English Canadian literature, Reginald Watters' Canadian anthology, 3rd ed., and Raymond Brazeau's An anthology of contemporary French Canadian authors.

Canadian literature has published a fairly comprehensive annual bibliography as has the Journal of Canadian fiction. There is a Canadian section included in the annual bibliographies of both the Journal of Commonwealth literature and the M.L.A. bibliography. Each bibliography, however, has a different format and scope, complicating research more than it need be.

Late in the decade the Centre de recherche en civilisation canadienne-française of the Université d'Ottawa published the multi-volume Bibliographie critique de la littérature québécoise dans les revues des XIXe siecles. There is, however, no truly bilingual work, covering as widely as possible both the Anglophone and Francophone literatures of Canada.

To simplify matters for Glendon students, a card file was organized along the lines of the Palmer and Dyson format using as a base the entries in Canadian literature and the M.L.A. bibliography French and English-Canadian sections.

The original intention was to expand the file to cover the years 1967 to 1978 for all forms of literature: fiction, drama, poetry and prose. It quickly became apparent that this was an enormous task and would have to be narrowed down. The E.C.W. Press was beginning its series of bibliographies on Canadian authors. Though this series creates a different type of research tool, it covers the most prominent Canadian novelists. It was therefore decided to restrict this work to Canadian poetry. As criticism in this field really began to flourish in the 1970s, the time period was restricted to criticisms published during that decade, with the hope that there would be a retrospective work, as well as subsequent editions.

The primary arrangement of this index is alphabetical by the poet whose work is criticized. Under each poet the subgroupings are: general works; bibliographies; book titles arranged alphabetically; individual poem titles. Under each subheading the entries are listed alphabetically by critic, or by title for unsigned articles.

Each entry has been checked for its contents, to place it in the most useful subgrouping(s). A large number of serials specializing in English and French Canadian literature have been checked. Articles have also been found in some foreign periodicals. Theses are included only if they could be checked for their contents by this author.

It was a pleasant surprise to find such a wealth of material, even though the scope of coverage was so restricted. It was, therefore, decided to exclude items that were too short to prove of much value to students or researchers.

Another problem arose in deciding who was Canadian. There have been poets who touched down briefly in Canada, and those who came and stayed longer. The final criteria in most cases were the York University Libraries' and Toronto's Metro Central Library's classification schemes. If their cataloguers considered them Canadian, they were included.

Many thanks must be given: to the students who helped me organize the original file; the York University Libraries Sabbatical Committee who granted me the time to work on this project; the York SSHRC and Glendon Minor Research Committee who supplied the finances for the research and typing; Toni Olshen who was part-time researcher; professors Clara Thomas, Elizabeth Waterston and Barry Olshen for their encouragement; Noli Swatman of York's Office of Research Assistance, Maria Dirner of Leslie Frost Library; and many others. I also must thank especially Irving Kalushner for his support and advice.

Collections analyzed for essays on Canadian Poetry
(Starred * items have been partially analyzed)

Bayard, Carole and David, Jack. Out-posts/Avant-postes; interviews,
poetry, bibliographies & a critical introduction to 8 major modern
poets Erin, Ont: Press Porcépic, 1978. Bayard 1978

*Bessai, Diane and Jackel, David, eds. Figures in a ground: Canadian
essays on modern literature collected in honor of Sheila Watson.
Saskatoon: Western Producer Prairie Books [c1978]. Bessai 1977

*Blais, Jacques. De l'ordre et de l'aventure: la poésie au Québec de 1934
a 1944. Québec: Presses de l'Univ. Laval, 1975. (Vie des lettres
québécoises, 14.) Blais 1975

*Bouchard, Denis. Une lecture d'Ann Hébert: la recherche d'une
mythologie. Montréal: Hurtubise HMH, 1977. (Cahiers du Québec.)
Bouchard 1977

*Boucher, Jean-Pierre. Instantanés de la condition québécoise: études
de textes. Montréal: Hurtubise HMH, 1977. (Cahiers du Québec.
Collection littérature.) Boucher 1977

*Bourassa, André-G. Surréalisme et littérature québécoise. Montréal:
Ed. l'Étincele, 1977. Bourassa 1977

*Brindeau, Serge, et. al. La poésie contemporaine de langue française
depuis 1945. Études critiques. Paris: Ed. Saint-Germain-des-Prés,
1973. Brindeau 1973

*Brown, E. K. Responses and evaluations: essays on Canada. Ed. with an
introduction by David Staines. Toronto: McClelland and Stewart,
1977. (New Canadian library, 137.) Brown 1977

*Bugnet, Georges. Poèmes. Edmonton: Ed. de l'Églantier, 1978.
Bugnet 1978

Cappon, Paul, ed. In our own house; social perspectives on Canadian
literature. Toronto: McClelland & Stewart, 1978. Cappon 1978

Colombo, John Robert. Rhymes and reasons: nine Canadian poets discuss
their work. Toronto: Holt, Rinehart, and Winston of Canada, 1971.
Colombo 1971

Crémazie, Octave. Oeuvres I: Poésies. Texte établi, annoté et présenté
par Odette Condemine. Ottawa: Éd. de l'Univ. d'Ottawa, 1972.
Crémazie 1972

Dallard, Sylvie. Trois poètes québécois exemplaires (1940-1970). Québec:
Université Laval, 1977. Dallard 1977

*Dudek, Louis. Selected essays and criticism. Ottawa: Tecumseh Press,
1978. Dudek 1978

*Le lieu et la formule: hommage à Marc Eigeldinger. Neuchatel: Baconniére, 1978. Eigeldinger 1978

*Fisette, Jean. Le texte automatiste. Montréal: P.U.Q., 1977. Fisette 1977.

Garcia, Juan. Corps de gloire. Montréal: Presses de l'Univ. de Montréal, 1971. (Collection du prix de la revue Etudes françaises.) Garcia 1971

*Heavysege, Charles. Saul and selected poems: including excerpts from Jephthah's daughter and Jezebel: a poem in three cantos. Toronto: University of Toronto Press, 1976. Heavysege 1976

*Helwig, David, ed. The human elements: critical essays. Ottawa: Oberon Press, 1978. Helwig 1978

Laroche, Maximilien. Deux études sur la poésie et l'idéologie québécoises. Québec: Inst. supérieur des sciences humaines, Univ. Laval, 1975. (Science de la culture. Cahiers de l'ISSH.) Laroche 1975

Lee, Dennis. Savage fields. Toronto: Anansi, 1977. Lee 1977

*Lewis, Merrill, and Lee, L. L., eds. The westering experience in American literature: bicentennial essays. Bellingham, WA: Bureau for Faculty Research, Western Washington University, 1977. Lewis 1977

*Littératures: mélanges littéraires publiés à l'occasion du 150e anniversaire de l'Université McGill de Montréal. Montréal: Hurtubise HMH, 1971. Littératures 1971

*Lortie, Jeanne d'Arc. La poésie nationaliste au Canada français (1606-1867) Québec: Presses de l'Univ. Laval, 1975. (Vie des lettres québécoises, 13.) Lortie 1975

MacKinnon, Kenneth, ed. Atlantic Provinces literature colloquium papers. Communications du colloque sur la littérature des provinces atlantiques. St. John: Atlantic Canada Inst., 1977. (Marco Polo papers, 1.) MacKinnon 1977

*Mandel, Eli. Another time. Erin, Ont.: Press Porcépic, 1977. (Three solitudes: contemporary literary criticism in Canada, 3.) Mandel 1977

*Marshall, Tom. Harsh and lovely land: the major Canadian poets & the making of a Canadian tradition. Vancouver: Univ. of British Columbia Press, 1979. Marshall 1979

*Miron, Gaton. L'homme rapaillé. Montréal: Presses de l'Univ. de Montréal, 1970. Miron 1970

Maugey, Axel. Poésie et société au Québec (1937-1970). Québec: Presses de l'Univ. Laval, 1972. (Vie des lettres canadiennes, 9.) Maugey 1972

*Missions et démarches de la critique: mélanges offerts au Professeur
    J. A. Vier. Paris: Klincksieck, 1973.   Missions 1973

Moisan, Clément. Poésie des frontiéres: étude comparée des poésies
    canadienne et québécoise. Cité de LaSalle, Qué.: Éd. HMH, 1979.
    (Constantes, 38.)   Moison 1979

Nepveu, Pierre. Les mots à l'écoute; poésie et silence chez Fernand
    Ouellette, Gaston Miron et Paul-Marie Lapointe. Québec: Presses de
    l'Univ. Laval, 1979. (Vie des lettres québecoises, 17.)
    Nepveu 1979

*New, William H. Articulating West. Toronto: New Press, 1972.
    New 1972

*O'Flaherty, Patrick. The rock observed: studies in the literature of
    Newfoundland. Toronto: University of Toronto Press, 1979.
    O'Flaherty 1979

Ottawa, Université d'. Centre de recherches de littérature canadienne-
    française. L'école littéraire de Montréal 2d ed. Montréal: Fides,
    1972. (Archives des lettres canadiennes, 2.)   Ottawa 1972

*Pageau, René. Gustave Lamarche: poète dramatique. Québec: Éd.
    Garneau, 1976.   Pageau 1976

Savard, Pierre, ed. Mélanges de civilisation candienne-français offerts
    au professor Paul Wyczynski. Ottawa: University d'Ottawa, 1977.
    (Centre du recherche en civilisation canadienne-française, 10.)
    Savard 1977

*Smith, A. J. M. On poetry and poets: selected essays. Toronto:
    McClelland and Stewart, 1977. (New Canadian library, 143.)
    Smith 1977

*Smith, A. J. M. Towards a view of Canadian letters: selected critical
    essays 1928-1971. Vancouver: Univ. of British Columbia, 1973.
    Smith 1973

Staines, David, ed. The Canadian imagination; dimensions of a literary
    culture. Ed. with an introductory essay by David Staines. Cambridge,
    Mass.: Harvard Univ. Press, 1977.   Staines 1977

*Sutherland, John. Essays, controversies and poems. Ed. and with an
    introduction by Miriam Waddington. Toronto: McClelland and Stewart,
    1972. (New Canadian library, 81.)   Sutherland 1972

*Tierney, Frank M., ed. The Crawford symposium. Ottawa: Univ. of Ottawa
    Press, 1979, c1978. (Reappraisals: Canadian writers.)   Tierney 1978

Woodcock, George, ed. Colony and confederation: early Canadian poets and
    their background. Vancouver: Univ. of British Columbia Press, 1974.
    Woodcock 1974

Woodcock, George, ed. Poets and critics: essays from Canadian literature
    1966-1974. Toronto: Oxford University Press, 1974.   Woodcock 1974b

Sources and authorities

Butterfield, Rita, comp. "Canadian Literature 1970: A Checklist." CanL 48:96-119.

"Canadian literature, 1971: an annotated bibliography/une bibliographie avec commentaire" ECW 9:190-326, Winter 1977/78.

Cantin, Pierre. Bibliographie de la critique de la littérature québécoise des XIXe et XXe siècles par Pierre Cantin, Normand Harrington, Jean-Paul Hudon. Ottawa: Centre de recherche en civilisation canadienne-française, 1979. (Documents de travail du centre de recherche en civilisation canadienne-française, 12-16).

Davey, Frank. From there to here; a guide to English-Canadian literature since 1960. Erin, Ont.: Press Porcépic, 1974, (Our nature-our voices, 2).

Hamel, Réginald. Dictionnaire pratique des auteurs québécois. Réginald Hamel, John Hare, Paul Wyczynski. Montréal: Fides, 1976.

James, Charles Cannill. A bibliography of Canadian poetry (English). Toronto: Victoria University Library, 1899. (Victoria University Library. Publication, 1).

League of Canadian Poets. Catalogue of members. Toronto: 1976.

Stevens, Peter. Modern English-Canadian poetry; a guide to information sources. Detroit: Gale Research Co., 1978. (American literature, English literature, and world literatures in English information guide series, 15.)

Thomas, Clara. Our nature-our voices; a guidebook to English-Canadian literature. Vol. 1. Toronto: New Press, 1972.

Union des écrivains québécois. Petit dictionnaire des écrivains. n.p.:1979.

Watters, Reginald Eyre. A checklist of Canadian literature and background materials 1628-1960. 2d ed. rev. and enl. Toronto: U of T Press, 1972.

Watters, Reginald Eyre. "Bibliography." Klinck, Carl F. Canadian anthology 3d. ed., rev. and enl. Toronto: Gage Educational Pub., 1974, p. 645-721.

Woodcock, George. Canadian poets 1960-1973, Ottawa: Golden Dog press, 1976.

Abbreviations of Periodical Titles

Académie	Académie canadienne-française. Cahiers.
ActN	L'action nationale.
AntigR	Antigonish review.
ApF	Applegarth's folly.
Ariel	Ariel: a review of international English literature.
AspG	Aspen grove.
BdJ	Barre du jour.
BForum	Book forum: an international transdisciplinary quarterly.
BiC	Books in Canada.
Boundary	Boundary 2: a journal of postmodern literature.
Brick	Brick: a journal of reviews.
CA&B	Canadian author and bookman.
CanD	Canadian dimension.
CanL	Canadian literature.
CanR	Canadian review.
CapR	Capilano review.
CC-R	Les cahiers de Cap-Rouge
CF	Canadian forum.
ChiR	Chicago review.
CMLR	Canadian modern language review. La revue canadienne des langues vivantes.
CN&Q	Canadian notes and queries.
Compass	The compass: a provincial review.
Compass(KSC)	Compass: of Kutztown State College.
Copperfield	Copperfield: an independent Canadian literary magazine of the land and the north.

Cp	Concerning poetry.
CRCL	Canadian review of comparative literature. Revue canadienne de littérature comparée.
CtV	Culture vivante
CVII	CVII: contemporary verse two.
Dix	Cahiers des dix.
DR	Dalhousie review.
ECW	Essays on Canadian writing.
EdCF	Ecrits du Canada français
EF	Etudes françaises
EJ	The English journal
ELit	Etudes littéraires
EngQ	English quarterly
ESC	English studies in Canada
FDP	Four decades of poetry; 1890-1930.
FPt	Far point
FR	French review: journal of the American Association of Teachers of French.
FS	French studies: a quarterly review
HAB	Humanities Association review. La revue de l'Association des humanités.
HiC	Humanist in Canada.
HudR	The Hudson review.
Inc	Incidences, nouvelle série.
JCL	The journal of Commonwealth literature
JCP	Journal of Canadian poetry
JD	Jewish dialog
LanM	Les langues modernes
LAQ	Livres et auteurs québécois
Laomedon	Laomedon review

LauURev	Laurentian University review. Revue de l'Université Laurentienne.
Lettres qué	Les lettres québécoises.
LHY	Literary half-yearly.
L&I	Literature and ideology.
Lit	Littérature.
LURev	Lakehead University review.
MLit	Magazine Littéraire.
Meanjin	Meanjin quarterly.
MHRev	Malahat review: an international quarterly of life and letters.
MLS	Modern language studies.
Mosaic	Mosaic: a journal for the comparative study of literature and ideas.
MPS	Modern poetry studies.
MQR	Michigan quarterly review.
NBdJ	La nouvelle barre du jour.
Nj	Northern journey.
NL	Northern light.
NwR	Northwest review.
Old nun	Old nun magazine.
OntR	Ontario review: a North American journal of the arts.
OV	Other voices
PFr	Présence francophones: revue littéraire.
PrS	Prairie schooner.
PTor	Poetry Toronto.
QuéFr	Québec français.
QQ	Queen's quarterly.
Q&Q	Quill and quire.

RNL	Review of national literatures.
RPac	Revue du Pacifique: études de littérature française.
RUM	Revue de l'Université de Moncton.
RUO	Revue de l'Universite d'Ottawa. University of Ottawa quarterly.
SatN	Saturday night.
SFQ	Southern folklore quarterly.
Sphinx	The sphinx: a magazine of literature and society.
SCL	Studies in Canadian literature.
TamR	Tamarack review.
TCL	Twentieth century literature: a scholarly and critical journal.
UTQ	University of Toronto quarterly: a Canadian journal of the humanities.
UWR	University of Windsor review.
V&I	Voix et images: études québécoises.
VieFr	Vie française.
VIP	Voix et images du pays.
WascanaR	Wascana review.
WCR	West coast review.
WLWE	World literature written in English.

Other abbreviations used

comp.	compiler; compileur
ed.	editor, edition; éditeur, édition
inst.	institute; institut
n.p.	no place, no paging; sans lieu, ni pagination
n.s.	new series; nouvelle série
tr.	translated by; traduit par
univ.	university; université

Periodicals used in the Index

Académie canadienne-française. Cahiers (Académie).

L'action nationale (ActN).

Alive.

Antigonish review (AntigR).

Applegarth's folly (ApF).

Ariel: a review of international English literature (Ariel).

Aspen grove (AspG).

Barre du jour (BdJ).

Blackfish.

Book forum: an international transdisciplinary quarterly (BForum).

Books in Canada (BiC).

Boundary 2: a journal of postmodern literature (Boundary).

Brêches.

Brick: a journal of reviews (Brick).

Les cahiers de Cap-Rouge (CC-R).

Cahiers des dix (Dix).

Canadian author and bookman (CA&B).

Canadian dimension (CanD).

Canadian forum (CF).

Canadian literature (CL).

Canadian modern language review. La revue canadienne des languages vivantes (CMLR).

Canadian notes and queries (CN&Q).

Canadian review (CanR).

Canadian review of comparative literature. Revue canadienne de littérature comparée (CRCL).

Capilano review (CapR).

Caterpillar.

Châtelaine.

Chicago review (ChiR).

Chroniques

Le chien d'or. The golden dog (Le chien d'or).

Compass: a provincial review (Compass).

Compass: of Kutztown State College (Compass (KSC)).

Co-incidences.

Concerning poetry (Cp).

CVII: contemporary verse two (CVII).

Copperfield: an independent Canadian literary magazine of the land and the north (Copperfield).

Cul Q.

Culture.

Culture vivante (CtV).

Dalhousie review (DR).

Delta.

Dérives.

Deutschkanadisches jahrbuch.

Deuxiéme mouvement.

Ecrits du Canada français (EdCF).

Ellipse.

English.

The English journal (EJ).

English quarterly (EngQ).

English studies in Canada (ESC).

Esprit.

Essays on Canadian writing (ECW).

Estuaire.

Etudes françaises (EF).

Etudes littéraires (ELit).

Event.

Far point (FPt).

Fiddlehead.

Forces.

Four decades of poetry; 1890-1930 (FDP).

French review: journal of the American Association of Teachers of French (FR).

French studies: a quarterly review (FS).

Hobo-Québec.

Humanities Association review. La revue de l'Association des humanités (HAB).

The Hudson review (HudR).

Humanist in Canada (HiC).

Incidences, nouvelle série (Inc.).

Inscape.

Jewish dialog (JD).

Journal of Canadian poetry (JCP).

The journal of Commonwealth literature (JCL).

Lakehead University review (LURev).

Les langues modernes (LanM).

Laurentian University review. Revue de l'Université Laurentienne (LauURev).

Laomedon review (Laomedon).

Les lettres nouvelles.

Les lettres québécoises (Lettres qué).

Liberté.

Literary half-yearly (LHY).

Literature and ideology (L&I).

Littérature (Lit).

Livres et auteurs québécois (LAQ).

Le maclean

Maclean's

Magazine littéraire (MLit).

Maintenant.

Malahat review: an international quarterly of life and letters (MHRev).

Meanjin quarterly (Meanjin).

Michigan quarterly review (MQR).

Modern language studies (MLS).

Modern poetry studies (MPS).

Mosaic: a journal for the comparative study of literature and ideas (Mosaic).

New.

Nord.

Northern light (NL).

Northern journey (Nj).

Northern review.

Northwest review (NwR).

La nouvelle barre du jour (NBdJ).

Old nun magazine (Old nun).

Ontario review: A North American journal of the arts (OntR).

Open letter. 2d, 3rd and 4th series.

Other voices (OV).

Poetry.

Poetry review.

Poetry Toronto (PTor).

Prairie Schooner (PrS).

Présence francophone: revue littéraire (PFr).

Presqu'amérique

Protée.

Quarry.

Québec français (QuéFr).

Québec histoire.

Queen's quarterly (QQ).

Quill and quire (Q&Q).

Relations.

Review of national literatures (RNL).

Revue de l'Université d'Ottawa. University of Ottawa quarterly (RUO).

Revue de l'Université de Moncton (RUM).

Revue du Pacifique: études de littérature française (RPac).

Room of one's own.

Saturday night (SatN).

Southern folklore quarterly (SFQ).

The sphinx: a magazine of literature and society (Sphinx).

Studies in Canadian literature (SCL).

Tamarack review (TamR).

Tuatara.

Twentieth century literature: a scholarly and critical journal (TCL).

University of Toronto quarterly: a Canadian journal of the humanities
(UTQ).

University of Windsor review (UWR).

Vie française (VieFr).

Voix et images: études québécoises (V&I).

Voix et images du pays (VIP).

Wascana review (WascanaR).

Waves.

West coast review (WCR).

White pelican.

World literature written in English (WLWE).

Index to Criticisms of Canadian Poetry

ABBEY, Lloyd

The antlered boy
Hornyansky, Michael. UTQ 40:376-70, 1971.

Flies
Edwards, Mary Jane. CF 54(643):42-3, 1974.

Levenson, Christopher. "Poetry review." CanR 1(2):12-3, 1974.

Stevens, Peter. "The perils of majority." UWR 9(2):100-9, 1974.

ACORN, Milton

General
Lever, Bernice. "Milton Acorn: poet as crusader." Alive 38:7-9, 1974.

Marshall, Tom. "Facts and dreams again." Marshall 1979:107-11.

The island means Minago
Cameron, Barry. "Poetic historians." CanL 75:106-7, 1977.

Gasparini, Leonard. "One Milton who is living at this hour." BiC 4(12):25 - 6, 1975.

McFadgen, Lynn. Q&Q 41(10):18, 1975.

Purdy, Al. "Our purple-faced conscience." CVII 2(1):4-5, 1976.

Spettigue, D. QQ 83:167-8, 1976.

I've tasted my blood: poems 1956 to 1968
Boyce, Murray. OV 6(4): poems 1956 to 1968, n.p., 1971.

Gibson, Kenneth. "Noises and signals." Quarry 13(3):58-9, 1970.

Hornyansky, Michael. UTQ 39:335, 1970.

Jackpine sonnets
Gibbs, Robert. Fiddlehead 118:159-62, 1978.

Hatfield, Stephen. "Sputters on the green fuse." Waves 7(2):74-7, 1979.

McFadgen, Lynn. Q&Q 43(12):12-3, 1977.

McKay, Jean. "Stubborn nutty words." ECW 9:66-9, (Winter 1977/78).

ACORN, Milton

    Jackpine sonnets (cont'd.)

      Purdy, Brian. PTor 21:n.p., 1977.

    More poems for people
      Oughton, John. "Straight left and right across." BiC 2(1):58, 1973.

      Ryan, W.S. Q&Q 39(1):11, 1973.

ADAM, Ian

    Encounter
      Watson, Wilfred. "Encountering Encounter." White pelican 4(1):56-7,
      1974.

ADAMSON, Arthur

    The inside animal
      Barbour, Douglas. "Canadian poetry chronicle: VII." DR 59:154-75,
      1979.

      Popham, Beth. Quarry 27(2):85-6, 1978.

ADILMAN, Mona Elaine

    Cult of concrete
      Isaacs, Fran. Room of one's own 3(4):39, 1978.

AIDE, William

    Middle C
      Barnes, W.J. Quarry 21(2):70-2, 1972.

ALLAN, George

    Landscapes
      Gasparini, Len. "Mythopoeic hits and Ms." BiC 4(1):21-2, 1975.

      Hamilton, Jamie. Brick 1:46-7, 1977.

ALLEN, Robert

    The assumption of private lives
      Linder, Norma West. "Tales well told." CA&B 54(1):34, 1978.

      McFadden, Dave. "Of newts and natural gold." BiC 8(1):14-5, 1979.

      Miles, Ron. "Boxed set." CanL 81:138-9, 1979.

      Whiteman, Bruce. Quarry 27(4):88-9, 1978.

    Valhalla at the OK
      Martineau, Stephen. CF 52(618-19):44, 1972.

ALLINE, Henry

    General
      Vincent, Thomas B. "Alline and Bailey." CanL 68-9, 124-33, 1976.

ALMON, Bert

    Taking possession
      Scott, Robert Ian. WCR 13(1):33, 1978.

AMABILE, George

    Blood ties
      Bailey, Don. "Take five." QQ 80:99-106, 1973.

      Boland, J.A. Heidi. Alive 41:35, 1975.

      Dickinson-Brown, Roger, "Personalism and poetry." MPS 4:122-5, 1973.

      Ditsky, John. CF 53(631):35, 1973.

      Dragland, Stan. "Ties and threads." CanL 62:118-21, 1974.

      Orr, George B. Q&Q 38(9):7, 1972

    Flower and song
      Barbour, Douglas. "Canadian poetry chronicle: VII." DR 59:154-75, 1979.

    Open country
      Barbour, Douglas. "Poetry chronicle: IV." DR 57:355-71, 1977.

      Cogswell, Fred. "Three Manitoba poets." Sphinx 7(v.2(3)):68-70, 1977

AMABILE, George

Open country (cont'd.)
Hickmore, G.L. Quarry 26(4):65-6, 1977.

Powell, Craig. "The disappointments of a poet's progress." CVII 3(4):18-9, 1978.

Pyke, Linda. "A mari usque ad mare: four poetic landscapes." Q&Q 42(17):29, 1976.

Scobie, Stephen. "Hill poems from the plain." BiC 6(3):41-2, 1977.

AMPRIMOZ, Alexandre

Against the cold
Saunders, Leslie. Quarry 27(4):75, 1978.

Selected poems
Billings, Robert. "Hounslow's poetry lists: quality & diversity." Waves 8(1):71-6, 1979.

Fletcher, Peggy. "Vision and the personal dark." CA&B 54(4):26-7, 1979.

10/11
Moisan, Clément. LAQ 1979:92.

AMYOT, Geneviève

La mort était extravagante
Bourque, Paul-André. LAQ 1976:170-1.

ANDERSON, Patrick

General
Mayne, Seymour. "A conversation with Patrick Anderson." Inscape 11(3):46-79, 1974.

Ringrose, Christopher Xerxes. "Patrick Anderson and the critics." CanL 43:10-23, 1970.

Sutherland, John. "The poetry of Patrick Anderson." Sutherland 1972: 119-28.

ANDERSON, Patrick

Return to Canada: selected poems
Barbour, Douglas. "Poetry chronicle V." DR 58:149-69, 1978.

Farmiloe, Dorothy. Q&Q 43(9):8, 1977.

Hornyansky, Michael. UTQ 47:350-1, 1978.

Scobie, Stephen: Quarry 26(3):78-80, 1977.

Smith, A.J.M. "Wandering Gentile, homebody Jew." BiC 6(6):18-9, 1977.

Woodcock, George. "Returns and distances." CanL 78:83-7, 1978.

A visiting distance: poems: new, revised, and selected.
Barbour, Douglas. "Poetry chronicle V." DR 58:149-69, 1978.

Dabydeen, Cyril. UWR 12(2):106-7, 1977.

Denham, Paul. "A cold and remote visitation." CVII 2(4):4-5, 1976.

Farmiloe, Dorothy. Q&Q 42(15):38, 1976.

Hornyansky, Michael. UTQ 46:374-5, 1977.

Woodcock, George. "Returns and distances." CanL 78:83-7, 1978.

"Railroad station"
Cole, Wayne. "The railroad in Canadian literature." CanL 77:124-30, 1978.

ANDRÉ, André

Viesna
Grant, Judith. Q&Q 40(7):21, 1974.

ANDREW, David

The lure of Lanark
Leigh, Simon. "Two minor talons and a tidal borealis: Part II." Fiddlehead 109:128-32, 1976.

ARMSTRONG, Duncan T.

Distant music
   Hamel, Guy. "Recent Fiddlehead poetry books." Fiddlehead 118:137-45, 1978.

ARNOLD, Les

Rhythms
   Barbour, Douglas. "Canadian poetry chronicle: III." DR 56:560-73, 1976.

   McCarthy, Dermot. "Ancestors, real or imaginative." ECW 4:73-5, 1976.

ARSENAULT, Angèle

Première
   Cloutier, Cécile. "Voix acadiennes." LAQ 1975:132-4.

ARSENAULT, Guy

Acadie rock
   Arcand, Pierre-André. "Poets from the end of the earth." Ellipse 16:76-82, 1973. (Tr. Barbara Kuritzky.)

ASFOUR, John

Nisan, a book of poetry
   Munton, Ann. DR 57:379, 1977.

ATHERTON, Stanley S.

Welcome to the Maritimes
   McGaughey, G.S. "Problems for poets: publishing poetry." CF 55(650):63, 1975.

ATWOOD, Margaret

Bibliography
Horne, Alan J., comp. "A preliminary checklist of writings by and about Margaret Atwood." CLJ 31:576-92, 1974; MHRev 41:195-222, 1977.

General
Ayre, John. "Margaret Atwood and the end of colonialism." SatN 87 (11):23-6, 1972.

Davey, Frank. "Atwood's gorgon tough." SCL 2:146-63, 1977.

Foster, John Wilson. "The poetry of Margaret Atwood." CanL 74:5-20, 1977.

Gibson, Mary Ellis. "A conversation with Margaret Atwood." ChiR 27(4):105-13, 1976.

Glicksohn, Susan W. "The martian point of view." Extrapolation 15:161-73, 1974.

Hastrup, Inger. Flame-tree and totem: a study of the pioneer in the works of Judith Wright and Margaret Atwood. Kingston, Ontario: Queen's Univ., 1975. (M.A. thesis.)

Irvine, Lorna. "The red and silver heroes have collapsed." Cp 12(2):59-68, 1979.

Jones, D.G. "Cold eye and optic heart: Marshall McLuhan and some Canadian poets." MPS 5:170-87, 1974.

Kaminski, Margaret. "Interview with Margaret Atwood." Waves 4(1):8-13, 1975.

Macri, F.M. "Survival kit: Margaret Atwood and the Canadian scene." MPS 5:187-95, 1974.

"A Margaret Atwood interview with Karla Hammond." Cp 12(2):73-81, 1979.

Marshall, Tom. "Les animaux de son pays: notes sur la poésie de Margaret Atwood." Ellipse 3:81-6, 1970. (Tr. Monique Grandmangin.)

Marshall, Tom. "Atwood under and above water." MHRev 41:89-94, 1977. (Also Marshall 1979:154-61.)

McCombs, Judith. "Atwood's nature concepts." Waves 7(1):68-77, 1978.

Moisan, Clément. "Poésie de la libération." Moisan 1979:167-218.

Oates, Joyce Carol. "A conversation with Margaret Atwood." OntR 9:5-18, 1978-79.

ATWOOD, Margaret

General (cont'd.)
Power, Linda Laporte. The reality of selfhood: a study of polarity in the poetry and fiction of Margaret Atwood. Montreal: McGill Univ., 1973. (M.A. thesis.)

Rogers, Linda. "Margaret the Magician." CanL 60:83-5, 1974.

Rosenberg, Jerome. "'For or such is the kingdom...': Margaret Atwood's Two-headed poems." ECW 16:130-9, 1979-80.

Sandler, Linda, ed. "Margaret Atwood: a symposium." MHRev 41, 1977. (whole issue.)

Scott, Andrew P. Margaret Atwood: a critical appreciation. Fredericton: Univ. of New Brunswick, 1975, c1976 (M.A. thesis.)

Sillers, Pat. "Power impinging: hearing Atwood's vision." SCL 4(1):59-70, 1979.

Slinger, Helen. "Interview with Margaret Atwood." Maclean's 89(15):4-7, 1976.

Struthers, J.R.(Tim). "An interview with Margaret Atwood." ECW 6:18-27, 1977.

Sullivan, Rosemary. "Breaking the circle." MHRev 41:30-41, 1977.

Van Varseveld, Gail. "Talking with Atwood." Room of one's own 1(2):66-70, 1975.

Weir, Lorraine. "'Fauna of mirrors': the poetry of Hébert and Atwood." Ariel 10(3):99-113, 1979.

Woodcock, George. "Margaret Atwood." LHY 13(2):233-42, 1972.

Animals in that country
Ross, Gary. "The divided self." CanL 71:39-47, 1976.

The circle game
Davidson, Arnold E. "Entering The circle game: Margaret Atwood's beginnings as a poet." Cp 12(2):47-54, 1979.

Garnet, Eldon. "For the poets, the landscape is the great Canadian myth." SatN 85(2):31-3, 1970.

Ross, Gary. "The circle game." CanL 60:51-63, 1974.

ATWOOD, Margaret

The journals of Susanna Moodie
   Allen, Carolyn. "Margaret Atwood: power of transformation, power of knowledge." ECW 6:5-17, 1977.

   Barbour, Douglas. CF 50:225-6, 1970.

   Barbour, Douglas. "The search for roots: a meditative sermon of sorts." LHY 13(2):1-14, 1972.

   Doyle, Mike. "Made in Canada?" Poetry 119:356-62, 1972.

   Hastrup, Inger. Flame-tree and totem: a study of the pioneer in the works of Judith Wright and Margaret Atwood. Kingston, Ontario: Queen's Univ., 1975. (M.A. thesis.)

   Hutcheon, Linda. "'Snow storm of paper': the act of reading in self-reflective Canadian verse." DR 59:114-26, 1979.

   Marshall, Tom. "Canpo: a chronicle." Quarry 19(4):50-4, 1970.

   Purdy, A.W. "Atwood's Moodie." CanL 47:80-4, 1971.

   Purdy, Al. Wascana R 5(2):57-8, 1970.

   Skelton, Robin MHRev 17:133-4, 1971.

   Stephen, Sid. "The journals of Susanna Moodie: a self portrait of Margaret Atwood." White Pelican, 2(2):32-6, 1972.

Power politics
   Allen, Dick. "Shifts." Poetry 120:235-45, 1972.

   Bowering, George. "Get used to it." CanL 52:91-2, 1972.

   Buri, S.G. "It's how you play the game." AspG 1:34-46, 1972.

   Doyle, Mike. "Made in Canada?" Poetry 119:356-62, 1972.

   Harcourt, Joan. Quarry 20(4):70-3, 1971.

   Hornyansky, Michael. UTQ 41:334-5, 1972.

   Onley, Gloria. WCR 8(3):45-6, 1974.

   Onley, Gloria. "Power politics in Bluebeard's castle." CanL 60:21-42, 1974. (Also Woodcock 1974b:191-214.)

   Pritchard, William H. "Poetry matters." HudR 26:579-97, 1973.

   Woodcock, George. "Margaret Atwood." LHY 13(2):233-42, 1972.

ATWOOD, Margaret

Procedures for underground
Barbour, Douglas. DR 50:437-9, 1970.

Gibbs, Jean. Fiddlehead 87:61-5, 1970.

Harcourt, Joan. Quarry 20(1):52-3, 1971.

Hornyansky, Michael. UTQ 40:378-9, 1971.

Johnson, Jane. OV 6(3):n.p., 1970.

Skelton, Robin. MHRev 17:133-4, 1971.

Stevens, Peter. "Dark mouth." CanL 50:91-2, 1971.

Wainwright, Andy. "Margaret Atwood's drowned world." SatN 85(12):33-5, 1970.

Selected poems
Bobak, E.L. DR 56:404-6, 1976.

Challis, John. Laomedon 3(1):73, 1977.

Clarkson, Stephen. "Marriage play." CF 56(667):58, 1976-77.

Dunn, Timothy. "Procedures for surfacing." CanR 4(1):58, 1977.

Fletcher, Peggy. CA&B 52(1);26, 1976.

Geddes, Gary. "Now you see it..." BiC 5(7):4-6, 1976.

Hosek, Chaviva. "Powerful images in two new collections." Q&Q 42(9):36, 1976.

Keitner, Wendy. Quarry 26(2):51-2, 1977.

Rogers, Linda. "Dirges to baby." Sphinx 7:78-80, 1977.

Sandler, Linda. "The exorcisms of Atwood." SatN 91(5):59-60, 1976.

Williamson, Alan. "'Fool', said my muse to me..." Poetry 133:100-7, 1978.

Woodcock, George. "Playing with freezing fire." CanL 70:84-91, 1976.

ATWOOD, Margaret

Two-headed poems

Barbour, Douglas. Fiddlehead 121:139-42, 1979.

Barbour, Douglas. "Canadian poetry chronicle: VII." DR 59:154-75, 1979.

David, Jack. UWR 14(2):100-3, 1979.

Fletcher, Peggy. "Dialogues and other voices." CA&B 54(2):36-7, 1979.

Friesen, Patrick. "Dualities, duets." CVII 4(3):23-4, 1979.

Gatenby, Greg. Q&Q 44(16):10, 1978.

Gatenby, Greg. "Poetry chronicle." TamR 77-78:77-94, 1979.

Gibbons, Reginald. "Hayden, Peck, and Atwood." OntarioR 10:87-94, 1979.

Hornyansky, Michael. UTQ 48:341-2, 1979.

Keitner, Wendy. Quarry 28(4):77-81, 1979.

Matson, Marshall. "Yoked by violence." BiC 8(1):12-3, 1979.

Prato, Edward. WCR 14(1):43-6, 1979.

Rosenberg, Jerome. "'For of such is the kingdom...':Margaret Atwood's Two-headed poems." ECW 16:130-9, 1979-80.

Sullivan, Rosemary. "Atwood's new directions." TamR 76:108-9, 1979.

You are Happy

Allen, Carolyn. "Margaret Atwood: Power of transformation, power of knowledge." ECW 6:5-17, 1977.

Amabile, George. "Consciousness in ambush." CVII 1(1):5-6, 1975.

Chalmers, John W. CA&B 50(3):28-9, 1975.

Chamberlin, J.E. "Poetry chronicle." HudR 28:119-35, 1975.

Dilliott, Maureen. "Emerging from the cold: Margaret Atwood's You are Happy." MPS 8:73-90, 1977.

Douglas, Charles. "Poetry: presence and presentation." LURev 7(2)/8(1&2):74-85, 1976 (?).

12

ATWOOD, Margaret

You are Happy (cont'd.)

Hornyansky, Michael. UTQ 44:334-5, 1975.

Jacobs, Ann. DR 54:790-2, 1974-75.

Lauder, Scott. "We are not so happy." CF 54(646):17-8, 1974.

Levenson, Christopher. QQ 82:297-8, 1975.

Mandel, Eli. "Atwood gothic." MHRev 41: 165-74, 1977. Also: Mandel 1977: 137-45.

Marshall, Tom. "Five poets from five countries." OntR 2:86-94, 1975.

Matson, Marshall. "Seize the day and the axe." BiC 4(2):24, 1975.

Musgrave, Susan. "Atwood." Open letter 3d ser, 2:103-5, 1975.

Oughton, John. "The encircled self game." Open letter 3d ser, 2:105-6, 1975.

Pritchard, William H. "Despairing at styles." Poetry 127:292-302, 1976.

Pyke, Linda Annesley. Q&Q 40(11):22, 1974.

Sandler, Linda. "Gustafson & others." TamR 64:89-94, 1974.

Scott, Andrew. "The poet as sorceress." ECW 3:60-2, 1975.

"A bus along St. Clair: December"
Hastrup, Inger. Flame-tree and totem: A study of the pioneer in the works of Judith Wright and Margaret Atwood. Kingston, Ontario: Queens Univ., 1975 (M.A. thesis.)

"Further arrivals"
Hastrup, Inger. Flame-tree and totem: a study of the pioneer in the works of Judith Wright and Margaret Atwood. Kingston, Ontario: Queens Univ., 1975 (M.A. thesis.)

AUBERT, Rosemary

Two kinds of honey
Barbour, Douglas. "Canadian poetry chronicle: VII." DR 59:154-75, 1979.

Bayard, Caroline. Q&Q 43(17):34, 1976.

Donnell, David. "Three newcomers." TamR 74:69-71, 1978.

Gotlieb, Phyllis. Quarry 27(1):84-5, 1978.

AUBERT, Rosemary

<u>Two kinds of honey</u> (cont'd.)
  Hosek, Chaviva. Fiddlehead 118:163-4, 1978.

  Mallison, Jean. "Linked fictions, nerve-ends, and faith in language."
  CVII 4(3):25-8, 1979.

AUSTIN, Pat

<u>A time for lilies</u>
  Harper, A.W.J. "Four reviews." OV 8(2):n.p., 1972.

AVISON, Margaret

  General
  Bowering, George. "Avison's imitation of Christ the artist." CanL
  54:56-69, 1972.

  Cohn-Sfetcu, Ofelia. "To live in abundance of life: time in Canadian
  literature." CanL 76:25-36, 1978.

  Jones, D.G. "Cold eye and optic heart: Marshall McLuhan and some
  Canadian poets." MPS 5:170-87, 1974.

  Marshall, Tom. "Major Canadian poets IV: Margaret Avison." CF
  58(687):21-3, 1979.

  Marshall, Tom. "Perspective: Margaret Avison." Marshall 1979:
  99-106.

  Merrett, Robert James. "'The ominous centre': the theological impulse
  in Margaret Avison's poetry." White pelican 5(2):12-24, 1976.

  New, William H. "The mind's (I's) (ice): the poetry of Margaret
  Avison." TCL 16:185-202, 1970.

  Redekop, Ernest. Margaret Avison. Toronto: Copp Clark, 1970.
  (Studies in Canadian literature, 9.)

  Zichy, Francis. "'Each in his prison/thinking of the key': images of
  confinement and liberation in Margaret Avison." SCL 3:232-43, 1978.

AVISON, Margaret

The dumbfounding

Cohn-Sfetcu, Ofelia. "Margaret Avison: the all-swallowing moment." ESC 2:339-44, 1976.

Doerksen, Daniel W. "Search and discovery: Margaret Avison's poetry." CanL 60:7-20, 1974. (Also Woodcock 1974b:123-37.)

Moisan, Clément. "Poésie de la clandestinité." Moisan 1979:91-127.

Moisan, Clément. "Rina Lasnier et Margaret Avison." Liberté 108:21-33, 1976.

New, William H. "The mind's eyes (I's)(ice): the poetry of Margaret Avison." New 1972:234-58.

Reigo, Ants. "Margaret Avison and the gospel of vision." CVII 3(2):14-9, 1977.

Sunblue

Johnston, G. "Avison's temple." CF 59 (689):30-1, 1979.

Linder, Norma West. "Starkness and sensibility." CA&B 54(3):28-9, 1979.

McNally, Paul. Fiddlehead 123:100-2, 1979.

Moritz, Albert. "Stalking the sacred asparagus." BiC 8(7):28-9, 1979.

Winter sun

Cohn-Sfetcu, Ofelia. "Margaret Avison: the all-swallowing moment." ESC 2:339-44, 1976.

Doerksen, Daniel W. "Search and discovery: Margaret Avison's poetry." CanL 60:7-20, 1974.

Hutcheon, Linda. "'Snow storm of paper': the act of reading in self-reflexive Canadian verse." DR 59:114-26, 1979.

Moisan, Clément. "Poésie de la clandestinité." Moisan 1979:91-127.

Moisan, Clément. "Rina Lasnier et Margaret Avison." Liberté 108:21-33, 1976.

New, William H. "The mind's eyes (I's)(ice): the poetry of Margaret Avison." New 1972:234-58.

Reigo, Ants. "Margaret Avison and the gospel of vision." CVII 3(2):14-9, 1977.

Smith, A.J.M. "Critical improvisations on Margaret Avison's Winter sun." Smith 1973:142-5. (Originally published TamR 18:81-6, 1961.)

AVISON, Margaret

"The Agnes Cleves papers"
   Kertzer, J.M. "Margaret Avison's portrait of a lady: 'The Agnes
   Cleves papers.'" Cp 12(2):17-24, 1979.

"Snow"
   Lecker, Robert. "Exegetical blizzard." SCL 4(1):180-4, 1979.

   Pollock, Zailig. "A response to Michael Taylor's 'Snow blindness.'"
   SCL 4(1):177-9, 1979.

   Reigo, Ants. "Margaret Avison and the gospel of vision." CVII 3(2):
   14-9,1977.

   Taylor, Michael. "Snow blindness." SCL 3:288-90, 1978.

   Zichy, Francis. "A response to Robert Lecker's 'Exegetical blizzard'
   and Michael Taylor's 'Snow blindness.'" SCL 4(2):147-54, 1979.

BACHAND, Denis

   Où vers
   Bisson-Henchiri, Michelle. LAQ 1972: 177.

   Roséfine la cristalline
   Bourque, Paul-André. LAQ 1973: 113-5.

BAGLOW, John

   Emergency measures
   Amprimoz, Alexandre. "The space of memory." CanL 80:72-4, 1979.

   Barbour, Douglas. "Poetry chronicle IV." DR 57:355-71, 1977.

   Bowering, Marilyn. Q&Q 42(13):44, 1976.

   Keitner, Wendy. Quarry 26(1):70-2, 1977.

   Scherzer, David. "Squint poetry." CVII 3(2):60-1, 1977.

BAILEY, Alfred Goldsworthy

General
Pacey, Desmond. "A.G. Bailey." CanL 68-9:49-61, 1976.

Smith, A.J.M. "The poetics of Alfred G. Bailey: 1974." Smith 1977:102-5.

Thanks for a drowned island
Arnason, David. Q&Q 40(1):14, 1974.

Cogswell, Fred. "Canadian essence." CanL 61:119-21, 1974.

Gutteridge, Don. QQ 81:149-50, 1974.

Lane, M. Travis. "The muskrat in his brook." Fiddlehead 100:95-101, 1974.

Smith, A.J.M. DR 53:752-5, 1973-74.

Werner, Hans. "Ripples and waves." BiC 2(5):6-7, 1973

BAILEY, Don

My bareness is not just my body
Adams, Richard G. Fiddlehead 93:111-2, 1972.

Helwig, David. Quarry 21(2):63-5, 1972.

Rogers, Linda. "Three trails." BiC 1(11):28-9, 1972.

Woodruff, Sandra. HAB 25:82-3, 1974.

The shapes around me
Crawford, Terry. Quarry 23(1):76-7, 1974.

Marcellin, Phil. Alive 35:10, 1974.

BAILEY, Jacob

General
Vincent, Thomas B. "Alline and Bailey." CanL 68-9:124-33, 1976.

BALDERSTONE, Greg

Where the words are unspoken
Lanczos, Elmar. WCR 8(2):61-3, 1973.

BALL, Helen

General
Ball, Helen. "Reminiscences." PTor 46:n.p., 1979.

BALL, Nelson

Water-pipes & moonlights
Barbour, Douglas. "The young poets and the little presses, 1969." DR 50:112-26, 1970.

BARBOUR, Douglas
He & she
Gasparini, Leonard. "Flat, muddled, and egotistical." BiC 4(10):27, 29, 1975.

Sandler, Linda. QQ 83:168-9, 1976.

Land fall
Jones, D.G. "Between mindscape and landscape." CanL 53:81-8, 1972.

Stevens, Peter. "Not a bang but a whimper?" UWR 7(2):103-8, 1972.

A poem as long as the highway
Bailey, Don. "A provincial look at ten volumes of Canadian poetry." QQ 79:242-54, 1972.

Jones, D.G. "Between mindscape and landscape." CanL 53:81-8, 1972.

MacDonald, Robert. Q&Q 38(6):11, 1972.

Pollack, Claudette. Quarry 22(2):68-70,1973.

Songbook
Powell, D. Reid. Q&Q 40(2):12, 1974.

Visions of my Grandfather
Aubert, Rosemary. Q&Q 43(10):39, 1977.

Whiteman, Bruce. "Big seeing & necessary as breath." ECW 10:57-60, 1978.

BARBOUR, Douglas

White
Bailey, Don. "Take five." QQ 80:99-106, 1973.

Estok, Michael. "All in the family: the metaphysics of domesticity." DR 52:653-67, 1973.

Nichol, bp. "Overwhelming colour." Open letter 2d ser, 8:110-2, 1974.

Pollack, Claudette. Quarry 22(2):68-70, 1973.

Woodruff, Sandra. HAB 25:79-80, 1974.

BARRETO-RIVERA, Rafael

Canadada
Oughton, John. Open letter 2d ser, 5:118-9, 1973.

The four horsemen alive in the west
bissett, bill. "What 4 voices can together say." ECW 12:241-2, 1978.

Horse d'oeuvres
Barbour, Douglas. "Canadian poetry chronicle 2." DR 55:748-59, 1975-76.

David, Jack. "Hoarse meet." ECW 3:55-7, 1975.

Lever, Bernice. Q&Q 41(8):32, 1975.

BATES, Maxwell

General
Skelton, Robin. "Maxwell Bates: experience and reality." MHRev 20:57-97, 1971.

BAUER, Walter

General
Beissel, Henry. "A few words of farewell to a friend." TamR 77&78:5-13, 1979.

Beissel, Henry. "A tribute to Walter Bauer." TamR 64:5-8, 1974.

Froeschle, Hartmut. "Walter Bauer. Seiner dichterisches Werk mit besonderer Berücksichtigung seines Kanada-Erlebnisses." Deutschkanadisches Jahrbuch 5:77-100, 1979. (Includes English abstract.)

Watt, F.W. "A different sun: Walter Bauer's Canadian poetry." CF 59(692):20-4, 1979.

A different sun
Amprimoz, Alexandre. "Mostly a migration of metaphors." Brick 2:20-2, 1978.

Amprimoz, Alexandre. Q&Q 42(8):35-6, 1976.

Barbour, Douglas. "Poetry chronicle IV." DR 57:355-71, 1977.

Bickmore, G.L. Quarry 26(2):64-6, 1977.

Dabydeen, Cyril. "Will to live." CanL 75:103-4, 1977.

Maurer, Karl W. "A particular genius: observations on Bauer and translation." CVII 2(4):34-5, 1976.

Riedel, Walter E. CRCL 4:384-6, 1977.

Thorpe, Michael. "Lebensraum at last." BiC 5(9):34, 1976.

BAUER, William

The terrible word
Barbour, Douglas. "Canadian poetry chronicle: VII. DR 59:154-75, 1979.

Oliver, Michael Brian. "Tantramar - and Saint John and Fredericton - revisited." Fiddlehead 122:115-24, 1979.

BAYLEY, Cornwall

"Canada, a descriptive poem"
Talman, James and Talman, Ruth. "A note on the authorship of 'Canada, a descriptive poem,' Quebec 1806." CN&Q 20:12-3, 1977.

BEARDSLEY, Doug

Going down into history
Barbour, Douglas. "Canadian poetry chronicle: III." DR 56:560-73, 1976.

Bowering, Marilyn. Q&Q 42(10):45, 1976.

Lillard, Charles. WCR 11(3):55-6, 1977.

The only country in the world called Canada
Browne, Colin. "Between fact and revelation." CVII 3(1):8-9, 1977.

McFadgen, Lynn. Q&Q 43(1):31, 1977.

Oliver, Michael Brian. "Raising Canada." Fiddlehead 114:141-5, 1977.

Play on the water
Barbour, Douglas. "Canadian poetry chronicle: VII." DR 59:154-75, 1979.

Brown, Allan. Quarry 28(4):81-4, 1979.

Daniel, Lorne. Q&Q 45(17):20, 1979.

Di Cicco, Pier Giorgio. "No man is an island, true, but there can be a circean catch to regionalism." BiC 8(1):21-2, 1979.

Hall, Phil. "Play on the water--a hard act to follow or drownproofing." UWR 14(2):109, 1979.

BEAUCHAMP, Germain

Le livre du vent quoi
Paradis, Suzanne. LAQ 1973: 111-3.

BEAUCHEMIN, Nérée

General
Arnould, Ivor A. "Nérée Beauchemin, poète de transition." RUO
42(2):279-93, 1972.

Guilmette, Armand. "Nérée Beauchemin, poète de la conciliation."
Académie 14:131-8, 1972.

BEAULIEU, Michel

Anecdotes
Bourassa, André-G. "Justice et Beaulieu." Lettres qué 10:12-5, 1978.

Hébert, Francois. "Lefrançois, Beaulieu, Nepveu, Vanier." Liberté
114:93-9, 1977.

Malenfant, Paul Chanel. LAQ 1977: 160-4.

Le cercle du justice
Bourassa, André-G. "Justice et Beaulieu." Lettres qué 10:12-5, 1978.

Malenfant, Paul Chanel. LAQ 1977:160-4.

Charmes de la fureur
Dallard, Sylvie. LAQ 1970: 137.

Dionne, René. "Ou va notre poésie?" Relations 357:55-7, 1971.

Major, Jean-Louis. UTQ 40:440, 1971.

Nepveu, Pierre. "Le poeme inachevé." EF 11:55-65, 1975.

Dérives
Bourassa, André-G. "Justice et Beaulieu." Lettres qué 10:12-5, 1978.

Malenfant, Paul Chanel. LAQ 1977: 160-4.

FM lettres des saisons III
Blais, Jacques. UTQ 45:348, 1976.

Bonenfant, Joseph. LAQ 1976: 167-9.

Indicatif présent
Beausoleil, Claude. NBdJ 66:74-5, 1978.

L'octobre
Bourassa, André-G. "Justice et Beaulieu." Lettres qué 10:12-5, 1978.

Malenfant, Paul Chanel. LAQ 1977:160-4.

22

BEAULIEU, Michel

Oracle des ombres
Gaudet, Gérald. LAQ 1979:94-5.

Paysage
Lacroix, Pierre. LAQ 1971:151.

Nepveu, Pierre. "Le poeme inachevé." EF 11:55-65, 1975.

Pulsions
Demers, Jeanne. LAQ 1973:133-6.

Variables
Demers, Jeanne. LAQ 1973:133-6.

Nepveu, Pierre. "Le poeme inachevé." EF 11:55-65, 1975.

BEAUREGARD, Alphonse

General
Rivard, Raymond. "Alphonse Beauregard." Ottawa 1972:255-79.

BEAUREGARD, André

Changer la vie
Blais, Jacques. UTQ 44:342-3, 1975.

Miroirs électriques
Mailhot, Laurent. LAQ 1972:179.

BEAUSOLEIL, Claude

Ahuntsic dream
Bauer, Christian. LAQ 1975:121-2.

Avatars du trait
Carrière, André. LAQ 1974:118-20.

Les bracelets d'ombre
Bourque, Paul-André. LAQ 1973:115.

Dead line
Carrière, André. LAQ 1974:118-20.

Journal Mobile
Carrière, André. LAQ 1974:118-20.

Now
Bauer, Christian. LAQ 1975:121-2.

BEAUSOLEIL, Claude

    Sens interdit
      Giguère, Richard. "Trois tendances de la poésie québécoise." LAQ
      1976:114-6.

    La surface du paysage
      Corriveau, Hugues. LAQ 1979:95-7.

    Le temps maya
      Girous, Robert. LAQ 1977:181-2.

    "Hypothèses"
      "Mise au point (à propos de 'Hypothèses' de C.B.)." Dérives 8:15-7,
      1977.

BÉDARD, Nicole

    L'en deça
      Cotnoir, Louise. LAQ 1979:98-9.

BEDWELL, Bill

    Satan in sackcloth
      Bailey, Don. Quarry 20(3):51-2, 1971.

BÉGIN, Luc A.

    Depuis silence
      Engel, Christiane. LAQ 1977:166-7.

BEISSEL, Henry

    Face in the dark
      Cogswell, Fred. "Lensmen and madmen." CanL 50:96-8, 1971.

    The salt I taste
      Amprimoz, Alexandre. "The space of memory." CanL 80:72-4, 1979.

      Di Cicco, Pier Giorgio. "Gay in not so jocund company." BiC
      5(5):15-6, 1976.

BÉLANGER, Marcel

General
Bourassa, André-G. "'Leur lieu est une île d'or': des poètes Paul Chamberland et Marcel Bélanger." Lettres qué 12:11-4, 1978.

Fragments paniques
Demers, Jeanne. LAQ 1978:90-3.

Infranoir
Bourassa, André-G. "'Leur lieu est une île d'or': des poètes Paul Chamberland et Marcel Bélanger." Lettres qué 12:11-4, 1978.

Demers, Jeanne. LAQ 1978:90-3.

Migrations
Guévremont, Lise. LAQ 1979:101-2.

Plein-vent
Le Grande, Éva. LAQ 1971:171.

Saisons sauvages
Bonenfant, Joseph. LAQ 1976:146-8.

Bourassa, André-G. "D'après peinture: Bélanger, Leblanc, Marteau, Ouellette, Girardin et Lapointe." Lettres qué 6:10-3, 1977.

Drolet, Bruno. "Marcel Bélanger: les quatre-saisons." CC-R 5(3):65-71, 1977.

BÉLANGER, Yrénée

Dans les plaies

Dionne, René. "Sur les voies de notre poésie - II." Relations 368:56-9, 1972.

Fournier, Gérard-Claude. LAQ 1971:163-4.

Là derrière le corps
Gallays, François. LAQ 1972:175.

BELFORD, Ken

The post electric cave man
Barbour, Douglas. "Play in the Western World." CanL 52:77-81, 1972.

BELL, Wade

   The North Saskatchewan River book
      David, Jack. Fiddlehead 118:170, 1978.

BELLEFEUILLE, Normand de

   Voir/see De Bellefeuille, Normand

BELLEMARE, Gaston

   Bleu-source de terre
      Bélanger, Yrénée. LAQ 1971:172-3.

BENNETT, Thea

   Yesterday's unicorn
      Barr, Arlee. Alive 35:11, 1974.

      Dragland, Stan. ApF 2:r13, 1975.

BERGERON, Louis

   Fin d'end
      Benoît, Monique. "Parti Pris." LAQ 1975:128-31.

BERLAND, Jayne

   Landscapes of kin
      Allison, Diane. "Kitsch and kin." BiC 5(5):16, 1976.

      Farmiloe, Dorothy. Q&Q 42(7):41, 1976.

BERRY, D.

   Pocket pool
      Barbour, Douglas. "Poetry chronicle IV." DR 57:355-71, 1977.

      Gasparini, Len. "Chips, nuts, and wafers." BiC 5(3):18, 1976.

      Jewinsky, Ed. Q&Q 42(1):25, 1976.

      Novak, Barbara. Quarry 25(3):75-6, 1976.

      Smith, Patricia Keeney. "A variety of voices." CanL 78:91-4, 1978.

BERTRAND, Pierre

L'homme incendié
Fournier, Gérard-Claude. LAQ 1972:182.

BESSETTE, Gérard

General
Robidoux, Réjean. "Le cycle créateur de Gérard Bessette ou le fond c'est la forme." LAQ 1971:11-28.

Poemes temporels
Kushner, Eva. LAQ 1973:131-3.

BILLINGS, Robert

Blue negatives
Malcolm, Ian. Quarry 27(1):79-82, 1978.

BIRCHARD, Guy

Baby grand
Kleinzahler, August. "The world well limned." BiC 8(9):14, 1979.

BIRNEY, Earle

Bibliography
Noel-Bentley, Peter C. and Birney, Earle. "Earle Birney: A bibliography in progress, 1923-1969." WCR 5(2):45-53, 1970.

General
Aichinger, Peter. Earle Birney. Boston: Twayne, 1979. (Twayne's world author series; TWAS 538: Canada.)

Bayard, Caroline and David, Jack. "Earle Birney" Bayard 1978:107-29.

Davey, Frank. Earle Birney. Toronto: Copp Clark, 1971. (Studies in Canadian literature, II.)

Davey, Frank. "The explorer in western Canadian literature." SCL 4(2):91-100, 1979.

BIRNEY, Earle

General (cont'd.)
David, Jack. "Visual poetry in Canada: Birney, bissett and bp." SCL 2:252-66, 1977.

Gray, William. "Earle Birney's concrete architecture." CVII 2(2):45, 1976.

Gray, William N. Ironic survival in the poetry of Earle Birney. Victoria, B.C.: Univ. of Victoria, 1976. (M.A. thesis.)

Marshall, Earle. "The mountaineer: Earle Birney." Marshall 1979:61-6.

McLeod, Les. The stagehand's dream: irony and affirmation in the poetry of Earle Birney. Calgary: Univ. of Calgary, 1975 (M.A. thesis.)

Nesbitt, Bruce, ed. Earle Birney. Toronto: McGraw-Hill Ryerson, 1974. (Critical views on Canadian writers, 9.)

New, William H. "Maker of order, prisoner of dreams: the poetry of Earle Birney." New 1972:259-69.

New, William H. "Prisoner of dreams: the poetry of Earle Birney." CF 52(620);29-32, 1972.

Nichol, bp "Some notes on Earle Birney's 'solemn doodles'." ECW 9: 109-11, 1977.

Robillard, Richard H. Earle Birney. Toronto: McClelland and Stewart, 1971. (New Canadian library, Canadian writers, 9.)

Slonim, Leon. "Exoticism in modern Canadian poetry." ECW 1:21-6, 1974.

Walker, Susan. "Earle Birney recalls ten lost years." Q&Q 42(13):27, 1976.

Wilson, Milton. "Poet without a muse: Earle Birney." Woodcock 1974b:26-32. (Originally published CanL 30:14-20, 1966.)

Alphabeings & other seasyours
bissett, bill. Q&Q 43(5):42, 1977.

David, Jack. Fiddlehead 114:145-7, 1977.

Scobie, Stephen. "Words and reality." CF 57(676):42, 1977.

BIRNEY, Earle

The bear on the Delhi road
Hill, Hugh Creighton. Outposts 100:47, 1974.

Seargeant, Howard. "Poetry review." English 24:28-31, 1975.

The collected poems of Earle Birney
Barbour, Douglas. "Canadian poetry chronicle 2." DR 55:748-59, 1975-76.

Casto, Robert Clayton. Waves 3(3):10-4, 1975.

Cooperman, Stanley. QQ 82:649-51, 1975.

David, Jack. Q&Q 41(3):24, 1975.

Fletcher, Peggy. CA&B 51(1):28, 1975.

Jones, D.G. "Eternally invisible stranger." CF 55(657):51-3, 1975-6.

Levenson, Christopher. "Towards universality." CanL 66:99-101, 1975.

MacCulloch, Clare. "Earle Birney on the spit." BiC 4(4):3-4, 1975.

Noel-Bentley, Peter C. "Collected Birney." CVII 2(1):27-9, 1976.

Fall by fury & other makings
Barbour, Douglas. "Canadian poetry chronicle: VII." DR 59:154-75, 1979.

Charlton, Brian. "Climbing the tree." Brick 7:45-7, 1979.

Gasparini, Len. "Of imagination all compact." BiC 7(10):36-7, 1978.

Gatenby, Greg. "Poetry chronicle." TamR 77&78:77-94, 1979.

Linder, Norma West. "Starkness and sensibility." CA&B 54(3):28-9, 1979.

Nicoll, Sharon. Fiddlehead 123:108-9, 1979.

Pyke, Linda. "New works from three seasoned poets." Q&Q 44(13):8, 1978.

BIRNEY, Earle

Ghost in the wheels: selected poems
    Barbour, Douglas. "Canadian poetry chronicle: VI." DR 58:555-78, 1978.

    Ditsky, John. UWR 14(1):86-7, 1978.

    Fletcher, Peggy. "Poetic travelling: some true/some new." CA&B 53(3):40-1, 1978.

    Gibson, Kenneth. "A poetry chronicle." Waves 7(2):57-60, 1979.

    Mandel, Eli. "Three modernists in perspective." BiC 7(10):35-6, 1978.

    Solecki, Sam. "Birney and Newlove selected." Fiddlehead, 118:146-52, 1978.

    West, David S. "Old wine, broken bottles, cut glass." CanL 80:109-12, 1979.

    Woodcock, George. "Birney's makings." OntR 9:95-8, 1978-79.

Memory no servant
    Scott, Peter Dale. "A Canadian chronicle." Poetry 115:353-64, 1970.

Rag and bone shop
    Ballstadt, Carl. CF 51(606-7):36-7, 1971.

    Barbour, Douglas. DR 51:290, 1971.

    Boyce, Murray. OV 7(1):n.p., 1971.

    Cogswell, Fred. "Nearer the bone." CanL 49:96-8, 1971.

    Gowda, H.H. Anniah. "Rich stylistic range." LHY 13(2):243-4, 1972.

    Hornyansky, Michael. UTQ 40:380-1, 1971.

    Meredith, Ralph. Outposts 90:26, 1971.

    Tsubouchi, David. "Rag & bone shop." Waves 1(1):8-11, 1972.

    Wainwright, Andy. "Two hoary old poets." SatN 86(5):25-8, 1971.

BIRNEY, Earle

<u>The rugging and the moving times: poems new and uncollected 1976</u>
  Jewinski, Ed. Q&Q 42(17):28, 30, 1976.

  MacEwen, Gwendolyn. "Chaos is beaten again." BiC 5(10):28-9, 1976.

  Noel-Bentley, Peter C. "Birney half-burning." CVII 3(2):6-7, 1977.

  Weldon, J.F.G. Quarry 26(4):63-5, 1977.

<u>Selected poems</u>
  Smith, A.J.M. "Earl Birney: a unified personality." Smith
  1973:125-33. (Originally published CanL 30:4-13, 1966, under title "A
  unified personality: Birney's poems.")

<u>What's so big about green?</u>
  Bowering, George. "Suitcase poets." CanL 61:95-100, 1974.

  Cogswell, Fred. "What's so good about Birney?" LURev 7(1):153-5,
  1974.

  Evans, J.A.S. Q&Q 39(9):7, 1973.

  Lacey, Edward. "Canadian bards and South American reviewers." Nj
  4:82-120, 1974.

  MacCulloch, Clare. "The emperor's new clothes." Alive 34:3, 1974.

  MacCulloch, Clare. "New clothes for an emperor." Fiddlehead
  100:87-91, 1974.

  Noel-Bentley, Peter C. NL 1:59-65, 1974.

  Stevens, Peter. "The perils of majority." UWR 9(2):100-9, 1974.

  Sutherland, Fraser. "Birney's journey." BiC 2(4):4, 1973.

  Vizinczey, Stephen. Fiddlehead 102:137-8, 1974. (Letter to the
  Editor)

"Anglosaxon street"
  Jakes, Lynn. "Old English influences in Earle Birney's 'Anglosaxon
  Street' and 'Mappemounde.'" JCP 2(1):67-75, 1979.

"David"
  Birney, Earle. <u>The cow jumped over the moon: the writing and reading
  of poetry</u>. Toronto: Holt, Rinehart and Winston of Canada, 1972.

  MacLulich, T.D. "Earle Birney's 'David': a reconsideration." CVII
  2(3):24-7, 1976.

  Pollock, Zailig and Jones, Raymond E. "The transformed vision: Earle
  Birney's 'David'." ESC 3:223-30, 1977.

  Sutherland, John. "Earle Birney's 'David'." Sutherland 1972:93-6.

BIRNEY, Earle

"Mappemounde"
Jakes, Lynn. "Old English influences in Earle Birney's 'Anglosaxon Street' and 'Mappemounde.'" JCP 2(1):67-75, 1979.

BISSETT, bill

General
Bayard, Caroline and David, Jack. "bill bissett." Bayard 1978:51-76.

David, Jack. "Visual poetry in Canada: Birney, Bissett, and bp." SCL 2:252-66, 1977.

Early, Len. "bill bissett / poetics, politics & vision." ECW 5:4-24, 1976.

Early, Len. "Subversive diversions." ECW 3:52-4, 1975.

McCaffery, Steve. "Bill Bissett: a writing outside writing." Open letter 3d ser, 9:7-23, 1978.

Twigg, Alan. "Poetry's bad boy bill bissett." Q&Q 44(14):27, 1978.

Wachtel, Eleanor. "Why b.b. into C.C. won't go." BiC 8(6):3-6, 1979.

An allusyun to Macbeth
David, Jack. Q&Q 43(2):43, 1977.

Dragon fly
Lacey, Edward. "Canadian bards and South American reviewers." Nj 4:82-120, 1974.

Drifting into war
Gibbs, Robert. Fiddlehead 94:133-4, 1972.

Scobie, Stephen. "A dash for the border." CanL 56:89-92, 1973.

Starkman, Harvey. Q&Q 38(7):11, 1972.

Living with th vishyun
David, Jack. "The Vankouvr establishment suks swans in Stanly Park." Open letter 3d ser, 2:106-7, 1975.

BISSETT, bill

Medicine my mouth's on fire
Barbour, Douglas. Fiddlehead 105:121, 1975.

Barbour, Douglas. "The poets and presses revisited: circa 1974." DR 55:338-60, 1975.

Dault, Gary Michael. "Garnet and other glows." BiC 4(2):24-5, 1975.

David, Jack. Q&Q 40(11):21-2, 1974.

Doyle, Mike. "Animate imaginings." CanL 66:94-7, 1975.

Henderson, Brian. "Negative capabilities." ECW 2: 65-7, 1975.

Nobody owns th earth
Barbour, Douglas. QQ 79:570-1, 1972.

Davey, Frank. CF 52(618-9):44-5, 1972.

Garnet, Eldon. "Five poets on the brink of consciousness." SatN 87(6):38-42, 1972.

Gill, Elaine. New 18:46, 1972.

Nichol, bp. "Deep frieze." BiC 1(4):6, 1971.

Purdy, Al. "The woman of Barrie." CanL 54:86-90, 1972.

Ryan, Tom. WLWE 13(2):293-5, 1974.

Tanaszi, Marg. Quarry 21(3):57-61, 1972.

Wynand, Derk. MHRev 26:238-9, 1973.

Of th land divine spirit
Barbour, Douglas. "The young poets and the little presses, 1969." DR 50:112-26, 1970.

Pass th food release th spirit book
David, Jack. Q&Q 40(3):19, 1974.

Garnet, Eldon. Open letter 2d ser, 8:128, 1974.

Wynand, Derk. MHRev 31:167-8, 1974.

Plutonium missing
Hamilton, Jamie. Q&Q 43(5):43, 1977.

Pomes for Yoshi
Scobie, Stephen. "bissett's best." CanL 60:120-2, 1974.

BISSETT, bill

S th story I to: trew adventure
Doyle, Mike. Notes on concrete poetry. CanL 46:91-5, 1970.

Garnet, Eldon. "Five poets on the brink of consciousness." SatN 87(6):38-42, 1972.

Sailor
Barbour, Douglas. "Canadian poetry chronicle: VII." DR 59:154-75, 1979.

Gatenby, Greg. "Poetry chronicle." TamR 77&78:77-94, 1979.

Lecker, Robert. Q&Q 45(2):46, 1979.

Space Travel
Billings, Robert. Quarry 24(4):63-4, 1975.

Cathers, Ken. Waves 4(2):27-30, 1976.

Stardust
David, Jack. Q&Q 42(16): 8, 1976.

Gatenby, Greg. "Dots, stars and diapasons." BiC 5(12):28-9, 1976.

Sunday work (?)
Gervais, C.H. "The west coast seen." Quarry 19(4):57-9, 1970.

Th wind up tongue
Scobie, Stephen. "Words and reality." CF 57(676):42, 1977.

Yu can eat it at th opening
McCaffery, Steve. "Standing almost falling into." CVII 2(2):41, 1976.

BITTLE, David

Touch
Bessai, Diane. "Poetry from Ottawa." CF 55(652):36-8, 1975.

Leigh, Simon. "Two minor talons and a tidal borealis." Fiddlehead 108:120-4, 1976.

BLANCHET, Jacques

> Tête heureuse
> Thério, Adrien. LAQ 1971:164.

BLODGETT, E.D.

> Sounding
> Aubert, Rosemary. Q&Q 44(8):47, 1978.
>
> Barbour, Douglas. "Canadian poetry chronicle: VI." DR 58:555-78, 1978.
>
> Davis, Frances. "Innovation and indebtedness." CVII 4(2):45-6, 1979.
>
> Hatch, R.B. "Time's motion." CanL 81:129-32, 1979.
>
> McNally, Paul. Fiddlehead 121:155-6, 1979.

> Take away the names
> Barbour, Douglas. "The poets and presses revisited: circa 1974." DR 55:338-60, 1975.
>
> Davis, Frances. "Hermetic journies and reductions." CVII 3(1):4-5, 1977.
>
> Pivato, Joseph. "Prairie and poem." CanL 70:107-9, 1976.

BOISVERT, Yves

> Code d'oubli
> Corriveau, Hugues, LAQ 1978:94-6.

> Manifeste: Jet/Usage/Résidu
> Fisette, Jean. "Parutions récentes: de Desrochers aux Écrits des forges." V&I 3:497-500, 1978.
>
> Nepveu, Pierre. "La poésie qui se fait et celle qui ne se fait pas." Lettres qué 9:15-7, 1978.
>
> Roy, Max. LAQ 1977:130-2.

> Mourir épuisé
> Paradis, Suzanne. "Écrits des forges." LAQ 1975:125-6.

> Pour Miloiseau
> Émond, Maurice. LAQ 1974:144.

> Simulacre dictatoriel
> Haeck, Philippe. LAQ 1979:168-9.

BONENFANT, Yvon

L'oeil de sang
Bélanger, Yrénée. LAQ 1971:172-3.

Transes-mutations
Laflèche, Guy. LAQ 1973:117.

BORENSTEIN, Itzi

Ancient music
Barbour, Douglas. "Aural possibilities." ECW 16:147-52, 1979-80.

BORSA, Victor

A search for the wild
Hornyansky, Michael. UTQ 41:338-9, 1972.

BORSON, Roo

Landfall
Jenoff, Marvyne. "Seven books from two small presses." CVII
3(4)40-5, 1978.

BOSCO, Monique

Jéricho
Dionne, René. "Sur les voies de notre poésie - III." Relations
370:122-4, 1972.

Gallays, François. LAQ 1971:158.

Schabbat 70-77
Michaud, Ginette. LAQ 1978:96-7.

BOULERICE, Jacques

Elie Elie pourquoi
Dionne, René. "Où va notre poésie?" Relations 357:55-7, 1971.

Fournier, Gérard-Claude. "Trois poètes." LAQ 1970:147.

Marcotte, Gilles. EF 7:110-1, 1971.

BOURAOUI, Hédi

Eclat module
La Charité, Virginia A. FR 47:486-7, 1973.

Welch, Liliane. DR 55:689-90, 1972-73.

Tremblé
La Charité, Virginia A. FR 45:189-90, 1971.

Welch, Liliane. DR 50:416-7, 1970.

Vesuviade
Baciu-Simian, Mira. FR 51:132, 1977.

Cloutier, Cécile. Waves 6(1):76-7, 1977.

Welch, Liliane. AntigR 34:104-5, 1978.

Without boundaries. Sans frontières (Tr: Keith Harrison.)
Welch, Liliane. DR 59:368-70, 1979.

BOURNEUF, Roland

Passage de l'ombre
Lemaire, Michel. LAQ 1978:97-9.

BOWERING, George

General
Acorn, Milton. "Bowering: the laws of language? Or of empire?"
Blackfish 4-5, 1972-73.

Allard, Kerry. "Conversation: Jewish Layton Catholic Hood
Protestant Bowering." Open letter 2d ser. 5:30-9, 1973.

Bayard, Caroline and David, Jack. "George Bowering." Bayard
1978:77-106.

Bowering, George. Colombo 1971:10-9.

Brown, Allan. "Beyond the crenel - a view of Bowering." Brick
6:36-9, 1979.

"14 plums." CapR 15:86-107.

Sandler, Linda. "Romantic irony in art and life." Q&Q 42(8):26,
1976.

BOWERING, George

<u>Allophanes</u>
Barbour, Douglas. "Poetry chronicle V." DR 58:149-69, 1978.

Lincoln, Bob. Q&Q 43(6):43, 1977.

Oliver, Michael Brian. "Clever, curious, sometimes composed George."
Fiddlehead 116:158-64, 1978.

Whiteman, Bruce. "A seat on his language." ECW 9:83-8, 1977-78.

<u>Another mouth</u>
Abley, Mark. "Poetry that fell from the sky." Maclean's 93(41):54-8,
1979.

Coles, Don. "Deeper origins." CF 59(695):37, 1979-80.

Pearson, Ian. QQ 45(14):28, 1979.

<u>At war with the U.S.</u>
Barbour, Douglas. "The poets and presses revisited: circa 1974." DR
55:338-60, 1975.

Beardsley, Doug. "War and other measures." CVII 2(1):21, 1976.

Leigh, Simon. "Two minor talons and a tidal borealis." Fiddlehead
108:120-4, 1976.

<u>The catch</u>
Barbour, Douglas. "Poetry chronicle IV." DR 57:355-71, 1977.

Brown, Allan. "Beyond the crenel - a view of Bowering." Brick
6:36-9, 1979.

Gervais, Marty. Q&Q 43(1):31, 1977.

McKay, Don. "Two voices: Purdy and Bowering." UWR 13(1):99-104,
1977.

Oliver, Michael Brian. "Clever, curious, sometimes composed George."
Fiddlehead 116:158-64, 1978.

Peirce, J.C. DR 57:381-3, 1977.

Rosenblatt, Joe. "No Bowering toady he." BiC 5(10):29-30, 1976.

Wagner, Linda W. "The most contemporary of poetics." OntR 7:88-95,
1977-78.

Whiteman, Bruce. "A seat on his language." ECW 9:83-8, 1977-78.

38

BOWERING, George

The concrete island: Montreal poems 1967-71
Barbour, Douglas. "Canadian poetry chronicle: VI." DR 58:555-78, 1978.

Boland, Viga. Q&Q 43(10):38, 1977.

Davies, Gwendolyn. "Something's happening in Montreal." ECW 10:82-7, 1978.

McAuley, John. "Poems from the bottom drawer." CVII 3(1):22-3, 1977.

Oliver, Michael Brian. "Clever, curious, sometimes composed George." Fiddlehead 116:158-64, 1978.

Curious
Alpert, Barry. "Procedures." Open letter 2d ser. 9:99-101, 1974.

Barnes, Elizabeth A. Quarry 23(4):79, 1974.

Bradbury, Maureen. Q&Q 40(7):20, 1974.

Douglas, Charles. "Between the landscape & the scene." LURev 7(1):123-30, 1974.

Lacey, Edward. "Canadian bards and South American reviewers." Nj 4:82-120, 1974.

Langmaid, Bob. Alive 36:15, 1974.

Powell, D. Reid. Alive 36:15, 1974.

The gangs of Kosmos
Barbour, Douglas. "The young poets and the little presses, 1969." DR 50:112-26, 1970.

Gibbs, Robert. Fiddlehead 85:108-10, 1970.

Marshall, Tom. "Canpo: a chronicle." Quarry 19(4):50-4, 1970.

Purdy, Al. WascanaR 5(2):55-7, 1970.

Genève
Alpert, Barry. "Procedures." Open letter 2d ser. 9:99-101, 1974.

Bailey, Don. "A provincial look at ten volumes of Canadian poetry." QQ 79:242-54, 1972.

Davey, Frank. "A note on Bowering's Genève." Open letter 2d ser. 1:42-4, 1971-72.

Garnet, Eldon. "Two Bowerings embrace past, present, future." SatN 86(11):46-50, 1971.

Scobie, Stephen. "You gotta have heart." BiC 1(11):31-2, 1972.

BOWERING, George

George, Vancouver: a discovery poem
Davey, Frank. "The explorer in western Canadian literature." SCL 4(2):91-100, 1979.

Doyle, Mike. "Perhaps profound." CanL 58:108-9, 1973.

In the flesh
Bradbury, Maureen. Q&Q 40(7):20, 1974.

Douglas, Charles. "Between the landscape & the scene." LURev 7(1):123-30, 1974.

Ireland, G.W. QQ 82:300, 1975.

Lacey, Edward. "Canadian bards and South American reviewers." Nj 4:82-120, 1974.

Musgrave, Susan. MHRev 31:164-5, 1974.

Thompson, Eric. "Between two worlds." CanL 63:111-2, 1975.

Poem and other baseballs
Brown, Allan. "Beyond the crenel - a view of Bowering." Brick 6:36-9, 1979.

McKay, Don. "Two voices: Purdy and Bowering." UWR 13(1):99-104, 1977.

Pearson, Ian. Q&Q 43(1):31, 1977.

Touch: selected poems 1960-1970
Garnet, Eldon. "Two Bowerings embrace past, present, future." SatN 86(11):46-50, 1971.

Nugent, John L. Fiddlehead 92:109-10, 1972.

Purdy, Al. "The woman of Barrie." CanL 54:86-90, 1972.

Scobie, Stephen. "You gotta have heart." BiC 1(11):31-2, 1972.

BOWERING, Marilyn

The killing room
Billings, Robert. UWR 13(2):101-2, 1978.

Barbour, Douglas. "Canadian poetry chronicle: VI." DR 58:555-78, 1978.

Darling, Michael. "West coast seen." CanL 82:91-3, 1979.

Donnell, David. "Three newcomers." TamR 74:69-71, 1978.

Hosek, Chaviva. Fiddlehead 118:162-3, 1978.

Isaacs, Fran. Room of one's own. 3(4):44, 1978.

Levenson, Christopher. Quarry 27(4):81-2, 1978.

Pearson, Ian. Q&Q 43(16):10, 1977.

One who became lost
Barbour, Douglas. "Poetry chronicle IV." DR 57:355-71, 1977.

Darling, Michael. "West coast seen." CanL 82:91-3, 1979.

Lane, M. Travis. "'The hidden dreamer's cry:' natural force as point-of-view." Fiddlehead 112:156-60, 1977.

Pearson, Ian. Q&Q 42(15):38, 1976.

BOWMAN, Louise Morey

General
Arnason, David. "Canadian poetry: the interregnum." CVII 1(1):28-32, 1975.

Precosky, Donald. "Louise Morey Bowman." CanL 79:108-11, 1978.

Moonlight and common day
Arnason, David. "Canadian poetry: the interregnum." CVII 1(1):28-32, 1975.

BOXER, Avi

No address
Adams, Richard G. Fiddlehead 94:122-3, 1972.

Barbour, Douglas. QQ 80:141-2, 1973.

Mayne, Seymour. "Reflecting window pane." CanL 56:119-21, 1973.

BOYCE, Murray

Woodstock
    Barbour, Douglas G. ApF 2:r21-2, 1975.

    Billings, R. Quarry 24(1):77-8, 1975.

    Van Kuren, Susan. Alive 35:11, 1974. (Reprinted from the Windsor Star, June 8, 1974.)

BRAULT, Jacques

General
    Emont, Bernard. "Au royaume d'amour et de mort, situation d'un poète: Jacques Brault." LAQ 1970:280-92.

    Lemaire, Michel. "Jacques Brault dans le matin." V&I 2:173-94, 1976.

    Maugey, Axel. "Hommage à un poète du Québec: Jacques Brault." ActN 59:592-604, 1970.

L'en dessous l'admirable
    Blais, Jacques. UTQ 45:350-1, 1976.

    Bouvier, Luc. LAQ 1976:135-8.

    Poulin, Gabrielle. "Des mémoires d'outre-neiges." Relations 36(417):221-2, 1976.

    Vachon, G.-André. "Jacques Brault, à la recherche d'un lieu commun." EF 13:181-8, 1977.

    Weiss, Jonathan M. FR 52:508-9, 1979.

Mémoire
    Belleau, André. "Quelques remarques sur la poésie de Jacques Brault." Liberté 12(2):85-93, 1970.

    Mailhot, Laurent. "Against time and death: Mémoire by Jacques Brault." Ellipse 7:30-60, 1971. (Tr. Jean Vigneault and Roger Tremblay.)

    Mailhot, Laurence. "Contre le temps et la mort: Mémoire de Jacques Brault." VIP 3:124-44, 1970.

    Maugey, Axel. "Jacques Brault." Maugey 1972:209-20.

BRAULT, Jacques

Poèmes des quatres côtés
Amprimoz, Alexandre. "Four writers and today's Quebec." TamR 70:72-80, 1977.

Audet, Noel. V&I 1(1):131-4, 1975.

Blais, Jacques. UTQ 45:349, 1976.

Bourque, Paul-André. LAQ 1975:110-2.

Godbout, Jacques. "Au nom du peuple." Le maclean 15(8):8, 1975.

Lefrançois, Alexis. "'Accueillir le plus profond rêve du temps.'" Liberté 100:57-65, 1975.

Lefrançois, Alexis. "Entretien avec Jacques Brault." Liberté 100:66-72, 1975.

Ricard, François. "Livres de poésie." Liberté 100:100-11, 1975.

La poésie ce matin
Major, Jean-Louis. UTQ 41:348, 1972.

Marcotte, Giles. "La poésie - pour l'âme." EF 8:92-4, 1972.

Sanderson, Gertrude Kearns. AntigR 8:100-2, 1972.

Wyczynski, Paul. LAQ 1971:148-51.

BRENNER, David Norman

Ability to cope
Barnes, W.J. Quarry 23(3):78-9, 1974.

Lever, Bernice. "Seven nearly alive books." Alive 40:18, 1974.

McMullen, Robert. Alive 36:10, 1974.

Vrieze, Kevin R. Alive 36:10, 1974.

Positions and senses
Gervais, C.H. "Staying true." CanL 76:104-7, 1978.

BRETT, Brian

Fossil ground at Phantom Creek
Barbour, Douglas. "Poetry chronicle V." DR 58:149-69, 1978.

Bowering, Marilyn. "Stages of poetry." CanL 74:102-4, 1977.

Novak, Barbara. Quarry 25(4):75, 1976.

BREWSTER, Elizabeth

General
Pacey, Desmond. "The poetry of Elizabeth Brewster." Ariel
4(3):58-69, 1973.

In search of Eros
Beardsley, Doug. "A trial of immortality: recent Canadian poetry."
Nj 6:118-27, 1976.

Buri, S. "Catullus's new poems." CVII 1(2):6-9, 1975.

Downes, G.V. MHRev 39:135-6, 1976.

Gibbs, Robert. "These abiding questions." CanL 72:83-4, 1977.

Hornyansky, Michael. UTQ 45:339, 1976.

Long, Tanya. Q&Q 41(1):26, 1975.

Marshall, Tom. "Five poets from five countries." OntR 2:86-94, 1975.

McGaughey, G.S. "Problems for poets: publishing poetry." CF
55(650):63, 1975.

Merrett, Robert James. QQ 83:165-6, 1976.

Milner, Phil. AntigR 27:90-1, 1976.

Monk, Patricia. Quarry 24(4): 61, 1975.

Ravel, Aviva. 105:116-8, 1975.

Wyatt, Louise. Brick 1:16-9, 1977.

BREWSTER, Elizabeth

Passage of summer

Brewster, Elizabeth. "Chronology of summer." HAB 21(i):34-9, 1970.

Gibbs, Robert. "Next time from a different country." CanL 62:17-32, 1974.

Harcourt, Joan. Quarry 13(2):63, 1970.

Hornyansky, Michael. UTQ 39:334, 1970.

Marshall, Tom. QQ 77:294-5, 1970.

Oates, Joyce Carol. "Three poets." FPt 4:77-81, 1970.

Sometimes I think of moving

Barbour, Douglas. "Poetry chronicle V." DR 58:149-69, 1978.

Cogswell, Fred. Fiddlehead 115:142-5, 1977.

Gibbs, Robert. "Necessary fictions: the poems and stories of Elizabeth Brewster." ECW 10:122-5, 1978.

Greene, Elizabeth. Quarry 27(1):82-4, 1978.

McNamara, Eugene. "Ghetto long little dogie." BiC 6(8):16-7, 1977.

Woods, Elizabeth. Q&Q 43(9):8, 1977.

Sunrise north

Bartlett, Brian. Fiddlehead 95:118-22, 1972.

Henry, Kathleen. CA&B 48(2):24, 1972.

Johnston, George. Quarry 21(3):55-7, 1972.

Solecki, Sam. QQ 80:312, 1973.

BRIEN, Roger

General

Blais, Jacques. "Grandiloquence de Roger Brien." Blais 1975:232-3.

Roschini, Gabrièle M. "Roger Brien, chantre de la foi." VieFr 27:33-7, 1972. (Tr. of an article in L'osservatore romano, March, 1972.)

BRINGHURST, Robert

Bergschrund
Barbour, Douglas. "Canadian poetry chronicle: VI." DR 58:555-78, 1978.

Biguenet, John. "Stones are to silence as darkness is to light." WCR 11(2):39, 1976.

Hornyansky, Michael. UTQ 45:340, 1976.

Lecker, Robert. Q&Q 42(5):46, 1976.

Smith, Raymond J. "Poetry chronicle." OntR 4:104-10, 1976.

BROCKWAY, Robert W.

A thin book of verse
Chope, Gordon. "Three humanist poets." HiC 10(4):31, 1977.

BROMIGE, David

Birds of the west
Alpert, Barry. "Procedures." Open letter 2d ser, 9:99-101, 1974.

Barbour, Douglas. "The poets and presses revisited: circa 1974." DR 55:338-60, 1975.

The ends of the earth
Dobyns, Stephen. "Five poets." Poetry 117:392-8, 1971.

Ten years in the making: selected poems, songs, & stories, 1961-1970
Alpert, Barry. "Procedures." Open letter 2d ser, 9:99-101, 1974.

Threads
Barbour, Douglas. QQ 79:570, 1972.

Coleman, Victor. Open letter 2d ser, 2:81-2, 1972.

Dragland, Stan. "Ties and threads." CanL 62:118-21, 1974.

BROSSARD, Nicole

General

Bayard, Caroline et David, Jack. "De Toronto Caroline Bayard et Jack David sont venus rencontrer Nicole Brossard." Lettres que 4:34-7, 1976.

Bayard, Caroline and David, Jack. "Nicole Brossard." Bayard 1978:57-91.

Bayard, Caroline. "Subversion is the order of the day." ECW 7/8:17-25, 1977.

Beausoleil, Claude et Roy, André. "Entretien avec Nicole Brossard." Hobo-Québec 14/15:12-21, 1974.

Kravetz, Marc. "Nicole Brossard: une revue, des livres, un journal." MLit 134:98-9, 1978.

Michon, Jacques. "Surréalisme et modernité." EF 11:121-9, 1975.

Moisan, Clément. "Écriture et errance dans les poésies de Gwendolyn MacEwen et Nicole Brossard." CRCL 2:72-92, 1975.

Moisan, Clément. "La 'nouvelle culture,' la contre-culture ou the brilliant minority." Moisan 1979: 219-68.

Rancourt, Jacques. "Vers une neutralisation du langage: Nicole Brossard." Brindeau 1973:608-9.

Van Schendel, Michel et Fisette, Jean. "Un livre à venir - rencontre avec Nicole Brossard." V&I 3:3-18, 1977.

L'amer ou le chapitre effrité
Giguère, Richard. UTQ 47:359-60, 1978.

A book
Morritt, Hope. CA&B 52(1):26, 1976.

Le centre blanc
Gallays, François. LAQ 1970:135-7.

Marcotte, Gilles. EF 7:107-10, 1971.

Le centre blanc: poèmes 1965 - 1975.
Bayard, Caroline. "Nicole Brossard: la theorie et la pratique." Lettres qué 13:19-22, 1979.

Bourassa, Andre-G. et Giroux, Robert. LAQ 1978:99-106.

Giguère, Richard. UTQ 48:355-7, 1979.

Hébert, François. "L'ombilic d'une nymphe." Liberté 121:124-7, 1979.

BROSSARD, Nicole

Extrait/fragment
Charron, François. "Nicole devant son miroir en papier."
Presqu'amérique 1(8):34-5, 1972.

Masculin grammaticale
Moisan, Clément. LAQ 1974:122-5.

Mécanique jongleuse
Laliberté, Yves. "Deux recueils de poèmes où supprimer l'excentricité
s'est s'abstenir: Nicole Brossard." Inc n.s. 2-3(1):77-97, 1979.

Moisan, Clément. LAQ 1974:122-5.

La partie pour le tout
Laliberté, Yves. "Deux recueils de poèmes où supprimer l'excentricité
s'est s'abstenir: Nicole Brossard." Inc 2-3(1):77-97, 1979.

Moison, Clément. LAQ 1975: 115-8.

Suite logique
Dionne, René. "Où va notre poésie?" Relations 357:55-7, 1971.

Gallays, François. LAQ 1970: 135-7.

BROUDY, Hart

A book of A
McCaffrey, Steve. "Language in space." CVII 2(3):28-9, 1976.

BROWN, Jim

Forgetting
Gervais, C.H. "The west coast seen. Quarry 19(4):57-9, 1970.

Northern light
Barbour, Douglas. "Canadian poetry chronicle: VII." DR 59:154-75,
1979.

Darling, Michael. "West coast seen." CanL 82:91-3, 1979.

Towards a chemistry of reel people
Barbour, Douglas. "Play in the western world." CanL 52:77-81, 1972.

Davey, Frank. CF 52(618-9):45, 1972.

BROWN, Paul Cameron

Eyeshine
Brown, Allan. Quarry 28(4):81-4, 1979.

Fletcher, Peggy. "Good things come in small packages." CA&B
54(3):31-2, 1979.

Whispers
Heckman, Grant. Quarry 27(3):79-80, 1978.

Toth, Nancy. "Organized decays." CVII 4(3):38-41,43, 1979.

BROWNLOW, Edward Burrough

General
Whitridge, Margaret Coulby. "A tribute to Edward Brownlow: Sarepta
and the fatal fascination of the sonnet." JCP 1(1):26-36, 1978.

BROWNSTEIN, William

Live at the Apollo
Powell, D. Reid. Q&Q 42(1):26, 1976.

BRUCE, Charles

The Mulgrave road
Davis, Richard C. "Tradition and the individual talent of Charles
Bruce." DR 59:443-51, 1979.

BRUNET, Yves-Gabriel

Poésies I
Kushner, Eva. LAQ 1973: 92.

BRUSSIÈRES, Arthur de

General
Condemine, Odette. "Arthur de Brussières, cet inconnu." Ottawa 1972:
110-30.

BUCKAWAY, Catherine Margaret

Catherine M. Buckaway: a collection of prairie haiku (Air,17)
Billings, R.   Quarry 23(2):72-4, 1974.

Lacey, Edward.   "Canadian bards and South American reviewers."   Nj
4:82-120, 1974.

The silver cuckoo; poems in Japanese verse forms: Haiku, Tanka
Hamilton, Jamie.   Q&Q 41(8):32, 1975.

Herringer, Barbara.   CVII 2(1):13, 1976.

Strangely the birds have come

Wilson, Betty.   CA&B 49(1):24, 1973.

BUGNET, Georges

General
Duciaume, Jean-Marcel.   "Présentation."   Bugnet 1978:7-23.

Poèmes
"À retenir pour vos lectures."   Lettres qué 13:73, 1979.

BULLOCK, Michael

Black wings white dead
Amprimoz, Alexandre L.   Quarry 27(3):74-8, 1978.

Stevenson, Warren.   "Move over Musgrave."   CanL 80:103-4, 1979.

Varney, Edwin.   WCR 13(1):26-7, 1978.

Green beginning black ending
Sutherland, Frazer.   "Foreign fabulous free."   BiC 1(10):19-21, 1972.

A savage darkness
Ditsky, John.   CF 50:406, 1971.

Sutherland, Frazer.   "Foreign fabulous free."   BiC 1(10):19-21, 1972.

World without beginning amen
Green, Paul.   NL 2:53-5, 1975.

Lillard, Charles.   WCR 10(1):55-7, 1975.

50

CABIAC, Pierre

Symphonie laurentienne
  VieFr 26:270, 1972.

CALLAGHAN, Barry

The Hogg poems and drawings
  Barbour, Douglas. "Canadian poetry chronicle: VII." DR 59:154-75,
  1979.

  Beckmann, Susan. "Hogg in the holy land." CVII 4(2):53-5, 1979.

  Daniel, Lorne. Q&Q 44(8):46-7, 1978.

  Ellenwood, Ray. "Some notes on Callaghan's Hogg poems and drawings."
  Brick 7:24-6, 1979.

  Elson, Brigid. QQ 85:708-9, 1978.

  Fletcher, Peggy. "The printed page their classroom." CA&B
  53(4):42-3, 1978.

  Gibson, Kenneth. "A poetry chronicle." Waves 7(2):57-60, 1979.

  MacSween, R.J. AntigR 33:95-6, 1978.

  Novak, Barbara. "Poetry chronicle." TamR 75:88-95, 1978.

CAMERON, George Frederick

Lyrics on freedom, love and death
  Ower, John. "Freedom, love and death in the poetry of George
  Frederick Cameron." JCP 1(2):5-26, 1978.

CAMPBELL, William Wilfred

Bibliography
  Wicken, George. "William Wilfred Campbell (1858-1918): an annotated
  bibliography. ECW 9:37-47, 1977-78.

General
  Klinck, Carl F. Wilfred Campbell: a study in late provincial
  Victorianism. Ottawa: Tecumseh Press, 1977. (Reprint of earlier ed.
  Toronto: Ryerson, 1942.)

  Whalen, Terry. "Wilfred Campbell: the poetry of celebration and
  harmony." JCP 1(2):27-41, 1978.

CAMPBELL, William Wilfred

    <u>Vapour and blue: Souster selects Campbell</u>
      Dempster, Barry. Q&Q 45(7):39, 1979.

      Whalen, Terry. "Too genteel" DR 59:176-9, 1979.

    "Pan the fallen"
      Bentley, D.M.R. "Pan and the Confederation poets." CanL 81:59-71, 1979.

CAMPION, Constance.

    <u>Poetic melange</u>
      Fletcher, Peggy. "Poetic travelling: some true/some new." CA&B 53(3):40-1, 1978.

CAMPO, Mario

    <u>L'anovulatoire</u>
      Monette, Pierre. "D'une pierre trois coups: <u>La nouvelle barre du jour</u> édite." Lettres qué 13:25-7, 1979.

    <u>Como laudanum</u>
      Corriveau, Hugues. LAQ 1979:102-3.

CANDELARIA, Fred

    <u>Liturgies</u>
      Barbour, Douglas. "Canadian poetry chronicle: VI." DR 58:555-78, 1978.

      Cogswell, Fred. Fiddlehead 110:130-1, 1976.

      Lillard, Charles. MHRev 40:138-42, 1976.

      McFadgen, Lynn. Q&Q 42(5):46, 1976.

      Reed, John R. "Narrative as poetic structure." OntR 5:84-92, 1976-77.

      Wilson, Jean. "Life and claustrophobia." CanL 75:88-90, 1976.

    <u>Passages</u>
      Cogswell, Fred. Fiddlehead 108:118-9, 1976.

CARLSON, Chuck

Scientific works, etc. an omnibus of dwgs, fictions, poems and found
  images
  Enemark, Brett. Open letter 2d ser, 5:109, 1973.

CARMAN, Bliss

General
  Eggleston, Wilfred. "Bliss Carman in the twenties." JCP 1(2):59-68,
  1978.

  Gibbs, Robert. "Voice and persona in Carman and Roberts." MacKinnon
  1977: 56-67.

  Gundy, H. Pearson. "Flourishes and cadences: letters of Bliss Carman
  and Louise Imogen Guiney." DR 55:211-26, 1975.

  Marshall, Tom. "Mountaineers and swimmers." CanL 72:21-8, 1977.

  Marshall, Tom. "Mountaineers and swimmers: Roberts and Carman
  revisited." Marshall 1979:9-16.

  Rogers, A. Robert. "American recognition of Bliss Carman and Sir
  Charles G.D. Roberts." HAB 22,(2):19-25, 1971.

  Sorfleet, John Robert. "Transcendentalist, mystic, evolutionary
  idealist: Bliss Carman, 1886-1894." Woodcock 1974: 189-210.

  Stephens, Donald. "Carman and tradition." Woodcock 1974:178-88.
  (Originally published CanL 9:38-48, 1961, under the title "A maritime
  myth.")

The pipes of Pan
  Bentley, D.M.R. "Pan and the Confederation poets." CanL 81:59-71,
  1979.

"Low tide on Grand Pré"
  Nause, John. "'Low tide on the Grand Pré': an explication." CVII
  3(2):30-2, 1977.

CARMICHAEL, M.

Oyster wine
  Barbour, Douglas. "Canadian poetry chronicle: VII." DR 59:154-75,
  1979.

CARSON, E.J.

Scenes: a book of poems
Barbour, Douglas. "Canadian poetry chronicle: VII." DR 59:154-75, 1979.

DiCicco, Pier Giorgio. "No man is an island, true, but can there be a circean catch to regionalism." BiC 8(1):21-2, 1979.

Fletcher, Peggy. "Humour and sadness." CA&B 54(1):36-7, 1978.

CARTIER, Georges

Chanteaux: poèmes 1954-1974
Bourassa, André-G. "Chanteaux ou les ravages de Cartier." Lettres qué 2:9-11, 1976.

Demers, Jeanne. LAQ 1976: 165-7.

Dionne, René. UTQ 46:378-9, 1977.

Poulin, Gabrielle. "Mourir en poésie." Relations 37(429);254-5, 1977.

CASSIDY, Carol Coates

General
New, William H. "Carol Coates Cassidy and the form dispute." CanL 48:51-60, 1971. Also published New 1972: 20-31.

CATANOY, Nicholas

The fiddlehead republic
Clever, Christine. JCP 2(1):101, 1979.

Fletcher, Peggy. "Vehicles of expression." CA&B 55(1):24, 1979.

Hic et nunc
Baciu, Mira. FR 45:193, 1971.

Yates, J. Michael. WascanaR 5(1):97-8, 1970.

CATHERS, Ken

Images on water
   Barbour, Douglas. "Canadian poetry chronicle: VI." DR 58:555-78, 1978.

   Purdy, Al. "A flooding past." CanL 76:126-7, 1978.

CHALMERS, Penny

   Voir/see KEMP, Penny.

CHAMBERLAND, Paul

General
   Bayard, Caroline and David, Jack. "Paul Chamberland." Bayard 1978: 93-125.

   Bayard, Caroline et David, Jack. "Paul Chamberland: la poésie, le vécu: recherche et expérimentation." V&I 2:155-72, 1976.

   Bélanger, Marcel. "Paul Chamberland: de l'anarchie à l'utopie." Estuaire 13:95-100, 1979.

   Bouchard, Jacques. "Paul Chamberland: inexlicablement restait la poésie." ELit 5:429-46, 1972.

   Bouchard, Jacques. La poésie comme volunté et comme représentation dans l'oeuvre poétique de Paul Chamberland. Quebec: Univ. Laval, 1972. (M.A. thesis.)

   Giguère, Richard. "D'un 'équilibre impondérable' a une 'violence élementaire': Évolution thématique de la poésie québécoise 1935-1965: Saint-Denys Garneau, Anne Hébert, Roland Giguère et Paul Chamberland." VIP 7:51-90, 1973.

   Giguère, Richard. "Love revolution." Ellipse 8/9:66-78, 1971. (Tr. Kathy Mezei.)

   Moisan, Clément. "Poésie de la libération." Moisan 1979: 167-218.

L'afficheur hurle
   Fabi, Thérèse. "Paul Chamberland: le Québécois hurlant." ActN 64:597-609, 1975.

CHAMBERLAND, Paul

Demain les dieux naîtront
Bourassa, André-G. "Un Perreault ancien et un Chamberland nouveau." Lettres qué 1:10-2, 1976.

Brochu, André. LAQ 1975: 100-101.

Godbout, Jacques. "La poésie les larmes aux yeux." Le maclean 15(6):10, 1975.

Ricard, François. "Livres de poésie." Liberté 100:100-11, 1975.

Éclats de la pierre noire d'où rejaillit ma vie
Bonenfant, Joseph. LAQ 1972: 152-4.

Bouchard, Jacques. "Paul Chamberland: inexplicablement restait la poésie." ELit 5:429-46, 1972.

Marcotte, Gilles. EF 9:83-4, 1973.

Extrême survivance extrême poésie
Bourassa, André-G. "Leur lieu est une île d'or. Des poètes Paul Chamberland et Marcel Bélanger." Lettres qué 12:11-4, 1978.

Fisette, Jean. "Sur le front de la poésie: des positions se délimitent." V&I 4:150-2, 1978.

Giguère, Richard. UTQ 48:358-9, 1979.

Roy, Max. LAQ 1978: 106-9.

Le prince de sexamour
Bourassa, André-G. "L'Hexagone au quart de tour." Lettres qué 9:11-4, 1978.

Hébert, François. "Robert Marteau, Guy Lafond, Jean-Marc Fréchette (et Paul Chamberland?)" Liberté 110:70-6, 1977.

Roy, Max. LAQ 1976: 148-51.

Terre-Québec
Maugey, Axel. "Paul Chamberland." Maugey 1972: 200-8.

CHAPMAN, Evangeline

Poems for people over 25
Linder, Norma West. "Crafted with care: more or less." CA&B 53(3):42, 1978.

CHARLEBOIS, Jean

  Conduite intérieure
    Nepveu, Pierre. "Robert Mélançon, Gilles Cyr, Jean Charlebois,
    Jean-Yves Théberge." Lettres qué 14:22-5, 1979.

  Hanches neige
    Giguère, Richard. UTQ 47:362-3, 1978.

    Giguère, Richard. LAQ 1977: 139-42.

  Tendresses
    Arcand, Pierre-André. LAQ 1975: 122-4.

    Blais, Jacques. UTQ 45:349, 1976.

  Tête de bouc
    Bourque, Paul-André. LAQ 1973: 113-5.

CHARLES, Barry

  You used to like my pies
    Garnet, Eldon. "For the poets, the landscape is the great Canadian
    myth." SatN 85(2):31-3, 1970.

CHARRON, François

  General
    Haeck, Phillipe et Straram le Bison ravi, Patrick. "Entretien:
    l'écriture change." Chroniques 1(3):8-26, 1975.

  Blessures
    Giguère, Richard. LAQ 1979:104-5.

  Du commencement à la fin
    Giroux, Robert. LAQ 1977: 137-9.

    Nepveu, Pierre. "Les herbes rouges...jusqu'à François Charron."
    Lettres qué 11:38-40, 1978.

  Feu
    Beaudet, André. LAQ 1978: 109-11.

  Interventions politiques
    Bouvier, Luc. LAQ 1975: 112-4.

  Littérature/obscénités
    Demers, Jeanne. LAQ 1974: 120-1.

CHARRON, François

   Persister et se maintenir dans les vertiges de la terre qui demeurent
   sans fin
      Demers, Jeanne. LAQ 1974: 120-1.

      Haeck, Philippe. "La poésie en 1974." Chroniques 1(3):42-5, 1975.

      Nepveu, Pierre. "Les herbes rouges...jusqu'à François Charron."
      Lettres qué 11:38-40, 1978.

   Pirouette par hasard poésie
      Bouvier, Luc. LAQ 1975: 112-4.

   Propagande
      Giroux, Robert. LAQ 137-9, 1977.

      Renaud, Jacques. "Propagande de François Charron: un ton dionysiaque,
      une intuition héraclitéene et un vieux manteau manichéen." Lettres
      qué 9:36, 1978.

CHÂTILLON, Pierre

   La mangeur de neige
      Blais, Jacques. UTQ 43:366-7, 1974.

      Giroux, Robert. LAQ 1973: 107-8.

CHIASSON, Herménégilde

   General
      Arcand, Pierre-André. "Imposer la sensation." RUM 8(2):129-37,
      1975. (Interview.)

   Mourir à Scoudouc
      Arcand, Pierre-André. "Poets from the end of the earth." Ellipse
      16:76-82, 1974. (Tr. Barbara Kuritzky.)

      Godbout, Jacques. "La poésie des larmes aux yeux." Le maclean
      15(6):10, 1975.

      Masson, Alain. "Chutes." RUM 8(2):139-49, 1975.

      Nepveu, Pierre. LAQ 1974: 139-40.

   Rapport sur l'état de mes illusions
      Nepveu, Pierre. LAQ 1977: 151-2.

CHILD, Philip

    General
      Muldowney, James S. <u>The poetry of Philip Child</u>. Halifax: Dalhousie
    Univ., 1973. (M.A. thesis.)

CHOLETTE, Marie

    <u>Lis-moi comme tu m'aimes</u>
      Pontbriand, Jean-Noel. "Poètes québécois publiés en France." LAQ
    1975:134-7.

CHOPIN, René

    General
      Deguire, René. "René Chopin." Académie 14:91-7, 1972.

CHRISTENSEN, Peter

    <u>Hail storm</u>
      Flick, Jane. "Prairie images." CanL 80:105-6, 108-9, 1979.

      Jenoff, Marvyne. "Seven books from two small presses." CVII
    3(4):40-5, 1978.

      Lemm, Richard. Quarry 28(2):81-2, 1979.

CHRISTY, Jim

    <u>Palatine cat</u>
      Daniel, Lorne. Q&Q 45(2):46, 1979.

CIVIL, Jean

    <u>Entre deux pays</u>
      Bélanger, Christian. LAQ 1979:107-8.

CLAIROUX, Jacques

    <u>Coeur de Hotdog</u>
      Duclos, Jocelyn-Robert. LAQ 1973: 108-9.

CLEVER, Glenn

Count down
Dailey, Ross. "Four from Borealis." CanR 1(4):26-7, 1974.

Leigh, Simon. "Two minor talons and a tidal borealis: Part II."
Fiddlehead 109:128-32, 1976.

CLIFFORD, Wayne

Glass passages
Barbour, Douglas. "Poetry chronicle: IV." DR 57:355-71, 1977.

Coates, Brian. Brick 2:60-1, 1978.

Di Cicco, Pier Giorgio. "One up, two down." BiC 5(9):33, 1976.

Lecker, Robert A. Q&Q 42(10):44, 1976.

Marshall, Tom. "The mythmakers." CanL 73:100-3, 1977.

O'Donoghue, Gregory. Quarry, 26(1)66-7, 1977.

Stuewe, Paul. QQ 84:334-5, 1977.

CLINTON, Eddie

Spoke
Barbour, Douglas. Q&Q 39(3):8, 1973.

CLOUTIER, Cécile.

Cablogrammes
Fournier, Gérard-Claude. LAQ 1972: 165.

Cannelles et craies
Blandford, Bianca Zagolin. LAQ 1970: 130-1.

Dionne, René. "Où va notre poésie?" Relations 357:55-7, 1971.

Chaleuils
Benoît, Monique. LAQ 1979:108-9.

Paupières
Blandford, Bianca Zagolin. LAQ 1971: 166-7.

60

COCKBURN, Robert

Friday night, Fredericton
Lane, Patrick. New 12:39-40, 1970.

CODERRE, Émile

Voir/see NARRACHE, Jean

COGSWELL, Fred

Against perspective
Amprimoz, Alexandre L. Quarry 27(3):74-8, 1978.

Oliver, Michael Brian. "Tantramar--and Saint John and Fredericton--revisited." Fiddlehead 122:115-24, 1979.

Pearson, Ian. Q&Q 44(6):39, 1978.

Stevenson, Warren. "Move over Musgrave." CanL 80:103-4, 1979.

The chains of Lilliput
Gustafson, Ralph. "Circumventing dragons." CanL 55:105-8, 1973.

Prouty, William. Fiddlehead 94:116-7, 1972.

Immortal plowman
Ditsky, John. CF 49:270-1, 1970.

Light bird of life: selected poems
Stevens, Peter. "Honesty and anarchy." CanL 65:98-101, 1975.

COHEN, Leonard

General
  Amiel, Barbara. "Leonard Cohen says that to all the girls."
  Maclean's 91(19):55-8, 1978.

  Bem, Jeanne. "Avec Leonard Cohen: magic is alive." LanM 65:110-7,
  1971.

  Djwa, Sandra. "Leonard Cohen: black romantic." Woodcock
  1974b:1979-90. Originally published CanL 34:32-42, 1967.)

  Djwa, Sandra. "Leonard Cohen, romantique noir." Ellipse 2:70-82,
  1970. (Tr. Jacques Baron-Rousseau.)

  Elson, Nicholas. Love in the writings of Leonard Cohen. Fredericton:
  Univ. of New Brunswick, 1969 c1970. (M.A. thesis.)

  Gnarowski, Michael, ed. Leonard Cohen: the artist and his critics.
  Toronto: McGraw-Hill Ryerson, 1976. (Critical views on Canadian
  writers.)

  Grant, Judith Skelton. "Leonard Cohen's poems--songs." SCL 2:102-7,
  1977.

  Jantzen, Dorothy Helen. The poetry of Leonard Cohen: "His perfect
  body." Downsview, Ontario: York Univ., 1971. (M.A. thesis.)

  Johnson, Lewis David. Bird on the wire: the theme of freedom in the
  works of Leonard Cohen. Halifax: Dalhousie Univ., 1974 c1975. (M.A.
  thesis.)

  Marshall, Tom. "A history of us all: Leonard Cohen." Marshall 1979:
  135-43.

  Lavigne, Yves. "Leonard Cohen: at the mercy of time." CanR
  2(2):36-7, 1975.

  Ondaatje, Michael. Leonard Cohen. Toronto: McClelland and Stewart,
  1970. (Canadian writers, 5.)

  Saltzman, Paul. "Famous last words from Leonard Cohen: the poet's
  final interview, he hopes." Maclean's 85(6):6, 77-80, 1972.

  Scobie, Stephen. Leonard Cohen. Vancouver: Douglas & McIntyre,
  1978. (Studies in Canadian literature.)

  Vassal, Jacques. Leonard Cohen. Paris: A. Michel, c1974. (Rock &
  folk.)

  Wainwright, J.A. "Leonard Cohen: the master's voice." DR 58:773-8,
  1978-79.

COHEN, Leonard

General (cont'd.)
Wetherell, Nancy B. "Leonard Cohen: poems set to music." EJ 62:551-5, 1973.

Death of a ladies' man (phono record)
Waxman, Ken. "Rebirth of a ladies' man." SatN 93(1):61-4, 1978.

Death of a lady's man
Ajzenstat, Sam. "The ploy's the thing." BiC 7(8):10-1, 1978.

David, Jack. UWR 14(2):100-3, 1979.

Fletcher, Peggy. "Dialogues and other voices." CA&B 54(2):36-7, 1979.

Gatenby, Greg. "Poetry chronicle." TamR 77&78:77-94, 1979.

Mandel, Eli. "Leonard Cohen's brilliant con game." SatN 93(9):51-3, 1978.

Marshall, Tom. "Self-indulgent Cohen." CF 58(686):33-4, 1979.

Martin, Sandra. "Don't be impatient: Leonard Cohen will let you see his new poems. Eventually." SatN 92(9):30-5, 1977.

McNally, Paul. QQ 86:343-5, 1979.

Oliver, Michael Brian. "Not much nourished by modern love." Fiddlehead 121:143-6, 1979.

Scobie, Stephen. Quarry 28(2):73-6, 1979.

Wainwright, J.A. "Leonard Cohen: the master's voice." DR 58:773-8, 1978-79.

The emperor has no clothes (phono record)
Baker Dean. ApF 2:r21, 1975.

The energy of slaves
Almon, Bert. New 20:59, 1973.

"Along the fingertip trail." TLS 3696:10, 1973.

Bagchee, Shyamal. Q&Q 38(12):8, 1972.

Estok, Michael. "All in the family: the metaphysics of domesticity." DR 52:653-67, 1973.

Healey, James. PrS 47:185, 1973.

Johnson, Rick. Quarry 22(2):66-8, 1973.

Lehman, David. "Politics." Poetry 123:173-80, 1973.

Levenson, Christopher. QQ 80:470-1, 1973.

COHEN, Leonard

The energy of slaves (cont'd.)
Mandel, Eli. "Cohen's life as a slave." Mandel 1977: 124-36.

Morley, Patricia. "Solitary adventure, or shared pain." LURev 6:262-5, 1973.

Rockett, W.H. "Leonard Cohen and the killer instinct." SatN 87(12)52-6, 1972.

Scobie, Stephen. HAB 24:240-3, 1973.

Smith, Beverley. "By self possessed." BiC 1(12):52-3, 1972.

Wayman, Tom. "Cohen's women." CanL 60:89-93, 1974.

The spice-box of earth
Dudek, Louis. "Three major Canadian poets - three major forms of archaism." Dudek 1978:153-6. (Originally published Delta 16:23-5, 1961.

COHEN, Matt

Peach Melba
Baxter, Marilyn. Quarry 24(3)75-7, 1975.

Ringrose, Christopher. "Assorted catch." CanL 71:102-4, 1976.

Sandler, Linda. QQ 83:168, 1976.

COLEMAN, Victor

General
"Interview/Victor Coleman." CapR 5:66-88, 1974.

Tallman, Warren. "In limbo: Victor Coleman as political poet. A quick note on his January 28, 1974 Vancouver reading at The Western Front." CapR 5:63-5, 1974.

America
Barbour, Douglas. "Hopes & trepidations." CanL 59:117-9, 1974.

Garnet, Eldon. "Five poets on the brink of consciousness." SatN 87(6):38-42, 1972.

COLEMAN, Victor

Light verse
Ditsky, John. CF 50:190-1970.

Sullivan, D.H. WCR 5(2):71-2, 1970.

Old friend's ghosts
Doyle, Mike. "Perhaps profound." CanL 58:108-9, 1973.

Parking Lots
Barbour, Douglas. "Hopes & trepidations." CanL 59:117-9, 1974.

Gervais, C.H. Quarry 22(2):77-8, 1973.

Gibbs, Robert. Fiddlehead 94:134, 1972.

Some plays: on words
Davey, Frank. Open letter 2d ser, 3:90-1, 1972.

Speech sucks
Barbour, Douglas. "The poets and presses revisited: circa 1974." DR
55:338-60, 1975.

David, Jack. Q&Q 41(5):44-5, 1975.

Leigh, Simon. "Two minor talons and a tidal borealis." Fiddlehead
108:120-4, 1976.

Stranger
Barbour, Douglas. "The poets and presses revisited: circa 1974." DR
55:338-60, 1975.

David, Jack. "Sitting around the Coleman." Open letter 3d ser,
2:107-9, 1975.

Doyle, Mike. "Animate imaginings." CanL 66:94-7, 1975.

Macskimming, Roy. "A quatrain of contenders." BiC 3(7):5-6, 9, 1974.

Solecki, Sam. "Political poetry." CF 54(647):46-7, 1975.

Strange Love
Hogg, Robert. Open letter 2d ser, 3:89-90, 1972.

Terrific at both ends
Dempster, Barry. "Collages, clips, and quirky pics." BiC 8(6):18,
1979.

COLES, Don

General
Moritz, Albert. "The private life of Don Coles, unprolific poet: things that matter are closest to home." BiC 8(7):36-7, 1979.

Anniversaries
Johnson, Rick. "Interfaces." CF 59(691):30, 1979.

Moritz, A.F. "Bone hurt and battle-weary." BiC 8(4):10-1, 1979.

Pearson, Ian. Q&Q 45(3):19, 1979.

Sometimes all over
Barbour, Douglas. "Canadian poetry chronicle 2." DR 55:748-59, 1975-76.

Gibson, Kenneth. "Horsepuckey & horsemen." Waves 4(1):22-5, 1975.

Jonas, George. "A certain magic in an unfamiliar poet." SatN 90(5): 76-8, 1975.

Solecki, Sam. QQ 82:647-8, 1975.

COLIN, Marcel

En écoutant la sève
Plamondon, Gaétan. LAQ 1979:109-10.

COLLETTE, Jean Yves

Une certain volonté de patience
Beaudet, André. LAQ 1978: 111-2.

COLOMBO, John Robert

General
Mallinson, Jean. "John Robert Colombo: documentary poet as visionary." ECW 5:67-71, 1976.

Ryval, Michael. "Colombo's 'edible' enterprises." BiC 6(3):8-10, 1977.

The great San Francisco earthquake and fire
Ringrose, Christoper Xerxes. "Fiddlehead's energy." CanL 52:87-90, 1972.

Sorfleet, John Robert. Fiddlehead 93:116-7, 1972.

66

COLOMBO, John Robert

John Toronto: new poems by Dr. Strachan
Purdy, Al. Quarry 19(3):60-1, 1970.

Skelton, Robin. MHRev 17:132-3, 1971.

Yates, Michael. WascanaR 5(1):101-2, 1970.

Mostly monsters
Barbour, Douglas. "Poetry chronicle V." DR 58:149-69, 1978.

Cogswell, Fred. "Monster makers." CanL 79:106-7, 1978.

Neo poems
Barbour, Douglas. DR 50:431, 1970

Christy, Jim. "Ornaments and embellishments." CanL 50:84-5, 1971.

Cogswell, Fred. Fiddlehead 88:106, 1971.

Ditsky, John. CF 50:406, 1971.

Doyle, Mike. "Made in Canada?" Poetry 119:356-62, 1972.

Helwig, David. Quarry 20(1):49, 1971.

Hornyansky, Michael. UTQ 40:374-5, 1971.

Skelton, Robin. MHRev 17:132-3, 1971.

Private Parts
Bartlett, Brian. "We dipped and we flipped." BiC 7(8):16, 1978.

Billings, Robert. "Hounslow's poetry lists: quality & diversity.
Waves 8(1):71-6, 1979.

Mallinson, Jean. Fiddlehead 120:140-1, 1979.

Pearson, Ian. Q&Q 44(8):47, 1978.

The sad truths: new poems
Bishop, A.G. Q&Q 41(4):39, 1975.

Dudek, Louis. QQ 82:475-7, 1975.

Dunlop, Donna. "Hello Colombo." BiC 4(8):24, 1975.

Newton, Stuart. WCR 10(2):66-8, 1975.

O'Flaherty, Patrick. "Casting shadows." CF 55(652):38, 1975.

Oliver, Michael Brian. Fiddlehead 111:123-4, 1976.

Sandler, Linda. "Columbus Colombo?" CanL 66:105-8, 1975.

COLOMBO, John Robert

Translations from the English: found poems
Bishop, A.G.   Q&Q 41(4):39, 1975.

Dudek, Louis. QQ 82:475-7, 1975.

Dunlop, Donna. "Hello Colombo." BiC 4(8):24, 1975.

Newton, Stuart. WCR 10(2):66-8, 1975.

O'Flaherty, Patrick. "Casting shadows." CF 55(652):38, 1975.

Quickenden, Robert. CVII 1(1):11, 1975.

Sandler, Linda. "Columbus Colombo?" CanL 66:105-8, 1975.

Variable cloudiness
Barbour, Douglas. "Canadian poetry chronicle: VI." DR 58:555-78, 1978.

David, Jack. Q&Q 44(1):32, 1978.

Fletcher, Peggy. "No two alike." CA&B 53(2):43-4, 1978.

Mallinson, Jean. Fiddlehead 120:140-1, 1979.

Plantos, Ted. "Mandel's past, Colombo's candy, Purdy's earth." BiC 7(2):16-7, 1978.

Sherman, Kenneth. A found found review." ECW 9:93, 1977-78.

CONN, David

Harbour light
Oughton, John. "Simple songs, tricky cycles." BiC 5(4):20-1, 1976.

CONSTANTINEAU, Gilles

Nouveaux poèmes
Henchiri, Sliman. LAQ 1972:148-9.

COOK, Michael J.

Reflecting the sun
Verstraade, Peter CA&B 52(3):41, 1977.

68

COOPERMAN, Stanley

Canadian gothic and other poems
Barbour, Douglas. "Poetry chronicle IV." DR 57:355-71, 1977.

David, Jack. Q&Q 43(6) 43-4, 1977.

Lillard, Charles. MHRev 40:136-8, 1976.

Safarik, Alan. "Cappelbaum's last bow." BiC 6(2):26-7, 1977.

Cannibals
André, Michael. QQ 80:471, 1973.

Bennett, Donna A. "Reunion: contemporary Canadian poetry." LURev 6:236-9, 1973.

Estok, Michael. "All in the family: the metaphysics of domesticity." DR 52:653-67, 1973.

Hornyansky, Michael. UTQ 42:373, 1973.

Sutherland, Fraser. "Rebel yells." BiC 1(12):53-4, 1972.

Cappelbaum's dance
Brewster, Elizabeth. CF 51(606-7):37, 1971.

Cogswell, Fred. "Lensmen and madmen." CanL 50:96-8, 1971.

Fetherling, Doug. "Poetic journal." TamR 57:80-4, 1971.

Guftafson, Ralph. QQ 78:140-2, 1971.

Pollack, Claudette. Quarry 20(1):42-4, 1971.

The owl behind the door
Magowan, Robin. "Pancakes for you and me." Poetry 116:193-202, 1970.

Yates, J. Michael. WascanaR 5(1):104-5, 1970.

COPPENS, Patrick

Pas de
Demers, Jeanne. LAQ 1976: 138-9.

CORDERRE Émile

Voir/see Narrache, Jean

CORRIVEAU, Hugues
   Les compléments directs
      Giguère, Richard. LAQ 1979:106.

   Le grégaire inefficace
      Giguère, Richard. LAQ 1979:106.

CÔTE, Michel

   Dixième lunaison
      Blais, Jacques. UTQ 44:341, 1975.

      Bourque, Paul-André. LAQ 1974: 131-2.

COUTURE, Jacques

   Roséfine la cristalline
      Bourque, Paul-André. LAQ 1973:113-5.

COUZYN, Jeni

   Christmas in Africa
      Barbour, Douglas. "Canadian poetry chronicle: III." DR 56:560-73,
      1976.

      Bolick, Merle Wallis. Quarry 25(4):71-2, 1976.

      Hoskins, Cathleen. Q&Q 42(8):35, 1976.

      MacEwen, Gwendolyn. "Heart of lightness." BiC 5(6):23, 1976.

      Oliver, Michael Brian. "Lost and found." Fiddlehead 119:106-16,
      1978.

      Sullivan, Rosemary. "A voice with fingers." CVII 2(3);17, 1976.

   Flying
      Shepherd, W.G. PRev 62:206-7, 1971.

   House of changes
      Barbour, Douglas. "Canadian poetry chronicle: VII." DR 59:154-75,
      1979.

CRAWFORD, Isabella Valancy

Bibliography
   Suo, Lynne. "Annotated bibliography on Isabella Valancy Crawford."
   ECW 11:289-314, 1978.

General
   Bessai, Frank. "The ambivalence of love in the poetry of Isabella
   Valancy Crawford." QQ 77:404-18, 1970.

   Dunn, Margo. "Valancy Crawford: the lifestyle of a Canadian poet."
   Room of one's own 2(1):11-9, 1976.

   Farmiloe, Dorothy. "I.V. Crawford: the growing legend." CanL
   81:143-7, 1979.

   Livesay, Dorothy. "Tennyson's daughter or wilderness child? The
   factual and literary background of Isabella Valancy Crawford." JCF
   2(3), 161-7, 1973.

   Martin, Mary F. "The short life of Isabella Valancy Crawford." DR
   52:390-400, 1972.

   Noonan, Gerald. "In search of Isabella Valancy Crawford." Q&Q
   43(13):24, 1977.

   Ross, Catherine Louise. Dark matrix: a study of Isabella Valancy
   Crawford. London, Ont: Univ. of Western Ontario, 1975. (Ph.D.
   thesis.)

   Ross, Catherine Sheldrick. "Isabella Valancy Crawford: solar
   mythologist." ESC 4:305-16, 1978.

   Tierney, Frank M., ed. The Crawford Symposium. Ottawa: Univ. of
   Ottawa Press, 1979 c1978.(Re-appraisals: Canadian authors.)

   Yeoman, Ann. "Towards a native mythology: the poetry of Isabella
   Valancy Crawford." CanL 52:39-47, 1972.

The collected poems
   Macgillivray, S.R. "Crawford Reprinted." CanL 61:116-7, 1974.

   Ricou, Laurence. Q&Q 39(3):8, 1973.

   Spettigue, D.O. "Literature of Canada series." QQ 81:311-3, 1974.

Fairy tales
   Godard, Barbara. "The forces of light." ECW 9:52-4, 1977-78.

Hugh and Ion
(Voir aussi/see also "The hunters twain.")
   Farmiloe, Dorothy. Q&Q 43(13):52, 1977.

   Godard, Barbara. "The forces of light." ECW 9:52-4, 1977-78.

CRAWFORD, Isabel Valancy

"The canoe"
  Ower, John B. "Isabella Valancy Crawford: 'The canoe.'" Woodcock 1974:78-86. (Originally published CanL 34:54-62, 1967.)

"The dark stag"
  Livesay, Dorothy. "The hunters twain." CanL 55:75-98, 1973.

"Gisli, the chieftain"
  Dunn, Margo. "Crawford's 'Gisli, the chieftain.'" CVII 2(2):48-50, 1976.

"The helot"
  Burns, Robert Alan. "Crawford and the Indians: allegory in 'The helot.'" SCL 4(1):154-61, 1979.

  Hughes, Kenneth. "'The helot' and the objective correlative: Ontario and Greece." Tierney 1978: 87-96.

"The hunters twain"
(Voir aussi/see also <u>Hugh and Ion.</u>)
  Livesay, Dorothy. "The hunters twain." CanL 55:75-98, 1973.

  Martin, Mary F. "Another view of 'The hunters twain'." CF 71:111-2, 1976.

"The lily bed"
  Livesay, Dorothy. "The hunters twain." CanL 55:75-98, 1973.

  Ower, John. "Isabella Valancy Crawford and 'The fleshly school of poetry.'" SSL 13:275-81, 1978.

"Malcolm's Katie"
  Brooks, Marshall. "'Malcolm's Katie': the interior view." CanL 76:134-5, 1978.

  Burns, Robert Alan. "Crawford and the Indians: allegory in 'The helot.'" SCL 4(1):154-61, 1979.

  Hughes, Kenneth James and Sproxton, Birk. "Crawford's 'Malcolm's Katie' and MacLachlan's 'The emigrant.'" CN&Q 19)10-11, 1977.

  Hughes, Kenneth J. "Democratic vision of 'Malcolm's Katie.'" CVII 1(2):38-46, 1975.

  Hughes, Kenneth J. "Isabella Valancy Crawford: the names in 'Malcolm's Katie.'" CN&Q 14:6, 1974.

  Hughes, Kenneth and Sproxton, Birk. "'Malcolm's Katie': images and songs." CanL 65:55-64, 1975.

CRAWFORD, Isabel Valancy

"Malcolm's Katie" (cont'd.)
Mathews, Robin. "'Malcolm's Katie': love, wealth and nation building." SCL 2:49-60, 1977.

Radu, Kenneth. "Patterns of meaning: Isabella Crawford's 'Malcolm's Katie.'" DR 57:322-31, 1977.

Rudzik, Orest. "Myth in 'Malcolm's Katie.'" Tierney 1978:49-60.

West, David S. "'Malcolm's Katie': Alfred as nihilist not rapist." SCL 3:137-41, 1978.

"Narrative II"
Ross, Catherine. "'Narrative II'--the unpublished long narrative poem." Tierney 1978:107-22.

"Said the canoe"
Cogswell, Fred. "Feminism in Isabella Valancy Crawford's 'Said the canoe.'" Tierney 1978:79-85.

Livesay, Dorothy. "The hunters twain." CanL 55:75-98, 1973.

CRAWFORD, Terry

Sorcerers cafe
Zieroth, Dale. Quarry 22(1):73-4, 1973.

The werewolf miracles
Bradbury, Maureen. QQ 42(9):36, 1976.

Di Cicco, Pier Giorgio. "One up, two down." BiC 5(9):33, 1976.

MacCulloch, Clare. Quarry 25(4):65-7, 1976.

Scobie, Stephen. "Shades of precision." CanL 79:89-90, 1978.

CRÉMAZIE, Octave

General
Arnold, I.A. "Sources françaises dans l'oeuvre d'Octave Crémazie." RUO 41:294-313, 1971.

Condemine, Odette. "La notion de la gloire chez Crémazie." Savard 1977, 79-91.

Condemine, Odette. "Octave Crémazie: homme et poète." Crémazie 1972: 17-241.

Lortie, Jeanne d'Arc. "Voyant national: Octave Crémazie." Lortie, 1975:303-18.

CRÉMAZIE, Octave

    Poésies (Oeuvres I)
      Dionne, René. "Poètes d'hier et d'avant-hier—la poèsie québécoise en 1972." Relations 381:122-4, 1973.

      Roden, Lethem Sutcliffe. QQ 80:313-4, 1973.

CREWE, Judith

    The ancient and other poems
      Daniel, Lorne. Q&Q 43(3):12, 1977.

CROSSLEY, Don

    I, Adam
      Hosein, Clyde. "As the world yearns." BiC 4(10):27, 1975.

CROWSHOE, Marilyn

    The immaculate white fence
      Barbour, Douglas. Q&Q 39(3):8, 1973.

      Zimmerman, Susan. "Musicales." BiC 2(4):27-30, 1973.

CRUSZ, Rienzi

    Flesh and Thorn
      Barbour, Douglas. Q&Q 40(7):20, 1974.

      Barnes, W.J. Quarry 24(1):78-80, 1975.

      McKay, Don. ApF 2:r8-9, 1975.

CURRIE, Robert

Diving into fire
  Barbour, Douglas. "Poetry chronicle V." DR 58:149-69, 1978.

  Daniel, Lorne. Q&Q 43(8):42, 1977.

  McNamara, Eugene. "Ghetto long little dogie." BiC 6(8):16-7, 1977.

  Nelson, Sharon H. Quarry 26(3):83-4, 1977.

  Oliver, Michael Brian. "Lost and found." Fiddlehead 119:106-16, 1978.

  Tefs, Wayne. "This paradoxical malady." CVII 3(2):56-7, 1977.

The halls of Elsinore
  Billings, R. Quarry 23(3):74-5, 1974.

  Fletcher, Peggy. "Good things come in small packages." CA&B 54(3):31-2, 1979.

  Liman, Claude. "Open sesame." CVII 3(4):25-8, 1978.

CYR, Gilles

Sol inapparent
  Cloutier, Guy. "'Cette phrase me surprend.'" NBdJ 78:89-91, 1979.

  Hébert, François. "Gilles Cyr: 'où il n'y a pas de route.'" Liberté 123:109-11, 1979.

  Nepveu, Pierre. LAQ 1978:112-3.

  Nepveu, Pierre. "Robert Mélançon, Gilles Cyr, Jean Charlebois, Jean-Yves Théberge." Lettres qué 14:22-5, 1979.

DABYDEEN, Cyril

Goatsong
  Miles, Ron. "Boxed set." CanL 81:138-9, 1979.

DAIGNEAULT, André

Le doux feu
  Blais, Jacques. UTQ 44:339, 1975.

DALE, Sharon

General
Basmajian, Shant. Old nun 1:61, 1975.

D'AMBOISE, Jacqueline

Mother Myths
Amprimoz, Alexandre L. Quarry 27(3):74-8, 1978.

Barbour, Douglas. "Canadian poetry chronicle: VI." DR 58:555-78, 1978.

DANIEL, Lorne

Towards a new compass
Barbour, Douglas. "Canadian poetry chronicle: VI." DR 58:555-78, 1978.

Di Cicco, Pier Giorgio. "No man is an island, true, but can there be a circean catch to regionalism." BiC 8(1):21-2, 1979.

Fernstrom, Ken. Q&Q 44(13):14, 1978.

DANTIN, Louis

General
Garon, Yves. "Louis Dantin aux premiers temps de l'École littéraire de Montreal." Ottawa 1972:301-14.

DARGIS, Daniel

Perce-neige
Paradis, Suzanne. "Écrits des forges." LAQ 1975:125-6.

DAVEY, Frank

General
Bowering, George. "Starting at our skins: an interview with Frank Davey." Open letter, 4th ser, 3:89-181, 1979.

Komisar, Elizabeth. "Frank Davey." White pelican 5(2):49-58, 1976. (Interview.)

DAVEY, Frank

L'an trentiesme: selected poems 1961-71
Barbour, Douglas. "Finding a voice to say what must be said." LURev 7(1):102-13, 1974.

Hornyansky, Michael. UTQ 42:373-4, 1973.

Arcana
André, Michael. QQ 80:658-9, 1973.

Barbour, Douglas. CF 53(632):42-3, 1973.

Barbour, Douglas. "Finding a voice to say what must be said." LURev 7:102-13, 1974.

Cooley, Dennis. "Davey's locker." CVII 2(2):42-4, 1976.

Quill, Patricia. Q&Q 39(10):13, 1973.

Rogers, Linda. "Medium or magician." CanL 62:121-4, 1974.

The clallam
Abbey, Lloyd. "Anti-epic and nostalgia." CanL 63:107-9, 1975.

Barbour, Douglas. "Finding a voice to say what must be said." LURev 7(1):102-13, 1974.

Lacey, Edward. "Canadian bards and South American reviewers." Nj 4:82-120, 1974.

Pyke, Linda Annesley. Q&Q 40(7):20, 1974.

Four myths for Sam Perry
Barbour, Douglas. DR 51:141,1971.

Barbour, Douglas "Play in the western world." CanL 52:77-81, 1972.

Garnet, Eldon. "Five poets on the brink of consciousness." SatN 87(6):38-42, 1972.

King of swords
Barbour, Douglas. CF 53(632):42-3, 1973.

Barbour, Douglas. "Finding a voice to say what must be said." LURev 7(1):102-13, 1974.

Marshall, Tom. Quarry 22(4):78-9, 1973.

Rogers, Linda. "Medium or magician." CanL 62:121-4, 1974.

DAVEY, Frank

Weeds
Barbour, Douglas. DR 51:141-3, 1971.

Garnet, Eldon. "Five poets on the brink of consciousness." SatN 87(6):38-42, 1972.

Helwig, David. Quarry 22(4):76-7, 1973.

Hornyansky, Michael. UTQ 40:374, 1971.

DAWSON, David

Ceremonial: poems 1961-1967
Bagchee, Shyamal. Q&Q 39(2):12, 1973.

Barbour, Douglas. "Three west coast poets and one from the east." LURev 6:240-5, 1973.

Garnet, Eldon. Open letter 2d ser, 4:113-5, 1973.

Rogers, Linda. "Medium or magician." CanL 62:121-4, 1974.

DAY, Bonnie

This life one leaf: collected poems
Bishop, Alan. Q&Q 39(7):19, 1973.

DAY, David

The cowichan
Cooley, Dennis. "To be clean as broken stone." CVII 3(2):26-7, 1977.

McFadyen, Lynn. Q&Q 43(1):31, 1977.

Oliver, Michael Brian. "Raising Canada." Fiddlehead 114:141-5, 1977.

Virgo, Sean. NL 3:47-9, 1976.

DE BELLEFEUILLE, Normand

La belle conduite
Corriveau, Hugues. LAQ 1978:93-4, 1978.

Cas
Giguère, Richard. "Les Herbes rouges: une grande 'petite revue.'"
LAQ 1975:118-21.

Les grandes familles
Bonenfant, Joseph. LAQ 1977:178-80.

Le texte justement
Nepveu, Pierre. "Sens interdit: poèmes de Normand de Bellefeuille,
Renaud Longchamps et Roger Magini." Lettres qué 3:11-3, 1976.

Trois
Giguère, Richard. "Les Herbes rouges: une grande 'petite revue.'"
LAQ 1975:118-21.

DEROME, Gilles

Savoir par coeur
Étienne, Gérard. LAQ 1973:102-4.

DÉRY, Francine

En beau fusil
Fisette, Jean. "Sur le front de la poésie: des positions se
délimitent." V&I 4:150-2, 1978.

Giguère, Richard. UTQ 48:360, 1979.

Lemaire, Michel. LAQ 1978:113-5.

Nepveu, Pierre. "L'antre et la sorcière: Madeleine Gagnon et Francine
Déry." Lettres qué 12:15-6, 1978.

DÉRY, Pierre-Justin

Topograhies I
Haeck, Philippe. LAQ 1979:169-70.

DESAUTELS, Denise

    Comme miroirs en feuilles
      Arcand, Pierre-André. "Le Noroît." LAQ 1975:122-4.

      Blais, Jacques. UTQ 45:348-9, 1976.

      Nepveu, Pierre. "Les vaches maigres." Lettres qué 2:12-4, 1976.

    Marie tou s'éteignait en moi...
      Delisle, Claude. LAQ 1977:156-7.

DESBIENS, Patrice

    L'espace qui reste
      Moisan, Clément. LAQ 1979:92-4.

DÉSILETS, Guy

    Ô que la vie est ronde
      Bouvier, Luc. LAQ 1977:168-70.

      Recurt, Myriam. "L'ame et l'absolu." CanL 80:98-100, 1979.

    Poëme pour un homme pygmée
      Henchiri, Michelle. LAQ 1971:161.

    Un violon nu
      Henchiri, Michelle. LAQ 1972:180.

DESJARDINS, Henry-Marie

    General
      Saint-Bernard-de-Clairvaux, Soeur. "Henri Marie Desjardins." Ottawa 1972:37-65.

DES MARCHAIS, Gilles

    Mobiles sur des modes soniques
      Bonenfant, Joseph. LAQ 1972:162-3.

    Ombelles verbombreuses Parcellaires
    Demers, Jeanne. LAQ 1974:125-6.

DESPRÉS, Ronald

    Bibliography
      "Bibliographie." RUM 5(1):94-5, 1972.

    General
      Lavoie, Laurent. "Le réel violenté et sanguinolent." RUM 5(1):87-91, 1972.

      "Les recueils." RUM 5(1):85-6, 1972.

    Paysages en contrebande
      Wyczynski, Paul. LAQ 1975:107-9.

DESROCHERS, Alfred

    General
      Bolduc, Yves. "Alfred DesRochers, poète québécois." Lettres qué 10:34-6, 1978.

      Royer, Jean. "Les poètes de 1930: entretiens avec Alfred DesRochers et Clément Marchand." Estuaire 5:88-102, 1977.

    Oeuvres poétiques
      Fisette, Jean. "Parutions récentes: de DesRochers aux Écrits des forges." V&I 3:497-500, 1978.

      Giguère, Richard. UTQ 47:364-5, 1978.

    Oeuvres poétiques I et II
      Giguère, Richard. LAQ 1977:115-8.

DES ROCHES, Roger

    General
      Beausoleil, Claude. LAQ 1979:110-4.

    Autour de Françoise Sagan indélébile
      Audet, Noël. "Une poésie de la rupture." V&I 1:289-90, 1975.

    Corps accessoires
      Dionne, René. "Où va notre poésie?" Relations 357:55-7, 1971.

      Fournier, Gérard-Claude. "Trois poètes." LAQ 1970:147.

      Marcottes, Gilles. EF 7:111, 1971.

DES ROCHES, Roger

Les lèvres de n'importe qui
Corriveau, Hugues. "Poésie: des lèvres et des vertiges." NBdJ 81:87-90, 1979.

Giguère, Richard. LAQ 1979:105.

Les problèmes du cinématographe
Carrière, André. "Trois auteurs en quête d'un langage." LAQ 1973:100-1.

La promenade du spécialiste
Roy, Max. LAQ 1977:122-5.

La publicité discrète; le corps certain
Giguère, Richard. "Les Herbes rouges: une grande 'petite revue.'" LAQ 1975:118-21.

La vie de couple
Roy, Max. LAQ 1977:122-5

Tous, corps accessories
Beausoleil, Claude. LAQ 1979:110-4

DESRUISSEAUX, Pierre

Lettres
Bourneuf, Roland. LAQ 1979:115.

DEWDNEY, Christopher

General
McFadden, David. "The twilight of self-consciousness." Helwig 1978:78-96.

Fovea centralis
Barbour, Douglas. "Canadian poetry chronicle 2." DR 55:748-59, 1975-76.

Bayard, Caroline. Q&Q 41(12):30, 1975.

Dunlop, Donna. QQ 84:128, 1977.

Henderson, Brian. "In the museum of language." CVII 2(3):30-1, 1976.

Hornyansky, Michael. UTQ 45:342, 1976.

McCaffery, Steve. "Strata and strategy: pataphysics in the poetry of Christopher Dewdney." Open letter 3d ser, 4:45-56, 1976.

DEWDNEY, Christopher

A palaeozoic geology of London, Ontario

Alpert, Barry. "Procedures." Open letter 2d ser, 9:99-101, 1974.

Alpert, Barry. "Written on the wind (of Lake Ontario)." Open letter 3d ser, 2:5-25, 1975.

Gairdner, William. "Geology." Open letter 2d ser, 9:102, 1974.

Henderson, Brian. "In the museum of language." CVII 2(3):30-1, 1976.

McCaffery, Steve. "Strata and strategy: pataphysics in the poetry of Christoper Dewdney." Open letter, 3d ser, 4:45-56, 1976.

Stevens, Peter. "The perils of majority." UWR 9(2):100-9, 1974.

DE WIEL, Alexa

Conversations with Bibi

Cavanagh, Dave. "Reports from the front." BiC 5(2):36, 1976.

Lever, Bernice. Q&Q 41(10:19, 1975.

R., G. "Room of one's own." 1(4):76-8, 1976.

DI CICCO, Pier Giorgio

A burning patience

Gatenby, Greg. "Poetry chronicle." TamR 77&78:77-94, 1979.

McFadden, Dave. "Of newts and natural gold." BiC 8(1):14-5, 1979.

Pearson, Ian. Q&Q 44(15):33, 1978.

The circular dark

Barbour, Douglas. "Canadian poetry chronicle:VI." DR 58:555-78, 1978.

Hatch, R.B. "Time's motion." CanL 81:129-32, 1979.

Johnson, Sam. "The poet's space." Waves 7(2):60-3, 1979.

Dancing in the house of cards

Daniel, Lorne. Q&Q 44(10):12, 1978.

McFadden, Dave. "Of newts and natural gold." BiC 8(1):14-5, 1979.

Trethewey, Eric. Fiddlehead 123:110-1, 1979.

DI CICCO, Pier Giorgio

The sad facts
  Oliver, Michael Brian. "Lost and found." Fiddlehead 119:106-16, 1978.

The tough romance
  Abley, Mark. "Poetry that fell from the sky." Maclean's 93(41):54-8, 1979.

  Barbour, Douglas. "Canadian poetry chronicle: VII." DR 59:154-75, 1979.

  Casto, Robert. "Exile as art: DiCicco's tough romance with life." Waves 8(1):61-6, 1979.

  Gustafson, Ralph. "Pull up your pants and fall in love." BiC 8(4):10, 1979.

  Hicks, Lorne. Q&Q 45(5):33, 1979.

  Linder, Norma West. "Voices of character." CA&B 54(4):30-1, 1979.

  Sherman, Kenneth. "Tasteful necrophilia." CF 59(690):42-3, 1979.

  Trethewey, Eric. Fiddlehead 123:111, 1979.

  Whiteman, Bruce. Quarry 28(4):88-9, 1979.

We are the light turning
  Farmiloe, Dorothy. Q&Q 43(1):32, 1977.

  Heath, Terrence. "Touching the man." CVII 3(1):35, 1977.

  Oliver, Michael Brian. "Lost and Found." Fiddlehead 119:106-16, 1978.

  Whiteman, Bruce. "Big seeing & necessary as breath." ECW 10: 57-60, 1978.

DI MICHELE, Mary

Tree of August
  McFarlane, David. "To fall is not to finish." BiC 8(2):25, 1979.

  Saunders, Leslie. Quarry 27(4):74, 1978.

DION, Serge

    Aubes mortes
      Thériault, Serge A. Lettres qué 13:28, 1979.

    Décors d'amour
      Bouvier, Luc. LAQ 1979:117-9.

      Thériault, Serge A. Lettres qué 13:28, 1979.

    Mon pays a la chaleur et l'hiver faciles
      Bouvier, Luc. LAQ 1979:117-9.

DIONNE, André

    Demain d'aujourd'hui
      Bonenfant, Joseph. LAQ 1977:178-80.

      Nepveu, Pierre. "La poésie qui se fait et celle qui ne se fait pas."
      Lettres qué 9:15-7, 1978.

    Dyke
      Bélanger, Yrénée. "Bleu-source de terre de Gaston Bellemare; L'oeil
      de sang d'Yvon Bonenfant; Dyke d'André Dionne." LAQ 1971:172-3.

    Envers
      Gallays, François. LAQ 1972:172.

    Gangue
      Gallays, François. LAQ 1972:172.

DITSKY, John

    Scar tissue
      Fletcher, Peggy. "Humour and sadness." CA&B 54(1):36-7, 1978.

DOMANSKI, Don

    The Cape Breton book of the dead
      Di Cicco, Pier Giorgio. "East and West dead and alive." BiC
      5(3):18-9, 1976.

      Gatenby, Greg. Q&Q 42(1):25, 1976.

      Scobie, Stephen. "Shades of precision." CanL 79:89-90, 1978.

DOMANSKI, Don

Heaven
Daniel, Lorne. "From screen gems to animal acts." BiC 8(4):11-2, 1979.

Fernstrom, Ken. Q&Q 45(5):33, 1979.

Gatenby, Greg. "Poetry chronicle." TamR 77&78:77-94, 1979.

Hall, Phil. "Heaven--on earth." UWR 14(2):107-8, 1979.

Trethewey, Eric. Fiddlehead 123:112-3, 1979.

DONNELL, David

The blue sky, poems 1974-1977
Barbour, Douglas. "Canadian poetry chronicle: VI." DR 58:555-78, 1978.

Brown, Allan. "Black moss: six offerings." Waves 7(2):68-71, 1979.

Gasparini, Len. "Urbanity and mean streets." BiC 7(6):19-20. 1978.

DOR, Georges

Je chante-pleure encore
Dionne, René. "Sur les voies de notre poésie--II." Relations 368:56-9, 1972.

Poèmes et chansons
Dionne, Rene. "Sur les voies de notre poésie--II." Relations 368:56-9, 1972.

Saint-Amour, Robert. LAQ 1971:164.

DORSEY, Candas Jane

This is for you
Mallinson, Jean. "Poetry miscellany." ECW 7/8:151-8, 1977.

DOSTIE, Gaëtan
Courir la galipote
Royer, Jean. LAQ 1974:141-2.

Poing commun
Royer, Jean. LAQ 1974:141-2.

DOUGHERTY, Dan

The national hen
Gervais, C.H. "Staying true." CanL 76:104-7, 1978.

DOYLE, Lawrence

General
Ives, Edward D. Lawrence Doyle, the farmer poet of Prince Edward
Island: a study in local songmaking. Orono, Maine: Univ. of Maine,
1971. (Univ. of Maine studies, 92.)

DOYLE, Mike

General
Doyle, Mike. "Arches abandonnées, hôtels incendiés et cabanes
désaffectées." Ellipse 19:68-76, 1976. (Tr. Jacques Michon.)

Green, John. "Le long voyage de Mike Doyle." Ellipse 19:77-81, 1976.

Earth meditations: one to five
Molesworth, Charles. "Some locals." Poetry 120:107-13, 1972.

Pollack, C.H. Quarry 21(3):62-6, 1972.

Russell, Lawrence. "International ideas." CanL 52:97-8, 1972.

Preparing for the ark
Gasparini, Len. "Six poets who found a critic." BiC 3(7):20-2, 1974.

Ringrose, Christopher. "Assorted catch." CanL 71:102-4, 1976.

Wallace, Bronwen. Quarry 24(1):68-9, 1975.

Stonedancer
Amprimoz, Alexandre. "Poetic journeys." CanL 79:92-4, 1978.

Heinzelman, Kurt. "Five poets of the Commonwealth." Poetry
131:225-35, 1978.

Novak, Barbara. Quarry 25(4):76, 1976.

DRAGISTIC, Peggy

> From the medley
>> Fletcher, Peggy. "Good things come in small packages." CA&B 54(3):31-2 1979.

DROUIN, Michèle

> La duègne accroupie
>> Bédard, Nicole. LAQ 1978:115.

DUBÉ, Marcel

> Poèmes de sable
>> Godbout, Jacques. "La poésie les larmes aux yeux." Le maclean 15(6):10, 1975.
>
>> Laroche, Maximilien. LAQ 1974:132-3.

DUBOIS, Michèle

> Gestuelle
>> Bourneuf, Roland. LAQ 1976:134-5.
>
>> Fisette, Jean. "Poésie récente, poésie diverse." V&I 2:440-3, 1977.

DUDEK, Louis

> Bibliography
>> Wenek, Karol W.J. Louis Dudek: a check-list. Ottawa: Golden Dog Press, 1975.
>
> General
>> Barbour, Douglas. "Poet as philosopher." CanL 53:18-29, 1972. (Also Woodcock 1974b:110-22.)
>
>> Darling, Michael. "An interview with Louis Dudek." ECW 3:2-14, 1975.
>
>> Frayne, Helen. "On Quebec: an interview with Louis Dudek." CVII 3(3):38-40, 1978.
>
>> Lee, Dennis. "Poetic gravity." BiC 1(3):14, 19-20, 1971.
>
>> McCormick, Marion. "Why Louis Dudek thinks modernism remains the central question in the arts." BiC 7(8):37-8, 1978.

DUDEK, Louis

    General (cont'd.)
     Nause, John and Heenan, J. Michael. "An interview with Louis Dudek."
     TamR 69:30-43, 1976.

     Seidner, Eva. "Modernism in the booklength poems of Louis Dudek."
     Open letter 3d ser, 7:14-40, 1977.

    Collected poetry
     Dagg, Mel. Fiddlehead 94:111-6, 1972.

     Heenan, J.M.H. "The voice of order in Louis Dudek's Collected
     poetry." Inscape 11(2):41-7, 1974.

     Hornyansky, Michael. UTQ 41:332-3, 1972.

     Levinson, Christopher. QQ 79:274, 1972.

     Watt, F.W. CF 51(612-3):82-3, 1972.

     Weaver, Robert. "A puritan Dudek; an inefficient Webb." SatN
     86(11):50-2, 1971.

    Epigrams
     Di Cicco, Pier Giorgio. "Gay in not so jocund company." BiC
     5(5):15-6, 1976.

     Hensley, Don H. Brick 2:6-7, 1978.

    Selected poems
     Barbour, Douglas. "Canadian poetry chronicle: III." DR 56:560-73,
     1976.

DUGAS, Marcel

    General
     Brouillette, Leonce. Marcel Dugas: sa vie et son oeuvre. Quebec
     Univ. Laval, 1970. (Ph.D. thesis.)

     "Marcel Dugas et son temps." EF 7, 1971. (Whole issue.)

DUGUAY, Calixte

    Les stigmates du silence
     Cloutier, Cécile. "Voix acadiennes." LAQ 1975:132-4.

DUGUAY, Raoul

General
Arbic, Thérèse. "Raoul Duguay s'en va-t-au ciel." Chroniques 1(5):35-8, 1975.

Bayard, Caroline and David, Jack. "Raoul Duguay." Bayard 1978: 15-36.

Bourassa, André-G. "Duguay ou l'envers et l'endroit." Lettres qué 4:12-15, 1976.

Giguère, Richard. "Poésie est Eiséop: une entrevue avec Raoul Duguay." V&I 1:157-70, 1975.

Giguère, Richard. "Raoul Duguay, poetry is yrteop: interview/conversation." Ellipse 17:80-97, 1975. (Tr. David Lobdell.)

Moisan, Clément. "La 'nouvelle culture,' la contre-culture ou the brilliant minority." Moisan 1979:219-68.

Nichol, bp. "Raoul Duguay/bp Nichol (en anglais): interview (en anglais)." Open letter 2d ser, 6:65-73, 1973.

Rancourt, Jacques. "Jazz pour toulmonde: Raoul Duguay." Brindeau 1973:596-601.

Alllô tôulmônd (phono record)
Taschereau, Yves. "Saint Raoul et Furey le méchant." Le maclean 15(8):6, 1975.

L'amour
Bourque, Paul-André. "Poètes et artistes du Québec LAQ 1975:139-45.

Lapokalipsô
Bonenfant, Joseph. LAQ 1971:145-7.

Marcotte, Gilles. EF 9:82, 1973.

M (phono record)
Bourassa, André-G. "Les poètes de la musique." Lettres qué 11:32-7 1978.

Manifeste de l'Infonie
Lacroix, Pierre. LAQ 1970:139-40.

DUGUAY, Raoul

    Vivante avec tôulllmônd (phono record)
      Bourassa, André-G. "Les poètes de la musique." Lettres qué 11:32-7,
    1978.

DUHAIME, André

    Peau de fleur
      Bouvier, Luc. LAQ 1979:116-7.

DUMONT, Fernand

    Parler de septembre
      Dionne, René. "Où va notre poésie?" Relations 357:55-7, 1971.

      Lapointe, Gatien. LAQ 1970:128-30.

      Marcotte, Gilles. EF 8:94, 1972.

DUNCAN, Sara Jeannette
    General
      Flitton, Marilyn G. "Noms-de-plume and Sara Jeannette Duncan."
    CN&Q 13:9-10, 1974.

DURNO, Janet
    Poems
      Malcolm Ian. Quarry 27(1):79-82, 1978.

DUTTON, Paul

    The four horsemen alive in the west
      bissett, bill. "What 4 voices can together say." ECW 12:241-2, 1978.

    Horse d'oeuvres
      David, Jack. "Hoarse meet." ECW 3:55-7, 1975.

DYROFF, Jan Michael

    Journies and shows
      Barbour, Douglas. "The poets and presses revisited: circa 1974." DR
    55:338-60, 1975.

      Gasparini, Leonard. "Applaudeth one in three." BiC 4(11):16-8, 1975.

EIBEL, Deborah

Kayak sickness
Bessai, Diane. "Simple complexities." CanL 60:124-6, 1974.

EISLER, Ken

Inch man
Gervais, C.H. "Staying true." CanL 76:104-7, 1978.

ELLENBOGEN, George

The night unstones
Barbour, Douglas. QQ 79:569-71, 1972.

S., N. "Baring and weaving." BiC 1(12):41, 1972.

ENRICO, Harold

Now, a thousand years from now
Stuewe, Paul. Q&Q 41(10:19, 1975.

ERBAS, Tullin

Snowbirds (Tr. Tom Brosnahan and Talat Sait Halman.)
Fletcher, Peggy. CA&B 52(3):42, 1977.

ETHIER-BLAIS, Jean

Petits poèmes presque en prose
Major, Robert. LAQ 1978:116-7.

EVANS, Hubert

Whittlings
Mathews, Robin. "Two B.C. harbingers." CVII 3(1):34-5, 1977.

EVERSON, Ronald Gilmour

General

Gibbs, Robert. Fiddlehead 84:118-21, 1970.

Marshall, Tom. "Major Canadian poets III: the modernists." CF 58(686):13-7, 1979.

Carnival

Barbour, Douglas. "Canadian poetry chronicle: VII." DR 59:154-75, 1979.

Gasparini, Len. "Pain, thunder, and rainbows." BiC 8(2):24, 1979.

Gatenby, Greg. "Poetry chronicle." TamR 77-78:77-94, 1979.

Hornyansky, Michael. UTQ 48:344-5, 1979.

The dark is not so dark

Ballstadt, Carl. CF 50:225, 1970.

Cogswell, Fred. Inscape 8(1):n.p., 1970.

Gibbs, Robert. Fiddlehead 84:118-21, 1970.

Gustafson, Ralph. QQ 78:140-2, 1971.

Jones, D.G. "Voices in the dark." CanL 45:68-74, 1970.

Pacey, Desmond. "A Canadian quintet." Fiddlehead, 83:79-86, 1970.

Purdy, Al. Quarry 19(3):61-2, 1970.

Thompson, Laurel. "Canadian poetry." UWR 6(1):86-90, 1970.

Indian summer

Barbour, Douglas. "Poetry chronicle: IV." DR 57:355-71, 1977.

Darling, Michael. "Poems new and selected: Everson and Howith." ECW 7/8:158-63, 1977.

Gervais, C.H. "Two reporters, one commentator." BiC 6(7):24, 1977.

Livesay, Dorothy. "The poet who came in from the cold." CVII 2(4):17, 1976.

Lochhead, Douglas. UWR 13(2):103-4, 1978.

Novak, Barbara. Q&Q 42(16):8, 1976.

Purdy, Al. "Tribute to Everson." CanL 72:80-82, 1977.

Scherzer, D.K. Quarry 26(2):57-9, 1977.

EVERSON, Ronald Gilmour

Selected poems 1920/1970
Cogswell, Fred. QQ 78:325-6, 1971.

Dickey, William. "The poem and the moment." HudR 24:159-70, 1971.

Fetherling, Doug. "Poetic journal." TamR 57:80-4, 1971.

Gustafson, Ralph. "Everson's half century." CanL 49:65-7, 1971.

McSweeney, Kerry. Quarry 20(2):58-60, 1971.

Molesworth, Charles. "Some locals." Poetry 120:107-13, 1972.

EWING, Patricia Renée

The other land
Keitner, Wendy. Quarry 24(3):77-8, 1975.

FAFARD, Jacqueline

The invisible ladder/L'échelle invisible
Farmiloe, Dorothy. Q&Q 42(9):36, 1976.

FAIRLEY, Barker

Poems
Pearson, Ian. Q&Q 43(9):8, 1977.

FALK, Stella

Ambergris, love and its fallout: selected poetry and verse
Chope, Gordon. "Three humanist poets." HiC 10(4):31, 1977.

FALUDY, George

General
Amiel, Barbara. "You should know something about George Faludy."
SatN 88(12):23-8, 1973.

FALUDY, George

    East and west
      Aubert, Rosemary. Q&Q 44(10):12, 1978.

      Dobbs, Kildare. "The police chief and the poet." SatN 93(6):66-7, 1978.

      Fletcher, Peggy. "Humour and sadness." CA&B 54(1):36-7, 1978.

      Levenson, Christopher. "A meeting of the twain." BiC 7(9):14, 16, 1978.

FANCOTT, Edmund

    Hymn to Isis
      Ness, Sally. Q&Q 39(11):12, 1973.

FARKAS, Andre

    Murders in the Welcome Cafe
      David, Jack. "Three from Montreal." CVII 3(3):23-4, 1978.

      Davies, Gwendolyn. "Something's happening in Montreal." ECW 10:82-7, 1978.

FARLEY, Tom

    The last spaceman
      Bessai, Diane. "Poetry from Ottawa." CF 55(652):36-8, 1975.

      Dailey, Ross. "Four from Borealis." CanR 1(4):26-7, 1974.

      Leigh, Simon. "Two minor talons and a tidal borealis." Fiddlehead 109:128-32, 1976.

FARMILOE, Dorothy

    Adrenalin of weather
      Bayard, Caroline. Q&Q 45(5):33, 1979.

    And some in fire
      Rogers, Linda. "Demeter on the frontier." BiC 3(7):27-8, 1974.

FARMILOE, Dorothy

> Blue is the colour of death
>> Gasparini, Len. "Known what to see." CanL 58:112-3, 1973.
>>
>> Lanczos, Elmar. "Three from Fiddlehead." WCR 10(2):49-50, 1975.
>>
>> Zimmerman, Susan. "Musicales." BiC 2(4):27-30, 1973.
>
> Elk Lake diary poems
>> Oliver, Michael Brian. "Raising Canada." Fiddlehead 114:141-5, 1977.
>
> Poems for apartment dwellers
>> Cameron, Allen Barry. CF 50:310-1, 1970.
>>
>> MacSween, R.J. AntigR 1(2):104, 1970.
>>
>> Thompson, Laurel. "Canadian poetry." UWR 6(1):86-90, 1970.

FAVREAU, Marc

> Les oeufs limpides
>> Bergeron, Bertrand. LAQ 1979:166-71.

FAWCETT, Brian

> General
>> "Interview." CapR 12:89-119, 1977.
>
> Creatures of state
>> Barbour, Douglas. "Canadian poetry chronicle: VII." DR 59:154-75, 1979.
>>
>> Bartlett, Brian. "Torn and tattered comparisons." CVII 4(3):42,44, 1979.
>>
>> McColm, Sheila. "An entirely new set." Brick 6:53-4, 1979.
>>
>> Persky, Stan. "Address to the Workers' Council of Prince George, B.C." CapR 12:151-62, 1977.
>
> Friends
>> Coleman, Victor. Open letter 2d ser, 1:77-8, 1971-72.
>
> Permanent Relationships
>> Lockhead, Gordon. "Summer goes." Open letter 3d ser, 3:94-5, 1975.

FAWCETT, Brain

Permanent Relationships (cont'd.)
McKinnon, Barry. "Breaking surface." Open letter 3d ser, 4:88-90, 1976.

Novak, Barbara. Quarry 25(4):74, 1976.

Stuewe, Paul. Q&Q 41(12):30, 1975.

FERLAND, Albert

General
Jeanne-Leber, Soeur. "L'esthétique de Ferland." Ottawa 1972:150-77.

FERLAND, Jean-Pierre

General
Bourgault, Pierre. "Jean-Pierre Ferland redécouvre l'Amérique." Le maclean. 12(8):14-17; 28-33, 1972.

FERNS, John

Henry Hudson or Discovery
Barbour, Douglas. "Canadian poetry chronicle: III." DR 56:560-73, 1976.

Engel, Howard. "Pleasing voices." CF 56(662):54, 1976.

Hamilton, Jamie. Q&Q 42(4):24, 1976.

Liman, Claude. "Open sesame." CVII 3(4):25-8, 1978.

Woodman, Ross. Brick 2:18-9, 1978.

The snow horses
Barbour, Douglas. "Canadian poetry chronicle: VII." DR 59:154-75, 1979.

FERRON, Jacques

La nuit
Imbert, Patrick. "Antithèses et bouleversement culturel dans La nuit de J. Ferron." RPac 4:68-81, 1978.

FERTIG, Mona

> Seasons that I am
> Newton, Stuart. "Review." Event 7(1):139-42, 1978.

FETHERLING, Doug

> Achilles' navel: throbs, laments and vagaries
> David, Jack. Q&Q 40(6):12, 1974.
>
> Gutteridge, Don. Brick 1:19-20, 1977.
>
> Marken, Ronald. "Poetic oozings from the navel." CVII 1(1):17-8, 1975.
>
> Scott, Chris. "Navel tactics." BiC 3(3):14, 17, 1974.
>
> Woodcock, George. "Playing with freezing fire." CanL 70:84-91, 1976.

> Our man in Utopia
> Helwig, David. "Four poets." QQ 79:404-7, 1972.
>
> Purdy, Al. "Personal effects." BiC 1(4):22, 1971.
>
> Purdy, Al. "The woman of Barrie." CanL 54:86-90, 1972.

FIAMENGO, Marya

> In praise of old women
> Almon, Bert. WCR 11(2):42, 1976.
>
> Barbour, Douglas. "Poetry chronicle IV." DR 57:355-71, 1977.
>
> Bowering, Marilyn. "Stages of poetry." CanL 74:102-4, 1977.
>
> Drage, M. CA&B 51(4):25, 1976.
>
> Gervais, Marty. Q&Q 42(7):40, 1976.
>
> Goldie, Terry. Quarry 26(4):68-9, 1977.
>
> Harvey, Roderick W. "Views of reality." ECW 5:86-9, 1976.
>
> Jordan, Kimberley. Brick 2:41, 1978.
>
> McFadgen, Lynn. "The way she says it." Bic 5(8):13-4, 1976.
>
> Wayne, Joyce. "An eastern European repast." CVII 3(1):46, 1977.

> Silt of iron
> Swann, Susan. "From minding to feeling." BiC 1(10):21-2, 1972.

FILION, Jean-Paul

    Chansons, poèmes et la grondeuse
      Cloutier, Cécile. LAQ 1973:98.

    Demain les herbes rouges
      Dudek, Louis. "Those damned visionary poets (Les poètes maudits visionnaires)." Dudek 1978:166-7. (Originally published Delta 18:5-6, 1962.)

    Sainte-Bénite de Sainte-Bénite de mémère
      Godbout, Jacques. "Ces voyages qui forment la jeunesse." Le maclean 16(4):12, 1976.

FILIP, Raymond.

    Somebody told me I look like Everyman
      Moritz, A.F. "Restless alien, ceaseless flux." BiC 8(5):23-4, 1979.

FINCH, Robert

    Poems
      Sutherland, John. "Robert Finch and the Governor General's award." Sutherland 1972:144-7.

FINLAY, Michael

    The harpo scrolls
      Gibbs, Robert. Fiddlehead 90:113, 1971.

FINNIGAN, Joan

    Entrance to the garden
      Barbour, Douglas. "Low key." CanL 44:93-4, 1970.

    Entrance to the greenhouse
      Marshall, Tom. QQ 77:294-5, 1970.

    In the brown cottage on Loughborough Lake
      Barbour, Douglas. Quarry 20(4):75, 1971.

      Barrie, B.D. Fiddlehead 93:102-3, 1972.

    It was warm and sunny when we set out
      Barbour, Douglas. DR 50:435-7, 1970.

FINNIGAN, Joan

It was warm and sunny when we set out (cont'd.)
Fiamengo, Marya. "Careful and careless." CanL 53:104-5, 1972.

Gustafson, Ralph. QQ 78:140-2, 1971.

Harcourt, Joan. Quarry 20(1):50-1, 1971.

Woods, Elizabeth. "Out of context." TamR 55:79-84, 1970.

Living together
Farmiloe, Dorothy. Q&Q 42(13):44, 1976.

Foster, Anne. "Tough and glorious days." CVII 3(4):29-31, 1978.

Goldie, Terry. Quarry 26(4):67-8, 1977.

Munton, Ann. DR 57:380-1, 1977.

Oliver, Michael Brian. "Miscellanies, metamorphosis, & myth." CanL 74:95-101, 1977.

FIRESTONE, Catherine

Daydream daughter
Barbour, Douglas. "Poetry chronicle IV." DR 57:355-71, 1977.

Brennan, Pegeen. "Striking imagery." CanL 82:113-5, 1979.

Dunn, Timothy. "Welcome to my nightmare." CanR 4(1):59, 1977.

Farmiloe, Dorothy. Q&Q 42(16):8, 1976.

Scherzer, David R. Fiddlehead 113:147-50, 1977.

FISCHER, Heinz

Gnu soup
Booth, Luella. QQ 77:295-6, 1970.

FITZGERALD, Judith

Lacerating heartwood
Barbour, Douglas. "Canadian poetry chronicle: VII." DR 59:154-75, 1979.

Donnell, David. "Three newcomers." TamR 74:69-71, 1978.

FITZGERALD, Judith

Lacerating heartwood (cont'd.)
Isaacs, Fran. Room of one's own. 3(4):43, 1978.

Mallinson, Jean. "Linked fictions, nerve-ends, and faith in language." CVII 4(3):25-8, 1979.

Victory
Barbour, Douglas. "Canadian poetry chronicle: III." DR 56:560-73, 1976.

Bartley, Jan. "Painter, word twister." ECW 3:58-9, 1975.

FLANAGAN, Robert

Body
Bailey, Don. Quarry 20(1):57-60, 1971.

Barbour, Douglas. DR 50:429, 1970.

Gravity
Aubert, Rosemary. Q&Q 45(3):19, 1979.

Barbour, Douglas. "Canadian poetry chronicle: VII." DR 59:154-75, 1979.

Brown, Allan. Quarry 28(4):81-4, 1979.

Incisions
Morozink, Mary. Quarry 22(2):72-4, 1973.

S., N. "Baring and weaving." BiC. 1(12):41, 1972.

Walker, Susan. Q&Q 39(2): 12, 1973.

Once you learn you never forget
Aubert, Rosemary. Q&Q 45(3):19, 1979.

FLEET, Brenda

Bullets and cathedrals
Bailey, Don. Quarry 21(2):54-6, 1972.

Barbour, Douglas. DR 52:165-7, 1972.

Ringrose, Christopher Xerxes. "Fiddlehead's energy." CanL 52:87-90, 1972.

FLEET, Brenda

Bullets and cathedrals (cont'd.)
Spray, Carole. Fiddlehead 92:114-6, 1972.

Weppler, Torry L. CF 52(618-9):47, 1972.

Some wild gypsy
Dabydeen, Cyril. UWR 12(2):107, 1977.

Gasparini, Len. "Gail and Anne, Tom and Gary, Brenda and Erica." BiC 6(2):24-6, 1977.

Oliver, Michael Brian. "Miscellanies, metamorphosis, & myth." CanL 74:95-101, 1977.

Pearson, Ian. Q&Q 42(15):38, 1976.

Sullen earth
Gasparini, Len. "One plus three." CanL 63:92-5, 1975.

Lloyd, Marie Myers. Quarry 24(1):67-8, 1975.

McCarthy, Dermot. Brick 1:29-30, 1977.

FLETCHER, Peggy

The hell seekers
Barbour, Douglas. DR 52:165, 1972.

Harper, A.W.J. "Four reviews." OV 8(2):n.p., 1972.

FLOOD, John

The land they occupied

Bayard, Caroline. Q&Q 43(6):44, 1977.

Barbour, Douglas. "Poetry chronicle V." DR 58:149-69, 1978.

Jones, D.G. "Born of the landscape." CanL 79:77-82, 1978.

FONES, Robert

General
McFadden, David. "The twilight of self-consciousness." Helwig 1978:78-96.

Anthropomorphiks
Sutherland, Fraser. "The effigies and agonies." BiC 2(3):44-5, 1973.

FONES, Robert

The forest city
Afanso, Rui. Q&Q 40(8):23, 1974.

Alpert, Barry. "Written on the wind (of Lake Ontario)." Open letter 3d ser, 2:5-25, 1975.

Barbour, Douglas. "The poets and presses revisited: circa 1974." DR 55:338-60, 1975.

Gasparini, Len. "Six poets who found a critic." BiC 3(7):20-2, 1974.

Keitner, Wendy. Quarry 23(4):76-7, 1974.

FORD, Cathy

General
"Interview" CapR 14:74-100, 1978.

Blood uttering
Barbour, Douglas. "Poetry chronicle V." DR 58:149-69, 1978.

Broten, Delores. "Inter medias res." ECW 9:94-6, 1977-78.

FORD, R.A.D.

Holes in space
Billings, Robert. "Hounslow's poetry lists: quality & diversity." Waves 8(1):71-6, 1979.

Fletcher, Peggy. "Vehicles of expression." CA&B 55(1):24, 1979.

The solitary city
Waddington, Miriam. "Poet without masks." CanL 48:68-70, 1971.

FOREST, Léonard

Saisons antérieures
Arcand, Pierre-André. "Poets from the end of the earth." Ellipse 16:76-82, 1973. (Tr. Barbara Kuritzky.)

Masson, Alain. "Étranglement étalement." RUM 7(2):165-95, 1974.

Poulin, Gabrielle. "L'Acadie et ses poétes." Relations 36(411):29-31, 1976.

FORGUES, Rémi-Paul

Poemes du vent et des ombres
Poulin, Gabrielle. "Une 'ombre enchanteresse': la poésie de Rémi-Paul Forgues." Relations 35(400):26-8, 1975.

FORSYTHE, Kathleen

The haircage
Booth, Luella Kerr. "Five book reviews." OV 8(3):n.p., 1972.

Time and untime
Hamel, Guy. "Recent Fiddlehead poetry books." Fiddlehead 118:137-45, 1978.

Isaacs, Fran. Room of one's own. 3(4):45, 1978.

Jenoff, Marvyne. "Seven books from two small presses." CVII 3(4):40-5, 1978.

FORTIER, Jacques

Nerfs et danse
Henchiri, Michelle. LAQ 1970:145.

Redondances
Paradis, Suzanne. LAQ 1973:111-13.

FOUR HORSEMEN
Voir/see BARRETO-RIVERA,
DUTTON, Paul,
MCCAFFERY, Steve,
NICHOL, bp.

FOURNIER, Gérard-Claude

Présages de la mer
Gallays, François. LAQ 1972:171.

FOX, Gail

Dangerous season
    Davis, Marilyn. CF 50:250-2, 1970.

    Gasparini, Len. Quarry 19(4):50-5, 1970.

    Mitcham, Allison. RUM 4(1):52, 1971.

    Rodriguez, Elizabeth. Fiddlehead 86:163-4, 1970.

    Woods, Elizabeth. "Out of context." TamR 55:79-84, 1970.

Flight of the pterodactyl
    Edwards, Mary Jane. CF 54(643):43, 1974.

    Levenson, Christopher. "Poetry review." CanR 1(2):12-3, 1974.

    Stevens, Peter. "The perils of majority." UWR 9(2):100-9, 1974.

God's odd look
    Atherton, Stan. "Echoes from within." CF 56(667):62, 1976-7.

    Barbour, Douglas. Fiddlehead 113:143-6, 1977.

    Barbour, Douglas. "Poetry chronicle IV." DR 57:355-71, 1977.

    Gasparini, Len. "Gail and Anne, Tom and Gary, Brenda and Erica."
        BiC6(2):24-6, 1977.

    Isaacs, Fran. Room of one's own 3(4):38-9, 1978.

    McFadgen, Lynn. Q&Q 42(17):28, 1976.

    Mallinson, Jean. "Poetry miscellany." ECW 7/8:151-8, 1977.

    Novak, Barbara. Quarry 26(1):67-9, 1977.

    Stuewe, Paul. QQ 85:152-4, 1978.

The royal collector of dreams
    Bailey, Don. Quarry 20(3):55-6, 1971.

    Mitcham, Allison. RUM 4(1):52, 1971.

FOX, William L.

Iron Wind
    Gibbs, Robert. Fiddlehead 90:111-2, 1971.

FRANCIS, Vincent

Creampuff waves
Linder, Norma West. "Crafted with care: more or less." CA&B
53(3):42,1978.

FRANCOEUR, Lucien

General
Royer, Jean. "Entretien: Lucien Francoeur dans sa peau de poète."
Estuaire 9-10:70-5, 1978.

Drive-in
Beausoleil, Claude. "Lucien Francoeur supertexte." NBdJ 67:74-8,
1978.

Giguère, Richard. "Trois tendances de la poésie québécoise." LAQ
1976:114-6.

Nepveu, Pierre. "La jeune poésie, la critique peut-être..." Lettres
qué 6:13-5, 1977.

Minibrixes réactés
Bélanger, Yrénée. LAQ 1972:162.

Les néons las
Beausoleil, Claude. "Lucien Francoeur supertexte." NBdJ 67:74-8,
1978.

Richard, Robert. "LAQ 1978:117-8.

5=10=15
Bélanger, Yrénée. LAQ 1972:162.

FRASER, Dawn

Echoes from labor's war: industrial Cape Breton in the 1920s
Boland, Vigo. Q&Q 43(12):12, 1977.

Linder, Norma West. "Strong words indeed." CA&B 53(2):41, 1978.

106

FRASER, Raymond

I've laughed and sung through the whole night long seen the summer sunrise in the morning
Bowering, George. Quarry 19(3):64, 1970.

Currie, Sheldon. AntigR 1(2):110-1, 1970.

Thompson, Laurel. "Canadian poetry." UWR 6(1):86-90, 1970.

The more I live
Bailey, Don. "A provincial look at ten volumes of Canadian poetry." QQ 79:242-54, 1972.

Currie, Sheldon. AntigR 2(3):118-9, 1971.

Johnson, Jane. OV 7(1):n.p., 1971.

FRÉCHETTE, Jean-Marc

L'altra riva
Hébert, François. "Robert Marteau, Guy Lafond, Jean-Marc Fréchette (et Paul Chamberland?)." Liberté 110:70-6, 1977.

Pageau, René. LAQ 1976:154-5.

Le retour
Nepveu, Pierre. "La poésie qui se fait et celle qui ne se fait pas." Lettres qué 9:15-7, 1978.

Paradis, Suzanne. "Écrit des forges." LAQ 1975:125-6.

FRÉCHETTE, Louis-Honoré

General
Séraphin, Marion. "Louis Fréchette et le Canada francais d'autrefois." Dix 37:123-57, 1972.

La voix d'un exile
Monette, Guy. "La polémique autour de La voix d'un exile ou le chant du cygne de l'immanentisme au Québec." V&I 2: 334-57, 1977.

FREEMAN, Elaine

Poems from hope
Currie, Sheldon. AntigR 2(1):99, 1971.

FREIBERG, Stanley K.

The Caplin-crowded seas: poems of Newfoundland
Jones, Elizabeth. JCP 2(1):104-7, 1979.

FRENKEL, Vera

Image spaces
Weppler, Torry L. CF 52(618-9):46, 1972.

FRIESEN, Pat

Bluebottle
Barbour, Douglas. "Canadian poetry chronicle: VI." DR 58:555-78,
1978.

The lands I am
Powell, Craig. "Locating the lands he is." CVII 3(1):36-7, 1977.

Rowland, Aaron. Q&Q 42(16):8, 1976.

Scobie, Stephen. "Hill poems from the plain." BiC 6(3):41-2, 1977.

FRITH, D.W.

The plastic undergrowth
Gibbs, Robert. Fiddlehead 90:112-3, 1971.

FUNCKEN, Eugen

General
Erb, Peter C. "The Canadian poems of Eugen Funcken, C. R."
Deutschkanadisches Jahrbuch 4:225-33, 1978.

FURBERG, Jon

>   Jonas
>   Oughton, John.   Q&Q 39(2):12, 1973.

GADD, Maxine

>   Westerns
>   Gatenby, Greg.   "Dots, starts and diapasons."   BiC 5(12):28-9, 1976.

GAGNÉ, Sylvie

>   La sourcière
>   Corriveau, Hugues,   LAQ 1977:170-1
>
>   De Bellefeuille, Normand.   "Le signifiant vorace."   NBdJ 66:75-6, 1978.

GAGNON, Madeleine

>   Antre
>   Bedard, Nicole.   LAQ 1978:118-20.
>
>   Bettinotti, Julia.   V&I 4:543-5, 1979.
>
>   Nepveu, Pierre.   "L'antre et la sorcière: Madeleine Gagnon et Francine Déry."   Lettres qué 12:15-6, 1978.

>   Poélitique
>   Fisette, Jean.   V&I 1:454-5, 1976.

>   Pour les femmes et tous les autres
>   Haeck, Philippe.   "La poésie en 1974."   Chroniques 1(3):42-5, 1975.

GALVIN, Elizabeth

>   The shuttered door
>   Lanczos, Elmar.   WCR 9(3):50-1, 1975.

GARCIA, Juan

    General
      Rancourt, Jacques. "A propos de Juan Garcia: vivre et une mission sacréé." Liberté 91:5-7, 1974.

    Corps de gloire
      Brault, Jacques. "Juan Garcia, voyageur de nuit." Garcia 1971, 81-93.

      Demers, Jeanne. "Corps de gloire de Juan Garcia ou la poésie salvatrice." LAQ 1971:126-31.

      Dionne, René. "Sur les voies de notre poésie - II." Relations 368:56-9, 1972.

      Major, Jean-Louis. UTQ 41:343-4, 1972.

      Vachon, G-André. "De Juan Garcia et de la poésie." EF 7:171-9, 1971.

GARDINER, Dwight

    A book of occasional
      Bowering, George. Open letter 2d ser., 3:81-3, 1972.

    A soul station in my ear
      Jones, D.G. "Born of the landscape." CanL 79:77-82, 1978.

GARIGUE, Philippe

    L'humaine demeure
      Moisan, Clément. LAQ 1974:143-4.

    Le temps vivant
      Wyczynski, Paul. LAQ 1973:99-100.

GARNEAU, François-Xavier

    General
      Lortie, Jeanne d'Arc. "Un héraut du nationalisme: F.-X. Garneau." Lortie 1975:253-71.

      Wyczynski, Paul. "François-Xavier Garneau et la Pologne." RUO 47:237-49, 1977.

110

GARNEAU, Hector de Saint-Denys

General

Arnold, Ivor, "Saint-Denys Garneau et la quête de la foi." RUO 44:346-53, 1974.

Audet, Noël. "Saint-Denys Garneau ou le procès métonymique." V&I 1:432-41, 1976.

Blais, Jacques. De St. Denys Garneau. Montréal: Fides, 1971. (Dossiers de documentation sur la littérature canadienne-francaise, 7.)

Blais, Jacques. Saint-Denys Garneau et le mythe d'Icare. Sherbrooke: Editions Cosmos, 1973. (Profile,8.)

Bonenfant, Joseph. "L'ombre de Mallarmé sur la poésie de Saint-Denys Garneau et de Miron." VIP 6:51-63, 1973.

D'Agostino, Saro. "Saint-Denys Garneau: 30th anniversary." Waves, 3(1):14-6, 1974.

Dionne, René. "Du nationalisme traditionnel au nationalisme personaliste--Saint Denys Garneau." Relations 365:312-5, 1971.

Gallant, Melvin. "Saint-Denys Garneau et l'éblouissement de la nuit." Eigeldinger 1978:203-15.

Giguère, Richard. "D'un 'équilibre impondérable' à une 'violence élémentaire': Évolution thématique de la poésie québécoise 1935-1965: Saint-Denys Garneau, Anne Hébert, Roland Giguère et Paul Chamberland." VIP 7:51-90, 1973.

Haeck, Philippe. "Pour Saint-Denys Garneau." NBdJ 83:60-70, 1979.

Kushner, Éva. "La poétique de l'espace chez Saint-Denys Garneau." RUO 43:540-56, 1973.

Levac, Roger. Les idées esthétiques de Saint-Denys Garneau. Montreal: McGill, 1972. (M.A. thesis.)

Major, Jean-Louis. "Petit exercise à propos du mythe de Saint-Denys Garneau." RUO 42(4):528-49, 1972.

Major, Jean-Louis. "Saint-Denys Garneau et la poésie." EF 8:176-94, 1972.

Savoie, Paul. Anne Hébert, Saint-Denys Garneau; maison vide, solitude rompue. Winnipeg:Univ. of Manitoba, 1970. (M.A. thesis.)

GARNEAU, Hector de Saint-Denys

Complete poems of Saint Denys Garneau (Tr. John Glassco)
Barbour, Douglas. "Canadian poetry chronicle: III." DR 56:560-73, 1976.

Beaver, John. Q&Q 41(12):30, 1975.

Dragland, Stan. Quarry 25(4):76-80, 1976.

Ellenwood, Ray, "Translation in Canada." Brick 2:52-4, 1978.

Jones, D.G. QQ 83:694-5, 1976.

Mezei, Kathy. "Like the wind made visible." CanL 71:83-7, 1976.

Walker, Micheline. "Poetic distinction." CF 56(663):39-40, 1976.

Woodcock, George. "Levels of translation." CVII 2(1):18-20, 1976.

Élégie ou génocide des nasopodes
Savard, Michel. LAQ 1979:121.

Oeuvres
Dionne, René. "ELit 4:391-5, 1971.

Gathercole, Patricia M. FR 45:506-7, 1971.

Hayne, David M. FrSt 28:117-8, 1974.

"The quiet revolution of Quebec." TLS 3658:399, 1972.

Vigneault, Robert. "Saint-Denys Garneau mis à jour." EF 7:389-97, 1971.

Regards et jeux dans l'espace
Berube, Renald. "Sur deux poèmes de Saint-Denys Garneau." VIP 6:91-102, 1973.

Blais, Jacques. "Le monologue ironique de Saint-Denys Garneau." Blais 1975: 141-64.

Dobbs, Bryan G. "A critical edition of Hector de Saint-Denys Garneau's Regards et jeux dans l'espace." DAI 31:753A-4A, 1970.

Pelletier, Albert. EdCF 34:115-6, 1972.

Vignault, Robert. Saint-Denys Garneau à travers Regards et jeux dans l'espace. Montreal: Presses de l'Univ. de Montréal, 1973. (Lignes québécoises.)

GARNEAU, Hector de Saint-Denys

"Accompagnement"
Haeck, Philippe. "Naissance de la poésie moderne au Québec."
EF 9(2):95-113, 1973.

Major, Jean-Louis. "Saint-Denys Garneau et la poésie." EF 8:176-94,
1972

"Autrefois"
Fisette, Jean. "La question de l'énonciation en poésie: Saint-Denys
Garneau." V&I 2:375-89, 1977.

Fisette, Jean. "The question of enunciation in poetry: Saint-Denys
Garneau." ECW 12:216-34, 1978. (Tr. Christine von Aesch.)

"Cage d'oiseau"
Bérubé, Renald. "Sur deux poèmes de Saint-Denys Garneau." VIP
6:91-102, 1973.

"C'est eux qui m'ont tué"
Guèvremont, Lise. "'C'est eux qui m'ont tué' de Saint-Denys Garneau."
BdJ 39-41:154-73, 1973.

"Jeu"
Bouygues, Claude. "Lecture du 'Jeu' ou illustration de la modernité
de Saint-Denys Garneau." PFr 9:65-71, 1974.

"Paysage en deux couleurs sur fond de ciel"
Laliberté, Yves. "Essai d'explication du poème 'Paysage en duex
couleurs sur fond de ciel' de Saint-Denys Garneau." Co-incidences
4(1):54-62, 1974.

Riser, Georges. "Le paysage métaphysique de Saint-Denys Garneau:
'Paysage en deux couleurs sur fond de ciel.'" Inc 2-3(1):5-22, 1979.

"Portrait"
Bérubé, Renald. 'Sur deux poèmes de Saint-Denys Garneau." VIP
6:91-102, 1973.

"Saules"
De Bellefeuille, Normand. "'Saules' de Saint-Denys Garneau: une
esquisse?" VIP 7:137-50, 1973.

"Spectacle de la danse"
Perron, Paul. "Essai d'analyse sémiotique d'un poème de Saint-Denys
Garneau." V&I 4:479-91, 1979.

"La vieille roue du moulin"
Turcotte, Lucie. "Inédits de Saint-Denys Garneau." EF 8:398-407,
1972.

GARNEAU, Jacques

    Les espaces de vivre à vif
       Benoît, Monique. LAQ 1973:121-3.

    Poèmes à ne plus dormir dans votre sang
       Benoît, Monique. LAQ 1973:121-3.

GARNEAU, Joseph-René-Sylvain

    Objets retrouvés (1965 ed.)
       Châtillon, Pierre. "Le 'Chateau d'eau' de Sylvain Garneau." VIP
       3:63-102, 1970.

GARNEAU, Michel

    General
       Harris, Michael. "Michel Garneau in conversation with Michael
       Harris." CVII 3(3):14-21, 1978.

       Ricard, François. "Michel Garneau poète et dramaturge." Liberté
       97-8:303-16, 1975.

       Saint-Jacques, Denis. "Michel Garneau, un prix mérité." Lettres qué
       11:48-50, 1978.

    J'ai une chanson qui gratte dans la gorge
       Bourassa, André-G. "Les poètes de la musique." Lettres qué 11:32-7,
       1978.

    J'aime la littérature elle est utile
       Blais, Jacques. UTQ 44:343, 1975.

    Langage
       Ricard, François. "Michel Garneau poète et dramaturge." Liberté
       97-8:303-16, 1975.

    Moments
       Ricard, François. "Michel Garneau poète et dramaturge." Liberté
       97-8:303-16, 1975.

    Les petits chevals amoureux
       Giguère, Richard. UTQ 47:363-4, 1978.

       Giroux, Robert. LAQ 1977:125-6.

    La plus belle île
       Benoît, Monique. "Parti Pris." LAQ 1975:128-31.

       Blais, Jacques. UTQ 45:349-50, 1976.

    Politique
       Blais, Jacques. UTQ 44:343, 1975.

GARNEAU, Saint Denys

    Voir/see GARNEAU, Hector de Saint-Denys.

GARNEAU, Sylvain

    Voir/see GARNEAU, Joseph-René-Sylvain.

GARNET, Eldon

Angel
Allan, M. CA&B 51(1):27, 1975.

Barbour, Douglas. "Petit four." BiC 1(11):19, 1972.

Dragistic, Peggy. Brick 1:37-40, 1977.

McNamara, Eugene. "The vatic upsurge." CanL 58:104-6, 1973.

Pyke, Linda Annesley. Q&Q 41(1)26, 1975.

Brebeuf: a martyrdom of Jean de
Barbour, Douglas. "Poetry chronicle V." DR 58:149-69, 1978.

David, Jack. Fiddlehead 118:168-9, 1978.

Fernstrom, Ken. Q&Q 43(17):34, 1977.

The last adventure
Barbour, Douglas. "The poets and presses revisited: circa 1974." DR 55:338-60, 1975.

Darling, Michael E. "Return of the monster." ECW 1:60-2, 1974.

Dault, Gary Michael. "Garnet and other glows." BiC 4(2):24-5, 1975.

Doyle, Mike. "Animate imaginings." CanL 66:94-7, 1975.

Gervais, C.H. Quarry 24(4):62-3, 1975.

Watt, F.W. "Why poetry? Eleven answers." CF 55(651):40-1, 1975.

Wieland, Sarah. Q&Q 41(1):26, 1975.

GASPARINI, Len

Cutty Sark
Brewster, Elizabeth. CF 51(606-7):37, 1971.

Gufstafson, Ralph. QQ 78:140-2, 1971.

Helwig, David. Quarry 20(1):39-40, 1971.

If you love
Di Cicco, Pier Giorgio. "From Chile con amor." BiC 4(12):29-9, 1975.

Globe, Alexander. "Three poets." CanL 75:85-8, 1977.

Hamilton, Jamie. Q&Q 42(3):6-7, 1976.

Moon without light
Dempster, Barry. Q&Q 45(3):19-20, 1979.

Macfarlane, David. "To feel is not to finish." BiC 8(2):25, 1979.

One bullet left
Beardsley, Doug. "A trial of immortality: recent Canadian poetry." Nj 6:118-27, 1976.

Carrington, John. Alive 35:11, 1974.

Lever, Bernice. "Seven nearly alive books." Alive 40:18, 1974.

McMullen, Robert. Alive 41:33, 1975.

Rogers, Linda. "Handful of dust." CanL 65:119-20, 1975.

Wallace, Bronwen. Quarry 24(2):56-7, 1975.

Tunnel bus to Detroit
Bailey, Don. Quarry 21(2):56-7, 1972.

Ringrose, Christopher Xerxes. "Fiddlehead's energy." CanL 52:87-90, 1972.

Stevens, Peter. QQ 78:627-8, 1971.

Van den Hoven, A. "Two Windsor poets: Len Gasparini & Don Polson." Alive 21:4-5, 1972.

GATENBY, Greg

> The salmon country
> Daniel, Lorne. "From screen gems to animal acts." BiC 8(4):11-2,
> 1979.

> Johnson, Sam. "The poet's space." Waves 7(2):60-3, 1979.

> Pearson, Ian. Q&Q 45(2):46, 1979.

GAULIN, Huguette

> Lecture en vélocipède
> Pressault, Guy. LAQ 1972:164.

GAUTHIER, Jacques

> À la rencontre de mai
> Chamberland, Roger. LAQ 1971:122-3.

> Degel en noir et blanc
> Chamberland, Roger. LAQ 1971:122-3.

> L'oraison des saisons
> Chamberland, Roger. LAQ 1971:122-3.

GAUTHIER, Serge

> Glottes
> Bouvier, Luc. LAQ 1977:144-6.

> De Bellefeuille, Normand. "La gageure du lisible." NBdJ 60:70-1,
> 1977.

GAUVREAU, Claude

> Bibliography
> Imbeau, Gaston. Bibliographie des écrits déjà publiés de Claude
> Gauvreau. Montreal: Bibliothèque Nationale du Québec, 1977.

GAUVREAU, Claude

General
  Bélanger, Marcel. "La lettre contre l'esprit ou quelques points de repères sur la poésie de Claude Gauvreau." ELit 5:481-97, 1972.

  Bourassa, André-G. "Claude Gauvreau. La fin d'une occultation." Mlit 134:83-5, 1978.

  Bourassa, André-G. "Claude Gauvreau: la poésie pure." Bourassa 1977:132-40.

  Bourassa, André-G. "The poetic design of Claude Gauvreau." ECW 9:70-82,1977-8. (Tr. Christine von Aesch.)

  Bourassa, André-G. "Le projet poétique de Claude Gauvreau." Lettres qué 7:12-7, 1977.

  Brunet, Yves-Gabriel. "Portrait d'un poète: Claude Gauvreau." Culture vivante 22:31-5, 1971.

  Marchand, Jacques. Claude Gauvreau, poète et mythocrate: essai. Montréal: VLB ed., 1979.

  Rancourt, Jacques. "Poésie exploréene: Claude Gauvreau." Brindeau 1973:558-61.

  Saint-Denys, Janou. Claude Gauvreau: le cygne. Montréal: Presses de l'Univ. de Québec, 1978.

  Saint-Denys, Janou. "Pour Gauvreau: un témoignage." V&I 3:32-9, 1977.

  Soublière, Roger. "Les inédits." BdJ 29:94-5, 1971.

Oeuvres créatrices complètes
  Mélançon, Robert. "La poésie de Claude Gauvreau." LAQ 1977:297-304.

  Nepveu, Pierre. "Note provisoire sur les Oeuvres créatrices complètes." Lettres qué 7:17-8, 1977.

  Théorêt, France. "Présentation des Oeuvres créatrices de Gauvreau." NBdJ 58:95-8, 1977.

  Vandendorpe, Christian. "Un forcené du langage, Gauvreau, Oeuvres créatrices complètes." QuéFr 28:52-3, 1977.

"Sentinelle-onde"
  Gervais, André. "Eaux retenues d'une lecture: 'Sentinelle-onde' de Claude Gauvreau." V&I 2:390-406, 1977.

"Sous nar"
  Hurtubise, Nicole. BdJ 39-41:174-205, 1973.

118

GAY, Michel

L'implicite 3 le filigrane
Monette, Pierre, "D'une Pierre trois coups: La nouvelle barre du jour
édite." Lettres qué 13:25-7, 1979.

GAYSEK, Fred

First scratches no blood eye down
Barbour, Douglas. "Poetry chronicle V." DR 58:149-69, 1978.

Hamel, Guy. "Recent Fiddlehead poetry books." Fiddlehead 118:137-45,
1978.

GEDDES, Gary

Black walnut
Johnson, Jane. OV 7(1):n.p., 1971.

Letter of the master of horse
Crawford, Terry. Quarry 23(2):75-6, 1974.

Denham, Paul. HAB 25:366-7, 1974.

Stevens, Peter. "The perils of majority." UWR 9(2):100-9, 1974.

Sullivan, D.H. WCR 9(3):46-8, 1975.

Rivers inlet
Gervais, C.H. Quarry 22(2):78-9, 1973.

Scobie, Stephen. "A dash for the border." CanL 56:89-92, 1973.

Snakeroot
Gasparini, Len. "One plus three." CanL 63:92-5, 1975.

War and other measures
Barbour, Douglas. "Poetry chronicle IV." DR 57:355-71, 1977.

Lane, M. Travis. "Making Canadian history." Fiddlehead 111:134-8,
1976.

McFadgen, Lynn. Q&Q 42(12):13, 1976.

Merrett, Robert James. "Winning a reader." CanL 79:96-8, 1978.

Niederman, Michael. "Bennies for the old guys: great crimes of
literature no. 477." Brick 2:9-10, 1978.

Stevens, Peter. QQ 84:688-90, 1977.

Tefs, Wayne. "Poetry's other leg: a revisioned vision." CVII 2(3):
42-3, 1976.

Woodcock, George. "Penny for the old guy." BiC 5(8):5-6, 1976.

GENEST, Guy

    Le parti pris de la vie
        Arcand, Pierre-André. RUM 7(3):109, 1974.

        Blais, Jacques. UTQ 44:341, 1975.

        Paradis, Suzanne. LAQ 1974:150-1.

GEOFFROY, Jacques

    La catoche orange
        Gallays, François.   LAQ 1970:147.

GEOFFROY, Louis

    Empire State coca blues
        Cloutier, Guy L.   LAQ 1971:152.

    L.S.D., voyage
        Bourque, Paul-André. "Avatars de l''underground' (?)!" LAQ 1974:146-7.

    Le saint rouge et la pécheresse
        Dionne, René. "Où va notre poésie?" Relations 357:55-7, 1971.

        Fournier, Gérard-Claude. "Trois poètes." LAQ 1970:147.

        Marcotte, Gilles. EF 7:111-2, 1971.

    Totem poing fermé
        Carrière, André. "Trois auteurs en quête d'un langage." LAQ 1973:100-1.

GÉRIN-LAJOIE, Antoine

    General
        Dionne, René. Antoine Gérin-Lajoie, homme de lettres. Sherbrooke: Ed. Naaman, 1978.

GERVAIS, André

    L'instance de l'ire
        Corriveau, Hugues. LAQ 1977:152-3.

    Trop plein pollen, fragments lucides
        Giguère, Richard. "Les Herbes rouges: une grande 'petite revue.'" LAQ 1975:118-21.

GERVAIS, C.H.

Bittersweet
Dale, Sharon Goodier. "In Canada and out." BiC 2(2):43-4, 1973.

Other marriage vows
Barbour, Douglas. DR 50:433-5, 1970.

Marshall, Tom. "Canpo: a chronicle." Quarry 19(4):50-4, 1970.

Poems for American daughters
Dempster, Barry. "Poetry from Porcupine's Quill: new publisher's first 3 books." Alive 50:19, 1976.

Gatenby, Greg. Q&Q 42(7):41-2, 1976.

Hosein, Clyde. Quarry 25(4):70-1, 1976.

Jones, D.G. "Born of the landscape." CanL 79:77-82, 1978.

McCarthy, Dermot. "Mosquitoes and mundane heroism." ECW 5:75-9, 1976.

McNamara, Eugene. "In a high clean style." CanL 78:88-90, 1978.

A sympathy orchestra
Bailey, Don. "A provincial look at ten volumes of Canadian poetry." QQ 79:242-54, 1972.

GERVAIS, Guy

Poésie I
Major, Jean-Louis. UTQ 39:427-8, 1970.

GIBBS, Robert

General
Lane, M. Travis. "Roads round about here: the poetry of Robert Gibbs." HAB 23(4):47-54, 1972.

All this night long
Barbour, Douglas. "Canadian poetry chronicle: VII." DR 59:154-75, 1979.

Oliver, Michael Brian. "Tantramar--and Saint John and Fredericton--revisited." Fiddlehead 122:115-24, 1979.

Earth Charms heard so early
Bailey, Don. Quarry 20(3):54-5, 1971.

The road from here
Lane, Patrick. New 12:41-3, 1970.

GIBSON, Shirley

I am watching
André, Michael. QQ 80:658, 1973.

David, Jack. Q&Q 39(6):13, 1973.

Zimmerman, Susan. "Musicales." BiC 2(4):27-30, 1973.

GIGNAC, Rodrigue

Opale
Dionne, René. "Sur les voies de notre poésie-II." Relations 368:56-9, 1972.

Suite...
Dionne, René. "Où va notre poésie?" Relations 357:55-7, 1971.

GIGUÈRE, Roland

General
Bourneuf, Roland. "Roland Giguère." Ellipse 2:30-7, 1970. (Tr. Cormac Gerrard Cappon.)

Gauthier, Judith L. L'expérience de la création littéraire dans la poésie de Roland Giguère. Montreal: McGill, 1975, c1976. (M.A. thesis.)

Gauvreau, Claude. "Les affinités surréalistes de Roland Giguère." ELit 5:501-11, 1972.

Giguère, Richard. "D'un 'équilibre impondérable' à une 'violence élémentaire': évolution thématique de la poésie québécoise 1935-1965: Saint-Denys Garneau, Anne Hébert, Roland Giguère et Paul Chamberland." VIP 7:51-90, 1973.

Giguère, Roland. "La poésie est une lampe d'obsidienne." Liberté 14(1-2):32-33, 1972.

Lajoie, Yvan. "Roland Giguère, à la recherche de l'essentiel." ELit 5:411-28, 1972.

Rancourt, Jacques. "Au centre du feu: Roland Giguère." Brindeau 1973:571-7.

Ricard, François. "Giguère et Ducharme revisited." Liberté 91:94-105, 1974.

Robert, Guy." Roland Giguère." Le maclean 11(7):40, 1971.

GIGUÈRE, Ronald

L'âge de la parole
Lajoie, Yvan. "Roland Giguère, à la recherche de l'essentiel." ELit 5:411-28, 1972.

Maugey, Axel. "Roland Giguère." Maugey 1972: 145-65.

Forêt vierge folle
Cloutier, Guy. "Pour nourrir les oiseaux il faut faire son propre pain." NBdJ 81:82-6, 1979.

Giguère, Richard. UTQ 48:354-5, 1979.

Hébert, François. "Roland Giguère: une poésie aux filets réversibles." Liberté 122:124-7, 1979.

Lemaire, Michel. "Multiple Giguère." Lettres qué 13:17-8, 1979.

Marchand, Jacques. LAQ 1978:121-3.

Le main au feu
Brochu, André. LAQ 1973:93-6.

Mirror and letters to an escapee (Tr. Shiela Fischman)
Barbour, Douglas. "Canadian poetry chronicle: VI." DR 58:555-78, 1978.

Downes, G.V. "Excellence that needs no defence." CVII 4(2):48-9, 1979.

Yeux fixes
Fisette, Jean. "Yeux fixes--de l'ambiguité à la double lecture." Fisette 1977: 103-29.

"L'homme à la paille"
Purdy, Anthony. "Rôland Giguère et l'espace de l'autre: commentaire de deux poèmes." V&I 4:217-32, 1978.

"Le magicien"
Purdy, Anthony. "Roland Giguère et l'espace de l'autre: commentaire de deux poèmes." V&I 4:217-32, 1978.

"La main de bourreau finit toujours par pourrir"
Langevin, Lysane. "La main du bourreau finit toujours par pourrir: analyse". BdJ 39-40-41:206-26, 1973.

"Les mots-flots"
Gervais, André. "Lecture/écriture de Roland Giguère: 'Les mots-flots.'" V&I 3:302-19, 1977.

"Pouvoir du noir"
Laroche, Maximilien. "'Pouvoir du noir' de Roland Giguère ou la poésie comme critique de l'idéologie." Laroche 1975:19-40.

GIGUÉRE, Ronald

"Vivre mieux"
Lajoie, Yvan. "Roland Giguère, à la recherche de l'essentiel." ELit 5:411-28, 1972.

GILBERT, Gerry

Grounds
Barbour, Douglas. "Poetry chronicle V." DR 58:149-69, 1978.

Fernstrom, Ken. Q&Q 43(10):38-9, 1977.

Fraser, Keath. "The pain of its own rejection." ECW 11:284-8, 1978.

Oliver, Michael Brian. "Lost and found." Fiddlehead 119:106-16, 1978.

Journal to the East
MacCulloch, Clare. "Th lly fadth & ltd r haikus to illuminate." BiC 4(11):19-22, 1975.

Money
Coleman, Victor. Open letter 2d ser., 1:76-7, 1971-72.

Skies
Barbour, Douglas. "The poets and presses revisited: circa 1974." DR 55:338-60, 1975.

White lunch
Dudek, Louis. "The new Vancouver poetry." Dudek 1978: 186-92. (Originally published Culture 25:323-30, 1964.)

GILL, M. Lakshmi

First clearing
Sundara, P.K., WCR 8(1):62-3, 1973.

Mind walls
Bailey, Don. "A provincial look at ten volumes of Canadian poetry." QQ 79:242-54, 1972.

Sundara, P.K. WCR 8(1):62-3, 1973.

Weppler, Torry L. CF 52(618-9):47, 1972.

GILL, Stephen M.

Reflections: (a collection of poems)
Turner, J. Garth. Q&Q 39(2):13, 1973.

Wounds: (a collection of poems)
Barr, Arlee. Alive 35:11, 1974.

GIRARDIN, Robert G.

Peinture sur verbe
Engel, Christiane.   LAQ 1976:161-3.

Fisette, Jean.   "Poésie récente, poésie diverse."   V&I 2:440-3, 1977.

GIST, T. Kenneth

Night
Bird, A.L.   Q&Q 39(3):9, 1973.

GLASSCO, John

General
Clark, Wayne.   "In the embrace of an erotic muse."   Maclean's 93(51):10-2, 1979.

Dobbs, Kildare.   "The great Glassco: memoirs of a gentleman of pleasure."   Maclean's 88(8):48-52, 1975.

Jamieson, MacLean.   "John Glassco: the eye of the stranger."   ApF 1:68-76, 1974.

Marshall, Tom.   "Major Canadian poets III: the modernists."   CF 58(686):13-7, 1979.

Murdoch, Charles.   "Essential Glassco."   CanL 65:28-41, 1975.

Murdoch, Charles.   "La poésie et la prose de John Glassco."   Ellipse 14-15:128-44, 1973. (Tr. Marc Lebel.)

Montreal
Beardsley, Doug.   "A trial of immortality: recent Canadian poetry."   Nj 6:118-27, 1976.

Shaw, Robert B.   "A voice from Canada."   Poetry 126:50-3, 1975.

Selected poems
Fetherling, Doug.   "An overqualified poet deserves our notice."   SatN 87(4):38-41, 1972.

Hornyansky, Michael.   UTQ 41:335-6, 1972.

Shaw, Robert B.   "A voice from Canada."   Poetry 126:50-3, 1975.

Ware, Randall.   "Diamond in the rough."   BiC 1(4):22, 1971.

GODIN, Gérald

    General
      Smith, Donald. "Gérald Godin. poète, éditeur, journaliste." Lettres
      qué 1:30-2, 1976.

    Les cantouques
      Maugey, Axel. "Gérald Godin." Maugey 1972:226-31.

    Libertés surveillées
      Benoît, Monique. "Parti Pris." LAQ 1975:128-31.

    "Retable"
      Pélosse, Cécile. "La recherche du pays chez Paul-Marie Lapointe et
      Gérald Godin--concerto pour arbres." V&I 1:80-8, 1975.

GODIN, Guy

    Iom
      Dionne, René. "Sur les voies de notre poésie - III." Relations
      370:122-4, 1972.

GODIN, Robert

    Les jumelles interdites
      Cloutier, Cécile. LAQ 1976:171-2.

GOLD, Artie

    Cityflowers
      Grady, Wayne. "Axioms, eroicas, and mirrors." Nj 7&8:108-20, 1976.

      Hamilton, Jamie. "Visual filters, pyrex forms." BiC 4(11):18-9,
      1975.

      Pyke, Linda. "Artie Gold, Artie Gold." CVII 3(4):11-2, 1978.

    Even yr photograph looks afraid of me
      Bayard, Caroline. Q&Q 42(15):38, 1976.

      Burgess, G. C. Ian. Fiddlehead 112:148-50, 1977.

      Di Cicco, Pier Giorgio. "One up, two down." BiC 5(9):33, 1976.

      Pyke, Linda. "Artie Gold, Artie Gold." CVII 3(4):11-2, 1978.

    Some of the cat poems
      McFadden, Dave. "Of newts and natural Gold." BiC 8(1):14-5, 1979.

    Wildflowers
      Powell, D. Reid. Q&Q 42(1):26, 1976.

GOLDSMITH, Oliver

"The Rising Village"
Fetherling, Doug. "The Canadian Goldsmith." CanL 68-9:121-4, 1976.

Hughes, K.J. "Oliver Goldsmith's 'The rising village.'" LURev 7(1)/8(1&2):35-53, 1976(?).

GOM, Leona

Kindling
Barbour, Douglas. QQ 80:142-3, 1973.

Lanczos, Elmar. WCR 8(2):61-3, 1973.

Zimmerman, Susan. "Musicales." BiC 2(4):27-30, 1973.

The singletree
Amprimoz, Alexandre. "The space of memory." CanL 80:72-4, 1979.

Barbour, Douglas. "Poetry chronicle V." DR 58:149-69, 1978.

Cogswell, Fred. Fiddlehead 110:130, 1976.

Fraser, Eleanor. "Dreaming of a dactyl." CVII 2(3):48-9, 1976.

Long, Kenneth. WCR 10(4):11-2, 1976.

Smith, Raymond J. "Poetry chronicle." OntR 4:104-10, 1976.

GOOL, Reshard

In Medusa's eye and other poems
Dyroff, Jan Michael. "Gulf strains." BiC 2(3):48,50, 1973.

GOTLIEB, Phyllis

Doctor Umlaut's earthly kingdom
Barbour, Douglas. "Canadian poetry chronicle 2." DR 55:748-59, 1975-76.

Bolick, Merle. Quarry 23(4):77-9, 1974.

Hornyansky, Michael. UTQ 44:335, 1975.

Marshall, Tom. "Inferno, paradise and slapstick." CanL 64:104-7, 1975.

McFadgen, Lynn. Q&Q 40(6):12, 1974.

GOTLIEB, Phyllis

Ordinary, moving
  Aldan, Daisy. "The words of the tribe." Poetry 118:35-40, 1971.

  Barbour, Douglas. Quarry 19(4):56, 1970.

  Barbour, Douglas. "Phyllis Gotlieb's children of the future: Sunburst and Ordinary,moving." JCF 3(2):72-6, 1974.

  Ditsky, John M. "The autobiography of Phyllis Gotlieb." UWR 5(2):111-3, 1970.

  Hornyansky, Michael. UTQ 39:334, 1970.

  Keyes, Mary. CF 49:243, 1970.

  Pacey, Desmond. "A Canadian quintet." Fiddlehead 83:79-86, 1970.

  Rapoport, Janis. "Challenging the game." TamR 54:85-7, 1970.

The works: collected poems
  Aubert, Rosemary. Q&Q 44(10):12, 1978.

  Barbour, Douglas. "A cornucopia of poems." TamR 76:101-7, 1979.

  Bartlett, Brian. "We dipped and we flipped." BiC 7(8):16, 1978.

  Hornyansky, Michael. UTQ 48:344, 1979.

GOUIN, Gaston

J'il de noir
  Dionne, René. "Sur les voies de notre poésie--II." Relations 368:56-9, 1972.

  Gervais, Marielle. LAQ 1971:160.

  Sanderson, Gertrude. AntigR 14:108-10, 1973.

GOURLAY, Elizabeth

Motions dreams & aberrations
  Barbour, Douglas. CF 49:242, 1970.

  Barbour, Douglas. "The young poets and the little presses, 1969." DR 50:112-26, 1970.

  Cogswell, Fred. "Lonely runners." CanL 44:86-8, 1969.

GRACE, Gregory

Heaven's door
Fraser, Wayne. "Made human by humour." CVII 3(1):40-1, 1977.

Gatenby, Greg. "Sur realism rampant." BiC 5(8):21-2, 1976.

Linder, Norma West. CA&B 52(1):26, 1976.

Solecki, Sam. Fiddlehead 112:151-5, 1977.

GRANDBOIS, Alain

Bibliography
Bibiothèque nationale du Québec. "Fonds Alain Grandbois: inventaire dressé par Danielle Rompré: préf. de Jean-Guy Pilon." Montreal 1977.

General
Beauchemin, Normand. Recherches sur l'accent d'après les poèmes d'Alain Grandbois: étude acoustique et statisque. Québec: Presses de l'Univ. Laval, 1970.(Langue et littérature francaises au Canada, 6.)

Beaver, John. "Alain Grandbois: a final note." JCF 4(1):144-5, 1975.

Blais, Jacques. Présence d'Alain Grandbois: avec quatorze poèmes parus de 1956 à 1969. Québec: Presses de l'Univ. Laval, 1974. (Vie des lettres québécoises, 11.)

Dallard, Sylvie. "Alain Grandbois et la conscience de son temps." Dallard 1977:23-99.

Dallard, Sylvie. L'univers poétique d'Alain Grandbois. Sherbrooke, Qué.: Éditions Cosmos, 1975.(Profils, 9.)

"Extracts from Liberté: critical appraisals of Alan Grandbois." Ellipse 14-5:69-81, 1973.

Fournier, Claude. Le paysage de l'amoreuse dans la poésie d'Alain Grandbois. Trois-Rivières:Univ. du Quebec, 1972, c1975. (M.A. thesis.)

Fournier, Gérard-Claude. "L'opposition des espaces dans l'oeuvre d'Alain Grandbois." Co-incidences 5(1):51-74, 1975.

Gallays, François. Les mots et les images dans la poésie d'Alain Grandbois. Ottawa: Univ. d'Ottawa, 1971. (Ph.D. thesis.)

Greffard, Madeleine. Alain Grandbois. Montreal: Fides, 1975. (Écrivans canadiens d'aujourd'hui, 12.)

Pageau, René. "Un visage d'Alain Grandbois." CC-R 5(4):54-67, 1977.

Poulin, Gabrielle. "La poésie d'Alain Grandbois." Relations 345:22-3, 1970.

GRANDBOIS, Alain

    L'etoile poupre
      Pageau, René. "Un visage d'Alain Grandbois." CC-R 5(4):54-67, 1977.

    Les îles de la nuit
      Audet, Noel. "Alain Grandbois ou le procès métaphorique." V&I
      2:60-70, 1976.

      Blais, Jacques. "L'initiation au surréalisme." Blais 1975:295-323.

      Gallays, Francois. "Les îles de la nuit: prestiges d'un titre."
      Inc 2-3(1):23-35, 1979.

      Laliberté, Yves. "Lecture structurale d'Alain Grandbois: Le poème 18
      des Iles de la nuit." V&I 1:89-105, 1975.

    Poèmes
      Lemaire, Michel. LAQ 1979:123-5.

    "Avec ta robe..."
      Bolduc, Yves. "Amour et expérience du temps, (Analyse du poème:
      'Avec ta robe...')." Inc 1(1-3):85-92, 1977.

      Haeck, Philippe. "Naissance de la poésie moderne au Québec." EF
      9:95-113, 1973.

    "Les glaïeuls..."
      Charron, Claude-Yves. "Petits prolégomènes." BdJ 39-41:48-57, 1973.

    "O tourments..."
      Audet, Noel. "Alain Grandbois ou le procès métaphorique." V&I
      2:60-70, 1976.

    "Pris et protégé"
      Major, Jean-Louis. "Relire 'Pris et protégé!" Inc 1(1-3):70-84, 1977.

GRASSER, Carolyn

    The great getting-away
      Sutherland, Fraser. Q&Q 40(5):18, 1974.

    Nine lives
      Jewinski, Ed. Q&Q 41(13)32-33, 1975.

GREEN, Jim

North book
    de Santana, Hubert. "Poetic torrents, erotic jewels." BiC 5(2):36-8, 1976.

    Fletcher, Peggy. CA&B 52(1):26, 1976.

    Gatenby, Greg. Q&Q 41(13):33, 1975.

    Lane, Patrick. "Born round here." CVII 2(2):26-7, 1976.

    MacKendrick, Louis K. "Small press review." OntR 8:106-12, 1978.

    Sarna, Lazar. "A southwesterner meandering while east meets west." ECW 5:108-9, 1976.

    Turner, Gordon P. "Northern poems." CanL 70:101-3, 1976.

"Seal hunt, Boothia Peninsula"
    Turner, Gordon P. "The breath of Arctic men: the Eskimo north in poetry from within and without." QQ 83:13-35, 1976.

GRIER, Eldon

The assassination of colour
    Barbour, Douglas, "Canadian poetry chronicle: VII." DR 59:154-75, 1979.

    McNally, Paul. Fiddlehead 120:131-3, 1979.

Selected poems 1955-1970
    Barbour, Douglas. QQ 80:472, 1973.

    Garnet, Eldon. "Five poets on the brink of our consciousness." SatN 87(6):38-42, 1972.

    Gasparini, Len. "Eldon Grier." CanL 50:79-81, 1971.

    Sutherland, Frazer. "Foreign fabulous free." BiC 1(10):19-21, 1972.

GUAY, Jean-Pierre

General
    Guay, Jean-Pierre. "Journal d'un écrivain." NBdJ 78:48-62, 1979.

Ô l'homme
    Pontbriand, Jean-Noël. "Poètes québécois publiés en France." LAQ 1975:134-7.

Porteur d'os
    Guay, Jean-Pierre. "Journal d'un écrivain." NBdJ 78:48-62, 1979.

    Pontbriand, Jean-Noël. "Poètes québécois publiés en France." LAQ 1975:134-7.

GUIMONT, Madeleine

Dans l'aura de l'absence
  Bouvier, Luc. LAQ 1977:168-70.

Le manège apprivoisé
  Henchiri, Sliman.   LAQ 1971:170-1.

Les roses bleues de la malombre
  Siguret, Françoise. LAQ 1975:127.

GUSTAFSON, Ralph

  Bibliography
    Alison, L.M. and Keitner, W.J.R. "Ralph Gustafson: a bibiliography in
    progress, 1929-1972." WCR 9(1):29-38, 1974.

  General
    Keitner, Wendy. "Gustafson's double hook." CanL 79:44-53.

    Keitner, Wendy Joan Robbins. Ralph Gustafson: heir of centuries in a
    country without myths. Kingston, Ont.: Queen's Univ., 1973. (Ph.D.
    thesis.)

    Marshall, Tom. "Major Canadian poets III: the modernists." CF
    58(686):13-7, 1979.

    Mullins, Stanley G. "Recent poetry of a non-sophisticate: Ralph
    Gustafson." LauURev 7(1):32-48, 1974.

    Pettigrew, Damien. "Interview with Ralph Gustafson." CVII
    4(2):26-30, 1979.

    Sandler, Linda. "Poets are the least liars." Q&Q 41(12):14-5, 1975.

  Corners in the glass
    Barbour, Douglas. "Canadian poetry chronicle: VI." DR 58:555-78,
    1978.

    Beardsley, Doug. "Crystal clear." ECW 10:55-6, 1978.

    Billings, Robert. Quarry 27(1):76-9, 1978.

    Daniel, Lorne. Q&Q 43(15)35-6, 1977.

    Fletcher, Peggy. "No two alike." CA&B 53(2):43-4, 1978.

    Hatfield, Stephen. Waves 6(1):69-72, 1977.

    Hornyansky, Michael. UTQ 47:349-50, 1978.

    Lecker, Robert. Fiddlehead 117:124-5, 1978.

    Lochhead, Douglas. UWR 13(2):104-5, 1978.

GUSTAFSON, Ralph

Corners in the glass (cont'd.)

Mandel, Eli. "Three modernists in perspective." BiC 7(10):35-6, 1978.

Millward, A.E. "The many faces of death." CVII 3(4):22-4, 1978.

West, David S. "Old wine, broken bottles, cut glass." CanL 80:109-12, 1979.

Fire on stone

Amabile, George. "Finding the elusive presence." CVII 1(2):11, 1975.

Bagchee, Shyamal. "Two poets and a half." ECW 3:65-9, 1975.

Beardsley, Doug. "A trial of immortality: recent Canadian poetry." Nj 6:118-27, 1976.

Casto, Robert C. "Visionary paradoxes: the poetry of Ralph Gustafson." Waves 4(2):17-24, 1976.

Cogswell, Fred. "Temperament versus technique." CanL 64:112-3, 1975.

Fraser, Keath. "Creative juices swift and slow." BiC 3(7):16, 1974.

Gibbs, Robert. "Presiding voices: Purdy, Layton and Gustafson." DR 56:356-65, 1976.

Gutteridge, Don. QQ 82:140, 1975.

Herringer, Barbara. WCR 10(3):32, 1976.

Jamieson, MacLean. ApF 2:r27, 1975.

Keitner, Wendy. HAB 27:73-4, 1976.

Keitner, Wendy. Quarry 24(2):52-3, 1975.

Lane, M. Travis. "The concrete paradise: the major theme of Ralph Gustafson's Fire on Stone." Fiddlehead 104:106-10, 1975.

Powell, D. Reid. Q&Q 40(11):21, 1974.

Rosenblatt, J. "Filet mignon poetry." CF 54(646):20, 1974.

Sandler, Linda. "Gustafson & others." TamR 64:89-94, 1974.

Skelton, Robin. "Ralph Gustafson: review and retrospect." Mosaic 8(2):167-79, 1975.

Flight in darkness

Sutherland, John. "Ralph Gustafson: poet and editor." Sutherland 1972:98-9.

GUSTAFSON, Ralph

Ixion's wheel

Barbour, Douglas. Quarry 19(4):56-7, 1970.

Hornyansky, Michael. UTQ 39:327-8, 1970.

Jones, D.G. "Voices in the dark." CanL 45:68-74, 1970.

Motyer, Arthur. QQ 77:129-30, 1970.

Pacey, Desmond. "A Canadian quintet." Fiddlehead 83:79-86, 1970.

Yates, J. Michael. WascanaR 5(1):105-7, 1970.

Zitner, S.P. CF 49:299, 1970.

Selected poems

Barbour, Douglas. QQ 80:472-3, 1973.

Fetherling, Doug. "A rare sense of the continuity of things." SatN 87(12):56-7, 1972.

Hare, Jannis. CA&B 49(1):24, 1973.

Hosein, Clyde. "Only the truth is true." BiC 1(11):26, 28, 1972.

Keitner, Wendy. Quarry 22(1):75-7, 1973.

Lane, M. Travis. "The fundamental question about poetry." Fiddlehead 96:106-14, 1973.

Purdy, Al. WascanaR 8(2):68-70, 1973.

Ringrose, Christopher Xerxes. "A tilting equipoise." CanL 58:82-6, 1973.

Thompson, Steve. Q&Q 38(11):12, 1972.

Soviet poems: Sept. 13 to Oct. 5, 1976.

Barbour, Douglas. "Canadian poetry chronicle: VI." DR 58:555-78, 1978.

Brown, Allan. "Playing parts: five from Turnstone Press." Waves 8(1):67-71, 1979.

Daniel, Lorne. Q&Q 44(11):40, 1978.

Folsom, Eric. Quarry 28(1):81-5, 1979.

Hornyansky, Michael. UTQ 48:343-4, 1979.

134

GUSTAFSON, Ralph

Soviet poems: Sept. 13 to Oct. 5, 1976 (cont'd.)
Levenson, Christopher. "A meeting of the twain." BiC 7(9):14, 16, 1978.

McNally, Paul. Fiddlehead 121:153-4, 1979.

Novak, Barbara. "Poetry chronicle." TamR 75:88-95, 1978.

Themes and variations for sounding brass
Fetherling, Doug. "A rare sense of the continuity of things." SatN 87(12):56-7, 1972.

Gervais, C.H. Quarry 22(2):79, 1973.

Lane, M. Travis. "The fundamental question about poetry." Fiddlehead 96:106-14, 1973.

Pokorny, Amy. Quarry 22(2):75, 1973.

Ringrose, Christopher Xerxes. "A tilting equipoise." CanL 58:82-6, 1973.

GUTTERIDGE, Don

Borderlands
Barbour, Douglas. "Canadian poetry chronicle 2." DR 55:748-59, 1975-76.

Cooley, Dennis. "Of that time, of this place." CVII 2(3):18-9, 1976.

Gervais, C.H. Quarry 24(4):62-3, 1975.

Hamilton, Jamie. Q&Q 41(6):30, 1975.

Lane, M. Travis. "Be bold, be bold, be not too bold: the subject in poetry." Fiddlehead 106:121-7, 1975.

Solecki, Sam. QQ 82:646-7, 1975.

Sullivan, D.H. WCR 10(3):36-8, 1976.

Coppermine: the quest for north
Cavanagh, David. "Mining for mythos." Fiddlehead 100:102-4, 1974.

Denham, Paul. HAB 25:366, 1974.

GUTTERIDGE, Don

Coppermine: the quest for north

Cavanagh, David. "Mining for mythos." Fiddlehead 100:102-4, 1974.

Denham, Paul. HAB 25:366, 1974.

Levenson, Christopher. "Poetry review." CanR 1(2):12-3, 1974.

MacLulich, T.D. "Inarticulate north." Open letter 2d ser, 7:119-20, 1974.

Spencer, Nigel. "Old and new trips." BiC 2(6):17-9, 1973.

Stevens, Peter. "The perils of majority." UWR 9(2):100-9, 1974.

Sullivan, D.H. WCR 9(3):46-8, 1975.

Death at Quebec

Bailey, Don. "A provincial look at ten volumes of Canadian poetry." QQ 79:242-54, 1972.

Riel: a poem for voices

Govier, Katherine. "Voice prints." BiC 1(11):35-6, 1972.

Gutteridge, Don. "Riel: historical man or literary symbol?" HAB 21(3):3-15, 1970.

McSweeney, Kerry. Quarry 20(1):60-2, 1971.

Tecumseh

Barbour, Douglas. "Poetry chronicle IV." DR 57:355-71, 1977.

Pyke, Linda. "A mari usque ad mare: four poetic landscapes." Q&Q 42(17):29, 1976.

Scobie, Stephen. Fiddlehead 114:140, 1970.

Sullivan, D.H. WCR 12(3):50-1, 1978.

Whiteman, Bruce. "Tecumseh: poet in his pure air." Brick 2:63-5, 1978.

A true history of Lambton County

Barbour, Douglas. "Canadian poetry chronicle: VI." DR 58: 555-78, 1978.

Donnell, David. "The frustrated cartographer." CVII 3(4):10-1, 1978.

Lane, M. Travis. Fiddlehead 117:140-3, 1978.

Sullivan, D.H. WCR 13(3):42-3, 1979.

The village within

Brewster, Elizabeth. Quarry 20(1):55, 1971.

HAAS, Maara

The street where I live
Fletcher, Peggy. CA&B 52(3):42, 1977.

HAECK, Philippe

General
Haeck, Philippe. "Le hasard et l'attention." NBdJ 71:24-51, 1978.
Extrait de Naissances: de l'écriture québecoise: essais

Car tendresse
Fisette, Jean. "L'écriture moderne. Encore. Enfin." V&I 4:148-50,
1978.

Polyphanie: roman d'apprentissage: poèmes
Bonenfant, Joseph. "Polyphonie. D'une écriture ouvrière." NBdJ
71:79-83, 1978.

Giguère, Richard. UTQ 48:355-8, 1979.

Krysinski, Wladimir et Roy, Max. LAQ 1978:123-9.

Nepveu, Pierre. "Philippe Haeck: 'une poéthique de la naiveté.'"
Lettres qué 13:22-4, 1979.

Tout va bien
Roy, Max. LAQ 1975:114-5.

HAEFFELY, Claude

Des nus et des pierres
Arcand, Pierre-André.   LAQ 1973: 106-7.

Glück
Bourassa, André-G. "Poésie automatiste; poésie surréaliste" LAQ
1975:104-6.

HALLAL, Jean

Le songe de l'enfant-satyre
Blais, Jacques. UTQ 43:367-9, 1974.

Bourque, Paul-André. LAQ 1973:113-5.

Sanderson, Gertrude. AntigR 15:100-3, 1973.

HALLAL, Jean

> Le temps-nous
> > Roy, Max.   LAQ 1977:146-9.

> La tranche sidéreale
> > Bourque, Paul-André.   LAQ 1974:127-8.

HAMELIN, Francine

> Et je serai orphée
> > Blandford, Bianca Zagolin.   LAQ 1971: 159.

> Intérieur des jours
> > Belisle, Marie. LAQ 1979:126-7.

HAMILTON, Jamie

> About face
> > David, Jack. "Old Spooks' Pass." ECW 7/8:165-8, 1977.

> Binocular
> > David, Jack. "Old Spooks' Pass." ECW 7/8:165-8, 1977.

> Night mares
> > David, Jack. "Old Spooks' Pass." ECW 7/8:165-8, 1977.

> > Gasparini, Len. "Six poets who found a critic." BiC 3(7):20-2, 1974.

> Oiseaux
> > Amprimoz, Alexandre. Quarry 28(2):82-5, 1979.

> > Hicks, Lorne. Q&Q 45(5):33, 1979.

> > Linder, Norma West. "Voices of character." CA&B 54(4):30-1, 1979.

HANNAN, Jack

> Peeling oranges in the shade
> > Moritz, A.F. "Restless alien, ceaseless flux." BiC 8(5):23-4, 1979.

HARDY, Jacques

> Poèmes du corps ameuté
> > Bouvier, Luc.   LAQ 1977:144-6.

HARRIS, Lawren

Contrasts
Arnason, David. "Canadian poetry: the interregnum." CVII 1(1):28-32, 1975.

HARRIS, Michael

Grace
Hornyansky, Michael. UTQ 48:351-2, 1979.

Linder, Norma West. "There for the digging." CA&B 53(4):41, 1978.

Miles, Ron. "Boxed set." CanL 81:138-9, 1979.

West, David S. "Graceful kindlings." Fiddlehead 121:157-60, 1979.

Whiteman, Bruce. Quarry 27(4):88, 1978.

Sparks
Barbour, Douglas. "Poetry chronicle V." DR 58:149-69, 1978.

David, Jack. "Three from Montreal." CVII 3(3):23-4, 1978.

Malcolm, Ian. Quarry 26(2):63-4, 1977.

Newton, Stuart. "Poets' effort." CanL 76:113-4, 1978.

West, David S. "Graceful kindlings." Fiddlehead 121:157-60, 1979.

Text for Nausikaa
Scobie, Stephen. "Poets en masse." CanL 50:75-8, 1971.

HARVEY, Rolf

The perfect suicide
Barbour, Douglas. Q&Q 39(1):11, 1973.

McCubbins, Marie. FPt 7/8:102-4, 1972-73.

HAUSER, Gwen

The fascist branding powers #2
Mallinson, Jean. "Poetry miscellany." ECW 7/8:151-8, 1977.

The ordinary invisible woman
Barbour, Douglas. "Canadian poetry chronicle: VII." DR 59:154-75, 1979.

Livesay, Dorothy. "Extra ordinary." CVII 4(1):31, 1979.

HAWKES, Robert

A place, a people
Dale, Sharon Goodier. "In Canada and out." BiC 2(2):43-4, 1973.

Spring that never freezes
McNally, Paul. Fiddlehead 118:167-8, 1978.

Stevenson, Warren. "Move over Musgrave." CanL 80:103-4, 1979.

HAWKINS, William

The gift of space, selected poems 1960-1970
Levinson, Christopher. CF 52(617):43, 1972.

Offstein, A. Open letter 2d ser, 2:52-6, 1972.

Swan, Susan. "Lyrically yours." BiC 1(7):6-7, 1972.

HAWLEY, Helen

Gathering fire
Cameron, Michael. "Muddy waters." CVII 4(2):34-5, 1979.

Flick, Jane. "Prairie images." CanL 80:105-6, 108-9, 1979.

HAYMAN, Robert

Quodlibets
Endres, Robin. "Robert Hayman's Quodlibets." CanL 73:68-78, 1977.

HEAVYSEGE, Charles

Bibliography
Djwa, Sandra. "Charles Heavysege, 1816-76." Heavysege
1976:viii-lxvii. (Includes "Bibliography" and "Review of Heavysege
criticism.")

General
Djwa, Sandra. "Charles Heavysege, 1816-76." Heavysege
1976:viii-lxvii. (Includes "Bibliography" and "Review of Heavysege
criticism.")

Jezebel: a poem in three cantos
Sorfleet, J.R. Q&Q 39(4):10, 1973.

Saul and selected poems
Hatch, Ronald, B. ESC 4:502-5, 1978.

140

HÉBERT, Anne

Bibliography
Émond, Maurice. "Bibliographie sommaire." QuéFr. 32:40, 1978.

General
Amar, Wenny. L'amour dans l'oeuvre d'Anne Hébert. Montreal:McGill Univ., 1975, c1976. (M.A. thesis.)

Blais, Jacques. "L'univers magique d'Anne Hébert." Blais 1975:253-68.

Bouchard, Denis. "Anne Hébert et la 'solitude rompue': tentative de démystification d'un des lieux communs de notre littérature." EF 13:163-79, 1977.

Bouchard, Denis. "Anne Hébert et le "Mystère de la parole": un essai d'anti-biographie." RPac 3:67-81, 1977.

Bouchard, Denis. Une lecture d'Anne Hébert: la recherche d'une mythologie. Montreal: Hurtubise HMH, 1977. (Cahiers du Québec.)

Bouchard, Denis. "Érotisme et érotologie: aspects de l'oeuvre poétique et romanesque d'Anne Hébert." RPac 1:152-67, 1975.

Chiasson, Arthur Paul. "The tragic mood in the works of Anne Hébert." DAI 35(6), 3729-A-3730-A. Tufts Univ., 1974. (Ph.D. thesis.)

Cloutier, Cécile. "L'influence de quelques poètes français sur quelques poètes québécois." PFr 9:44-51, 1974.

Dubé, Cécile; Émond, Maurice et Vandendorpe, Christian."Anne Hébert: entrevue." QuéFr 32:33-5, 1978.

Émond, Maurice. "Introduction à l'oeuvre d'Anne Hébert." QuéFr. 32:37-40, 1978.

Féral, Josette. "Clôture du moi, clôture du texte dans l'oeuvre d'Anne Hébert." V&I 1:265-83, 1975.

Féral, Josette. "Clôture du moi, clôture du texte dans l'oeuvre d'Anne Hébert." Lit 20:102-17, 1975.

Giguère, Richard. "D'un 'équilibre impondérable' à une 'violence élémentaire': évolution thématique de la poésie québécoise 1935-1965: Saint-Denys Garneau, Anne Hébert, Roland Giguère et Paul Chamberland." VIP 7:51-90, 1973.

Major, Jean-Louis. Anne Hébert et le miracle de la parole. Montreal: Presses Univ. de Montréal, 1976.

Marmier, Jean. "Du Tombeau des rois à Kamouraska: vouloir-vivre et instinct de mort chez Anne Hébert." Missions 1973:807-14.

HÉBERT, Anne

General (cont'd.)

Miller, Joanne Elizabeth. <u>Le passage du désir a l'acte dans l'oeuvre poétique et romanesque d'Anne Hébert.</u> London, Ont.:Univ. of Western Ontario, 1975. (M.A. thesis.)

Moisan, Clément. "Poésie de la clandestinité." Moisan 1979:91-127.

Monette, Pierre. "À propos du prix David 1978. Anne Hébert: poésie rompue." Lettres qué 12:49-51, 1978.

Nahmiash, Robert. <u>L'oppression et la violence dans l'oeuvre d'Anne Hébert.</u> Montreal: McGill Univ., 1972, c1973. (M.A. thesis.)

Savoie, Paul. <u>Anne Hébert, Saint-Denys Garneau; maison vide, solitude rompue.</u> Winnipeg: Univ. of Manitoba, 1970. (M.A. thesis.)

Weir, Lorraine. "'Fauna of mirrors': the poetry of Hébert and Atwood." Ariel 10(3):99-113, 1979.

Mystère de la parole

Macri, F.M. "Anne Hébert: story and poem." CanL 58:9-18, 1973.

Voir aussi/see also her <u>Poèmes</u>

Poèmes

Jones, D.G. "Cold eye and optic heart: Marshall McLuhan and some Canadian Poets." MPS 5:170-87, 1974."

Marta, Janet. "Déchiffrage du code biblique dans les <u>Poémes</u> d'Anne Hébert." PFr 16:123-30, 1978.

Poems (Tr. Alan Brown.)

Barbour, Douglas. "Canadian poetry chronicle: III." DR 56:560-73, 1976.

Downes, G.V. "Hébert in English." CanL 71:87-9, 1976.

Ellenwood, Ray. "Translation in Canada." Brick 2:52-4, 1978.

Garebian, Keith. Q&Q 41(12):31, 1975.

Godard, Barbara. Waves 4(2):13-6, 1976.

Jones, D.G. QQ 85:151-2, 1978.

Micros, Marianne. "Rape and ritual." ECW 7/8:31-5, 1977.

Pyke, Linda. "Living and dying rooms." BiC 4(12):24, 1975.

Walker, David. "Exorcising demons." CF 56(663):38-9, 1976.

Woodcock, George. "Levels of translation." CVII 2(1):18-20, 1976.

142

HÉBERT, Anne

Les songes en équilibre
Blais, Jacques. "L'univers magique d'Anne Hébert." Blais
1975:253-68.

Le tombeau des rois
Macri, F.M. "Anne Hébert: story and poem." CanL 58:9-18, 1973.

"La fille maigre"
Giroux, Robert. "Lecture de 'La fille maigre' d'Anne Hébert." PFr
10:73-89, 1975.

"Il y a certainement quelqu'un"
De Bellefeuille, Normand. "Tel qu'en lui-même." BdJ 39-41:104-23,
1973.

"Marine"
Haeck, Philippe. "Naissance de la poésie moderne au Québec." EF
9:95-113, 1973.

"Neige"
Adam, Jean-Michel. "Sur cinq vers de Mystère de la parole: lire
aujourd'hui 'Neige' d'Anne Hébert." ELit 5:463-80, 1972.

"Le tombeau des rois"
Bouchard, Denis. "'Le tombeau des rois.'" Bouchard 1977:73-130.

Hébert, Anne et Scott, Frank. Dialogue sur la traduction: à propos du
"Tombeau des rois." Montréal: HMH, 1970. (Sur parole.)

Kunstmann, Pierre. "'Le tombeau des rois' ou la progression
régressive." V&I 2:255-64, 1976.

Lemieux, Pierre-H. "La mort des rois: commentaire du poème-titre 'Le
tombeau des rois' d'Anne Hébert." RUO 45:133-61, 1975.

Lemieux, Pierre-Hervé. Entre songe et parole: structure du "Tombeau
des rois" d'Anne Hébert. Ottawa, Ed. de l'Univ. d'Ottawa, 1978.

Voir aussi/see also her Poèmes

HÉBERT, François

Barbarie
Bourassa, André-G. LAQ 1978:130.

Ricard, François. "Tryptique de François Hébert." Liberté
118-9:240-5, 1978.

HÉBERT, Louis-Philippe

Les mangeurs de terre
Bélanger, Yrénée.   LAQ 1970:140-1.

HÉBERT, Marie-Francine

Slurch
Beaulieu, Michel. BdJ 24:76, 1970.

Bélanger, Yrénée. LAQ 1970:148.

HELWIG, David

General
Helwig, David. Colombo 1971:20-30.

Marshall, Tom. "Bourgeois and arsonist: David Helwig." Marshall 1979:162-70.

Atlantic crossings
Barbour, Douglas.   "The poets and presses revisited: circa 1974."   DR 55:338-60, 1975.

Johnston, George. QQ 82:295-7, 1975.

Levenson, Christopher. "Origins and lemons." BiC 3(8)26-7, 1974.

MacLulich, T.D. "All trad not bad." ECW 2:62-4, 1975.

Nelson, Joyce. Quarry 24(2):63-4, 1975.

Ricou, Laurie. "Another world." CanL 77:120-2, 1978.

Smith, Ron. TamR 66:106-8, 1975.

Watt, F.W. "Why poetry? Eleven answers." CF 55(651):40-1, 1975.

Wieland, Sarah. Q&Q 40(12):26, 1974.

The best name of silence
André, Michael. QQ 80:472, 1973.

Estok, Michael. "All in the family: the metaphysics of domesticity." DR 52:653-67, 1973.

Everard, Doris. "Landscape with Arsonist." CanL 60:110-2, 1974.

HELWIG, David

The best name of silence (cont'd.)

Fetherling, Doug. "The cities within." SatN 88(1):36-8, 1973.

Friesen, Ronald. Q&Q 38(11):11, 1972.

Jones, D.G. "David Helwig's new timber: notes on 'The best name of silence.'" QQ 81:202-14, 1974.

McWhirter, George. MHRev 26:235-6, 1973.

Sutherland, Fraser. "Rebel yells." BiC 1(12):53-4, 1972.

A book of the hours

Daniel, Lorne. Q&Q 45(7):39, 1979.

Precosky, Don. Fiddlehead 122:131-4, 1979.

The sign of the gunman

Atwood, Margaret. Quarry 19(2):61-2, 1970.

Barbour, Douglas. "The young poets and the little presses, 1969." DR 50:112-26, 1970.

Denny, Carolyn Struthers. OV 6(4):n.p., 1971.

Gasparini, Len. QQ 77:130-1, 1970.

Pacey, Desmond. "A Canadian quintet." Fiddlehead 83:79-86, 1970.

"The best name of silence"

Jones, D.G. "David Helwig's new timber: notes on 'The best name of silence'." QQ 81:202-14, 1974.

HEMSLEY, Stuart Davidson

Up Parnassus!

Leigh, Simon. "Two minor talons and a tidal borealis." Fiddlehead 109:128-32, 1976.

HÉNAULT, Gilles

General

Dallard, Sylvie. "Gilles Hénault et la volonté de vivre." Dallard 1977:100-92.

Haeck, Philippe; Piotte, Jean-Marc, et Straram le Bison ravi, Patrick. "Entretien: 30 ans après Le refus global." Chroniques 1(1):12-26, 1975.

HÉNAULT, Gilles

General (cont'd.)
Hallé, Paul-André. "Le 'cri nu' dans la poésie de Gilles Hénault."
Co-incidences 1(2)46-55, 1971.

Mailhot, Laurent. "La poésie de Gilles Hénault." VIP 8:149-61, 1974.

Allégories
Fisette, Jean. "Gilles Hénault between simplification and analogy."
Ellipse 18:62-71, 1976. (Tr. F.M. Macri.)

Kushner, Eva. "La poétique de Gilles Hénault." Savard 1977:137-48.

Sémaphore
Corriveau, Hugues. Gilles Hénault: lecture de Sémaphore. Montréal:
Presses de l'Univ. de Montréal, 1978.

Dudek, Louis. "Those damned visionary poets (Les poètes maudits
visionnaires)." Dudek 1978:166-7.

Fisette, Jean. "Gilles Hénault between simplification and analogy."
Ellipse 18:62-71, 1976. (Tr. F.M. Macri.)

Signaux pour les voyants
Kushner, Eva. "Signaux pour les voyants de Gilles Hénault." LAQ
1972:136-40.

Poulin, Gabrielle. "La poésie québécoise en 1972: II--Gilles Hénault
à l'Hexagone." Relations 383:188-90, 1973.

"Défense de toucher"
Corriveau, Hugues. BdJ 39-40-41:58-84, 1973.

HENDERSON, Brian

The expanding room
Archer, Anne. Quarry 28(1):75-7, 1979.

Brown, Allan. "Black Moss: six offerings." Waves 7(2):68-71, 1979.

Bruce, John. "For keeps." Brick 7:44-5, 1979.

Cook, John. "Singing toad." CF 59(688):32-3, 1979.

Jones, D.G. "The meeting of poles and latitudes: a review of Brian
Henderson." ECW 11:266-75, 1978.

146

HENDERSON, Brian

Paracelsus a poem in forty parts, with a prologue
Barbour, Douglas. "Canadian poetry chronicle: VI." DR 58:555-78, 1978.

Cook, John "Singing toad." CF 59(688):32-3, 1979.

Jones, D.G. "Born of the landscape." CanL 79:77-82, 1978.

Jones, D.G. "The meeting of poles and latitudes: a review of Brian Henderson." ECW 11:266-75, 1978.

The viridical book of the silent planet
Bruce, John. "For keeps." Brick 7:44-5, 1979.

HERTEL, François

General
Giroux, Robert. "François Hertel: le surhomme noyé." PFr 6:29-43, 1973.

O'Donnell, Kathleen. "François Hertel: the unprecedented voice." CanL 66:80-6, 1975.

Axe et parallaxes
Blais, Jacques. "L'extravagant François Hertel." Blais 1975:239-52.

Mystère cosmique et condition humaine
Thérien, Gilles. "François Hertel, curieux homme." V&I 2:47-59, 1976.

Strophes et catastrophes
Blais, Jacques. "L'extravagant François Hertel." Blais 1975:239-52.

HICKS, John V.

Now is a far country
Di Cicco, Pier Giorgio. "No man is an island, true, but there can be a circean catch to regionalism." BiC 8(1:)21-2, 1979.

HINE, Daryl

General
Martin, Robert K. "Coming full circle: Daryl Hine's recent poems." MPS 8:60-73, 1977.

McClatchy, J.D. "Winter's tale." Poetry 134:167-76, 1979.

HINE, Daryl

    Daylight Saving
     McClatchy, J.D. "Winter's tale." Poetry 134:167-76, 1979.

    The devil's picture book
     Dudek, Louis. "Three major Canadian poets--three major forms of archaism." Dudek 1978:153-6. (Originally published Delta 16;23-5, 1961.)

    Resident alien
     Cameron, Barry. "Alien world." CanL 71:108-10, 1976.

HOGG, Robert L.

    Standing back
     Barbour, Douglas. "Hopes & trepidations." CanL 59:117-9, 1974.

     Marlatt, Daphne. Open letter 2d ser, 3:83-6, 1972.

     McWhirter, George. MHRev 26:237-8, 1973.

HOLDEN-LAWRENCE, Monica

    Mad about the crazy lady
     Levy, Eric P. "Strategies." CanL 82:89-91, 1979.

HORIC, Alain

    Les coqs égorgés
     Gallays, François.   LAQ 1972:167-8.

HORNBY, Jim

    Pommes de terre: an album of pommes
     Dyroff, Jan Michael. "Gulf strains." BiC 2(3):48, 50, 1973.

HORNSEY, Richard

    Going in
     Barbour, Douglas. QQ 80:143, 1973.

HOWE, Joseph

Poems and essays
Gibbs, Robert. "Joseph Howe the writer." CanL 67:102-4, 1976.

Parker, George L. DR 54:769-71, 1974-75.

Sorfleet, J.R. Q&Q 40(2):12, 1974.

HOWELL, Bill

The red fox
Barbour, Douglas. DR 52:169-70, 1972.

Fetherling, Doug. "Can't wait to get home and be hugged by mom."
SatN 87(2):34, 1972.

McNamara, Eugene. Quarry 21(1):64-6, 1972.

Purdy, Al. "Personal effects." BiC 1(4):22, 1971.

Purdy, Al. "The woman of Barrie." CanL 54:86-90, 1972.

Wynand, Derk. MHRev 26:239-40, 1973.

HOWITH, Harry

Fragments of the dance
Barbour, Douglas. "The young poets and the little presses, 1969." DR
50:112-26, 1970.

Davis, Marilyn. CF 50:252-3, 1970.

Purdy, Al. Quarry 19(3):61, 1970.

Multiple choices: new and selected poems 1961-1976
Amprimoz, Alexandre. "Dusted inside." CanL 82:99-101, 1979.

Barbour, Douglas. "Poetry chronicle V." DR 58:149-69, 1978.

Darling, Michael. "Poems new and selected: Everson and Howith." ECW
7/8:158-63, 1977.

The stately homes of Westmount
Cameron, A.A. Brick 1:43-4, 1977.

Mayne, Seymour. "Other Montrealers." CanL 64:98-101, 1975.

HUTCHISON, Alexander

Deep-tap-tree
   Fletcher, Peggy. "Dialogues and other voices." CA&B 54(2):36-7, 1979.

   Kleinzahler, August. "The world well limned." BiC 8(9):14, 1979.

HUTCHMAN, Laurence

Explorations
   Di Cicco, Pier Giorgio. "Gay in not so jocund company." BiC 5(5):15-6, 1976.

   Globe, Alexander. "Three poets." CanL 75:85-8, 1977.

   Sandler, Linda. QQ 83:169, 1976.

INKSTER, Tim

General
   "Tim Inkster: poet and publisher; Porcupines Quill, Erin. Ontario." Alive 49:11-3, 1976.

The crown prince waits for a train
   Dempster, Barry. "Poetry from Porcupine's Quill: new publisher's first 3 books." Alive 50:19, 1976.

   Gatenby, Greg. Q&Q 42(7):41-2, 1976.

   Hosein, Clyde. Quarry 25(4):69-70, 1976.

   Jones, D.G. "Born of the landscape." CanL 79:77-82, 1978.

   McCarthy, Dermot. "Mosquitoes and mundane heroism." ECW 5:75-9, 1976.

Mrs. Grundy
   Dutton, Paul. "An old house." Open letter 2d ser, 9:105-6, 1974.

   Marcellin, Phil. Alive 35:10, 1974.

INKSTER, Tim

   Mrs. Grundy (cont'd.)
      Pomeroy, Graham. Alive 35:10, 1974.

      Powell, D. Reid. Q&Q 40(8):24, 1974.

   Letters
      Dutton, Paul. "Dear Tim." ECW 7/8:177-8, 1977.

   The topolobampo poems and other memories
      Barbour, Douglas. "Petit four." BiC 1(11):19, 1972.

      McNamara, Eugene. "The vatic upsurge." CanL 58:104-6, 1973.

IWANIUK, Waclaw

   Dark times
      Moritz, Albert. "Lessons of catastrophe." BiC 8(10):26-7, 1979.

JABARA, Albert M.

   The sonnet gate and the poem cell
      Linder, Norma West. CA&B 52(2):36, 1976.

JACOB, Louis

   Avant-serrure
      Roy, Max. " LAQ 1977:130-2.

   Double tram
      Haeck, Philippe. LAQ 1979:169.

   Manifeste: jet/usage/résidu
      Fisette, Jean. "Poésie. Parutions récentes: de Desroches aux Écrits
      des forges." V&I 3(3):497-500, 1978.

      Nepveu, Pierre. "La poésie qui se fait et celle qui ne se fait pas."
      Lettres qué 9:15-7, 1978.

      Roy, Max. LAQ 1977:130-2.

JAHN, Penelope

Long tall weeds
    Barr, Arlee. Alive 35:12, 1974.

JAMES, Christopher

Two sides
    Sutherland, Fraser. "Group groping and singular sensing." BiC
    1(10):30, 1972.

JAMES, Kit

On the eleventh line in the first house
    Gasparini, Leonard. "Applaudeth one in three." BiC 4(11):16-18,
    1975.

JANKOLA, Beth

Girl of the golden west
    Barbour, Douglas. "Canadian poetry chronicle: VII." DR 59:154-75,
    1979.

Jody said
    Toth, Nancy. "Organized decays." CVII 4(3):38-41,43, 1979.

JAQUES, Edna

Prairie born, prairie bred
    Rose, Mildred A. Q&Q 45(6):47, 1979.

JENOFF, Marvyne

Hollandsong
    Globe, Alexander. "Three poets." CanL 75:85-8, 1977.

    Gutteridge, Don. QQ 84:128-9, 1977.

    Oughton, John. Q&Q 41(13)32, 1975.

No lingering peace
    Fleet, Brenda. Fiddlehead 97:121-3, 1973.

    Zimmerman, Susan. "Musicales." BiC 2(4)27-30, 1973.

JEWINSKI, Hans

General
Waxman, Ken. "Poet cop." Q&Q 42(1):12, 1976.

Poet cop
Bemis, Virginia. "One poet in two parts: a study of Hans Jewinski."
UWR 14(2):16-24, 1979.

Grady, Wayne. "Axioms, eroicas, and mirrors." Nj 7&8:108-20, 1976.

Granatstein, J.L. "All hail poet and cop." CF 56(665):32, 1976.

Oughton, John. "The feet of the law." BiC 5(1):30-1, 1976.

JILES, Paulette

Waterloo express
Brown, S. "Waterloo express." CanR 1(1):16-7, 1974.

Edwards, Mary Jane. CF 54(643):42, 1974.

Lane, Travis M. "Travelling with Saint Theresa: the poetry of
Paulette Jiles." ECW 10:61-72, 1978.

Lee, Dennis. "The new poets: fresh voices in the land." SatN
88(12):33-5, 1973.

Long, Tanya. Q&Q 40(4):21, 1974.

Rogers, Linda. "Magical music." CanL 61:121-2, 1974.

JOHN, Godfrey

Five seasons
Johnson, Sam. Q&Q 44(17):33, 1978.

JOHNSON, Brian

Marzipan lies
Bowering, Marilyn. "Stages of poetry." CanL 74:102-4, 1977.

Dempster, Barry. "Poetry from Porcupine's Quill: new publisher's
first 3 books." Alive 50:19, 1976.

JOHNSON, Brian

Marzipan lies (cont'd.)
Hamilton, Jamie. "Marzipan lies." CanR 3(5):49, 1976.

Hosein, Clyde. Quarry 25(4):69, 1976.

Kiverago, Ron A. "Negative vision." ECW 6:93-5, 1977.

Power, Nick. Q&Q 42(5):46, 1976.

JOHNSON, Jane

The heart must know
Linder, Norma West. CA&B 52(1):26, 1976.

The listener
Boland, Viga. CA&B 52(1):28, 1976.

London letter
Boland, Viga. CA&B 52(1):28, 1976.

Fletcher, Peggy. CA&B 51(4):26, 1976.

Mills, Sparling. OV 10(2):n.p., 1975.

Never the sun
Bailey, Don. Quarry 20(3):50-1, 1971.

Hill, Bruce. OV 7(2):n.p., 1971.

JOHNSON, Pauline

General
Beker, Marilyn. Pauline Johnson: a biographical, thematic and stylistic study. Montreal: Sir George Williams Univ., 1974. (M.A. thesis.)

JOHNSTON, George

Cruising auk
Danys, Milda. "The poetry of George Johnston." Inscape 10(1):40-5, 1972.

Jones, Lawrence W. "The cruising auk and the world below." CanL 48:28-36, 1971. (Also Woodcock 1974b:71-9.)

JOHNSTON, George

> The Greenlanders' saga
>> Gervais, C.H. "Two reporters, one commentator." BiC 6(7):24, 1977.
>
> Happy enough: poems 1935-1972
>> Galassi, Jonathan. "Dealing with tradition." Poetry 123:113-9, 1973.
>>
>> Jones, D.G. "George Johnston." CanL 59:81-7, 1974.
>>
>> Hornyansky, Michael. UTQ 42:375, 1973.
>>
>> Nynych, Stephanie J. "At home with the world." BiC 1(12):10, 12, 1972.
>>
>> Scobie, Stephen. QQ 80:310-1, 1973.
>
> Home free
>> Danys, Milda. "The poetry of George Johnston." Inscape 10(1):40-5, 1972.
>>
>> Jones, Lawrence W. "The cruising auk and the world below." CanL 48:28-36, 1971. (Also Woodcock 1974b:71-9.)

JOHNSTON, Grant

> A compass of open veins
>> Chambers, D.D.C. CF 51(610):53, 1971.

JOHNSTON, Neville

> Songs of my seasons
>> Thompson, Kent. "Editorial." Fiddlehead 102:1-3, 1974.

JONAS, George

> General
>> Jonas, George. Colombo 1971:35-45.
>>
>> Sandler, Linda. "George Jonas." CanL 73:25-38, 1977.
>
> The absolute smile
>> Schroeder, Andreas. "The poetry of George Jonas: a critical map." CanL 48:37-50, 1971.

JONAS, George

Cities

MacLulich, T.D. "All trad not bad." ECW 2:62-4, 1975.

Macskimming, Roy. "A quatrain of contenders." BiC 3(7):5-6, 9, 1974.

McKay, Don. Brick 1:41-2, 1977.

Powell, D. Reid. Q&Q 40(4):20, 1974.

Thompson, Kent. "A sensibility of quality." Fiddlehead 101:79-81, 1974.

Watt, F.W. "Why poetry? Eleven answers." CF 55(651):40-1, 1975.

The happy hungry man

Barbour, Douglas. DR 50:429, 1970.

Ditsky, John. CF 50:190, 1970.

Doyle, Mike. "Where Prufrock was." CanL 45:85-6, 1970.

Marshall, Tom. "Canpo: a chronicle." Quarry 19(4):50-4, 1970.

Schroeder, Andreas. "The poetry of George Jonas: a critical map." CanL 48:37-50, 1971.

JONES, D.G.

General

Blodgett, E.D. "The masks of D.G. Jones." CanL 60:64-82, 1974. (Also Woodcock 1974b:159-78.)

Bowering, George. "Coming home to the world." CanL 65:7-27, 1975.

Bowering, George. "D.G. Jones: 'être chez soi dans le monde.'" Ellipse 13:82-103, 1973. (Tr. Rodolphe Lacasse.)

Under the thunder the flowers light up the earth

Barbour, Douglas. "Canadian poetry chornicle: VI." DR 58:555-78, 1978.

Cook, John. "Special relationship." CF 58(682):47-8, 1978.

David, Jack. Q&Q 44(10):12, 1978.

Lane, M. Travis. "The Canadian gardener." Fiddlehead 118:152-6, 1978.

JONES, D.G.

Under the thunder the flowers light up the earth (cont'd.)
Mandel, Eli. QQ 86:170-2, 1979.

Marshall, Tom. "Keeping up with the Smiths and the Joneses." BiC 7(4):16-7, 1978.

Mullins, Stanley G. UWR 14(1):73-4, 1978.

Novak, Barbara. "Poetry chronicle." TamR 75:88-95, 1978.

Whiteman, Bruce. "A riot of flowers." Brick 4:58-9, 1978.

Woodcock, George. "Not this or that." ECW 11:276-9, 1978.

JONES, Elizabeth

Castings
Woodruff, Sandra. HAB 25:80-1, 1974.

Flux
Hatch, R.B. "Time's motion." CanL 81:129-32, 1979.

JORDAN, Jane

I smoke black Russian cigarettes with Turkish papers
Saunders, Brenda. Old nun 1:17, 1975.

KEARNS, Lionel

General
Kearns, Lionel. Colombo 1971:46-64.

About time
McCaffrey, Steve. "Time grooves." CVII 2(2):40, 1976.

By the light of the silvery McLune; media parables, poems, signs, gestures, and other assaults on the interface
Davey, Frank. "The limitations of wit." CanL 44:91-2, 1970.

Fulford, Robert. "Parables & fantasies." SatN 85(3):38-40, 1970 .

Marshall, Tom. "Canpo: a chronicle." Quarry 19(4):50-4, 1970.

Thomas, Peter. Fiddlehead 84:113-4, 1970.

Tuatara 2:46, 1970.

KEARNS, Lionel

Practicing up to be human
Dempster, Barry. "Collages, clips and quirky pics." BiC 8(6):18, 1979.

Fernstrom, Ken. Q&Q 45(6):47, 1979.

KEATING, Diane

In dark places
Barbour, Douglas. "Canadian poetry chronicle: VII." DR 59:154-75, 1979.

Brown, Allan. "Black moss: six offerings." Waves 7(2):68-71, 1979.

Dunlop, Donna. Q&Q 44(9):40, 1978.

KEELER, Wally

Walking on the greenhouse roof
Barbour, Douglas. DR 51:135, 1971.

KEMP, Penny

General
"Circumlocution." JCP 1(1):71-6, 1978.

Bearing down
Huggan, Isabel. "Notes on Penny Chalmers' work (Bearing down and Tranceform)." Brick 2:3-4, 1978.

Ramsay, Jocelyn. Q&Q 39(3):8, 1973.

Tranceform

Barbour, Douglas. "Canadian poetry chronicle: III." DR 56:560-73, 1976.

"Circumlocution." JCP 1(1):71-6, 1978.

David, Jack. Q&Q 42(10):45, 1976.

Huggan, Isabel. "Notes on Penny Chalmers' work (Bearing down and Tranceform)." Brick 2:3-4, 1978.

KENNEDY, Leo

The shrouding
Barbour, Douglas. "Canadian poetry chronicle: III." DR 56:560-73, 1976.

Bentley, D.M.R. "Modernist." CanL 79:90-2, 1978.

Gasparini, Len. "Exile and exhumanation." BiC 5(4):21-2, 1976.

McMullen, Lorraine. "Leo Kennedy." Le chien d'or/The golden dog 1: n.p., 1972 (13p.).

Stubbs, Roy St. George. "This man of April." CVII 2(2):20-2, 1976.

KENNY, George

Indians don't cry: poems and stories
Norman, Richard. PTor 27:n.p., 1978.

KERR, Luella

Tenth muse
Hamel, Guy. "Recent Fiddlehead poetry books." Fiddlehead 118:137-45, 1978.

Jenoff, Marvyne. "Seven books from two small presses." CVII 3(4):40-5, 1978.

KINSELLA, John

Weeds and other flowers
Linder, Norma West. "Crafted with care: more or less." CA&B 53(3):42, 1978.

KISHKAN, Theresa

Arranging the gallery
Barbour, Douglas. "Poetry chronicle V." DR 58:149-69, 1978.

Brown, Allan. "3 Fiddlehead books." Brick 3:12-4, 1978.

Lane, M. Travis. "'The hidden dreamer's cry': natural force as point-of-view." Fiddlehead 112:156-60, 1977.

Munton, Ann. DR 57:378-9, 1977.

KISHKAN, Theresa

> Ikons of the hunt
>> Barbour, Douglas. "Canadian poetry chronicle: VII." DR 59:154-75, 1979.
>>
>> Moritz, A.F. "Lost glories, found clichés." BiC 8:(1):14, 1979.

KIYOOKA, Roy

> General
>> "With Roy Kiyooka." White pelican 1(1):18-35, 1971.
>
> The fountainebleu dream machine, 18 frames from a book of rhetoric
>> Barbour, Douglas. "Canadian poetry chronicle: VI." DR 58:555-78, 1978.
>
> Kyoto airs
>> Dudek, Louis. "The new Vancouver poetry." Dudek 1978:186-92. (Originally published Culture 25:323-39, 1964.)
>
> Stoned gloves
>> Barbour, Douglas. White pelican 1(1):64, 1971.
>>
>> Chambers, D.D.C. CF 51(610):53, 1971.
>
> Transcanada letters
>> Barbour, Douglas. "Canadian poetry chronicle: III." DR 56:560-73, 1976.

KLASSEN, Jean-Marie

> L'étoile
>> Amprimoz, Alexandre. Quarry 28(2):82-5, 1979.

KLEIN, Abraham Moses

> Bibliography
>> Siebrasse, Glen. "A.M. Klein: a bibliography." JD Passover 1973:60-4.

160

KLEIN, Abraham Moses

General
"A.M. Klein--a tribute." JD Passover 1973. (Whole issue)

Dudek, Louis. "A.M. Klein" Dudek 1978:4-10. (Originally published CF 30(351):10-2, 1950)

Duran, Gillian. "A.M. Klein and working-class poetry." L&I 17:25-30, 1974.

Esco, Helen E. Judaic tradition and the poetry of A.M. Klein. Kingston, Ont.: Queen's Univ. 1973. (M.A. thesis.)

Fischer, Gretl Krans. A.M. Klein: religious philosophy and ethics in his writing. Montreal: McGill Univ., 1972. (Ph.D. thesis.)

Fischer, Gretl K. In search of Jerusalem: religion and ethics in the writings of A.M. Klein. Montreal: McGill-Queen's University Press, 1975.

Fisher, Esther Safer. "A.M. Klein: portrait of the poet as Jew." CanL 79:121-7.

Gustafson, Ralph. "A.M. Klein." JD Summer 1973:6.

Kertzer, J.M. "A.M. Klein's meditation on life." JCL 13(i):1-19, 1978.

Marshall, Tom, ed. A.M. Klein. Toronto: Ryerson, 1970.

Marshall, Tom. "The nth Adam: A.M. Klein." Marshall 1979:55-60.

Marshall, Tom. "Portrait of a people: some afterthoughts about the landscape of A.M. Klein." JD Rosh hashanah 1972: 32-3.

Mayne, Seymour, ed. The A.M. Klein symposium. Ottawa: Univ. of Ottawa Press, 1975.

Nadel, Ira Bruce. "A.M. Klein on literature." JD Hanukah 1974:4-7.

Pollock, Zailig. "Sunflower seeds: Klein's hero and semagogue." CanL 82:48-58, 1979.

Pomeroy, Graham. "The Klein symposium." CanR 1(3):3-4, 1974.

Popham, E.A. "A.M. Klein: the impulse to define." CanL 79:5-17.

Russell, Kenneth C. "The blasphemies of A.M. Klein." CanL 72:59-66, 1977.

Still, Robert Ernest. The early poetry of A.M. Klein. London, Ont.: Univ. of Western Ontario, 1974. (M.A. thesis.)

KLEIN, Abraham Moses

    General (cont'd.)
    Waddington, Miriam. <u>A.M. Klein</u>. Toronto, Copp Clark, 1970.

    Waddington, Miriam. "The function of folklore in the poetry of A.M. Klein." Ariel 10(3):5-19, 1979.

    Waddington, Miriam. "On A.M. Klein." CF 52(621-2):4-5, 1972.

    Weir, Lorraine. "Portrait of the poet as Joyce Scholar: an approach to A.M. Klein." CanL 76:47-55.

<u>The collected poems (comp. Miriam Waddington)</u>
    Denham, Paul. "Taking a greener inventory." CVII 2(3):14-5, 1976.

    Dudek, Louis. "Waddington's Klein." CanR 2(1):26-7, 1975.

    Edel, Leon. "Mirrorings of A.M. Klein." TamR 66:94-8, 1975.

    Lewis, David. "Oscillations of integrity." BiC 3(7):20, 1974.

    Marshall, Tom. "Klein's poet surfacing." CanL 63:81-5, 1975.

    Rosenthal, Helene. "Of frolicks, jousts and wailing walls." WCR 11(2):34-6, 1976.

    Steinberg, M.W. QQ 8:648-9, 1975.

    Warkentin, Germaine. Q&Q 40(10):24, 1974.

    Watt, F.W. "Fruits of stifled genius." CF 54(646):18, 1974.

<u>Hath not a Jew</u>
    Still, Robert Ernest. <u>The early poetry of A.M. Klein</u>. London, Ont.: Univ. of Western Ontario, 1974. (M.A. thesis.)

    Sutherland, John. "The poetry of A.M. Klein." Sutherland 1972:128-38.

    Waddington, Miriam. "The function of folklore in the poetry of A.M. Klein." Ariel 10(3):5-19, 1979.

<u>Hershel of Ostropol</u>
    Fischer, G.K. "A.M. Klein's forgotten play." CanL 43:42-53, 1970.

<u>The Hitleriad</u>
    Sutherland, John. "The poetry of A.M. Klein." Sutherland 1972:128-38.

<u>The rocking chair and other poems</u>
    Sutherland, John. "A.M. Klein: the laughter of seriousness." Sutherland 1972:139-44.

KLEIN, Abraham Moses

The second scroll
Pollack, Zailig. "The myth of exile and redemption in 'Gloss gimel'."
SCL 4(1):26-42, 1979.

"Gloss gimel"
Pollack, Zailig. "The myth of exile and redemption in 'Gloss gimel'."
SCL 4(1):26-42, 1979.

"Portrait of the poet"
Stephen, Sidney J. "Adam in exile: A.M. Klein's portrait of the poet
as landscape." DR 51:553-8, 1971-72.

KLIMOV, Alexis

Des arcanes et des jeux, XXII ordonnances pour une fête baroque
Mauranges, Jean Paul. LAQ 1976:163-5.

KNIGHT, David

The army does not go away
Barbour, Douglas. "The young poets and the little presses, 1969." DR
50:112-26, 1970.

KNISTER, Raymond

Bibliography
Burke, A. "Raymond Knister: an annotated checklist." ECW 16:20-61,
1979-80.

General
Arnason, David. "Canadian poetry: the interregnum." CVII 1(1):28-32,
1975.

Givens, Imogen. "Raymond Knister--man or myth?" ECW 16:5-19,
1979-80.

"Special Knister issue." JCF 4(2):1975.

KOEHN, Lala

Portraits
Barbour, Douglas. "Poetry chronicle V." DR 58:149-69, 1978.

Jenoff, Marvyne. "Seven books from two small presses." CVII
3(4):40-5, 1978.

KOGAWA, Joy

    General
      Dabydeen, Cyril. "Deepening the enigma: interview with Joy Kogawa."
      CVII 4(3):31-3, 1979.

      Marchand, Blaine. "The quiet voice of Joy Kogawa." CanR 1(3):9-10,
      1974.

    A choice of dreams
      Almon, Bert. WCR 9(2):53-5, 1974.

      Lacey, Edward. "Canadian birds and South American reviewers." Nj
      4:82-120, 1974.

      Marshall, Tom. "Dorothy's daughters: three more Emilys." CVII
      2(2):29, 1976.

      Musgrave, Susan. MHR 31:163-4, 1974.

      Sandler, Linda. "Gustafson & others." TamR 64:89-94, 1973.

      Thompson, Eric. "Between two worlds." CanL 63:111-2, 1975.

    Jericho road
      Barbour, Douglas. "Poetry chronicle V." DR 58:149-69, 1978.

      Farmiloe, Dorothy. Q&Q 43(6):44, 1977.

      Purdy, Al. "A flooding past." CanL 76:126-7, 1978.

KONYVES, Tom

    No parking
      Fletcher, Peggy. "Vehicles of expression." CA&B 55(1):24, 1979.

KOSTER, Rolf

    Suddenly this season, years ago
      Johnson, Jane. OV 9(2):n.p., 1974.

KROETSCH, Robert

    Bibliography
      Lecker, Robert. "An annotated bibliography of works by and about
      Robert Kroetsch." ECW 7-8:74-96, 1977.

    General
      Wood, Susan. "Reinventing the word: Kroetsch's poetry." CanL
      77:28-39, 1978.

KROETSCH, Robert

The ledger
Carpenter, David. "Balanced account." CVII 2(1):12, 1976.

McCarthy, Dermot. "Ancestors, real or imaginative." ECW 4:73-5, 1976.

Thomas, Peter. Fiddlehead 108:114-7, 1976.

Seed catalogue
Barbour, Douglas. "Poetry chronicle V." DR 58:149-69, 1978.

Daniel, Lorne. Q&Q 43(13):52, 1977.

Johnson, Jay. "Kroetsch in bloom!" ECW 9:89-92, 1977/78.

Mulhallen, Karen. "Book of life." CF 58(685):46-7, 1978.

Popham, Beth. Quarry 27(2):86-7, 1978.

Thomas, Peter. "How much story can a song take?" Fiddlehead 117:108-17, 1978.

The stone hammer poems
Carpenter, David. "Stone chipped and hammered." CVII 2(2):38-9, 1976.

Engel, Howard. "Prose-flawed poems." CF 56(665):33, 1976.

Gasparini, Len. "Chips, nuts and wafers." BiC 5(3):18, 1976.

MacKendrick, Louis K. UWR 12(2):92-5, 1977.

Tidler, Charles. Q&Q 42(2):45, 1976.

KRYSINSKI, Wladimir

Formotropie
Beaudet, André. LAQ 1978:130-3.

LABELLE, Edmond

Récitatifs
Blais, Jacques. "Les Récitatifs d'Edmond Labelle." Blais 1975:237-9.

LABERGE, Albert

Hymnes à la terre
Lebel, Maurice. "Albert Laberge (1871-1960) et ses Hymnes à la terre (1955.)" MLS 6(2):22-37, 1976.

LABERGE, Marie

Les chants de l'éperrière
Pontbriand, Jean-Noel. LAQ 1979:129-30.

Soleil d'otage
Blandford, Bianca Zagolin. LAQ 1970:146.

LABERGE, Pierre

Au lieu de mourir
Gaulin, André. LAQ 1979:131-2.

Nepveu, Pierre. "Du corps et de quelques poètes." Lettres qué 16:21-3, 1979-80.

Dedans dehors
Gaulin, André. LAQ 1977:153-5.

La fête
Bonenfant, Joseph. LAQ 1973:109-11.

La guerre promise
Arcand, Pierre-André. "Le noroît" LAQ 1975:122-4.

Nepveu, Pierre. "Les vaches maigres." Lettres qué 2:12-4, 1976.

L'oeil de nuit
Bonenfant, Joseph. LAQ 1973:109-11.

Point de repère
Gaulin, André. LAQ 1977:153-5.

Le vif du sujet
Arcand, Pierre-André. "Le noroît" LAQ 1975:122-4.

Nepveu, Pierre. "Les vaches maigres." Lettres qué 2:12-4, 1976.

Vue du corps
Gaulin, André. LAQ 1979:131-2.

Nepveu, Pierre. "Du corps et de quelques poètes." Lettres qué 16:21-3, 1979-80.

LABINE, Marcel

Les allures de ma mort
Giguère, Richard. LAQ 1979:106.

Les lieux domestiques
Giguère, Richard. LAQ 1977:150-1.

LACELLE-BOURDON, Andrée

Au soleil du souffle
Chamberland, Roger. LAQ 1979:145.

LACEY, E.A.

Later: poems 1973-1978
Fernstrom, Ken. Q&Q 45(8):51, 1979.

Path of snow
Hamilton, Jamie. "Diamonds in the rough." CanR 3(2):59, 1976.

Sutherland, Fraser. "Muy hombre." CanL 65:104-18, 1975.

LACHANCE, Bertrand

Bertrand Lachance: Poems (Air, 13)
Amprimoz, Alexandre. "Poetry & vulgarity:--Bertrand Lachance." Brick
1:32-7, 1977.

Billings, R. Quarry 23(2):74-5, 1974.

Lacey, Edward. "Canadian bards and South American reviewers." Nj
4:82-120, 1974.

Cock tales
Amprimoz, Alexandre. "Poetry & vulgarity:--Bertrand Lachance." Brick
1:32-7, 1977.

Street flesh
Amprimoz, Alexandre. "Poetry & Vulgarity:--Bertrand Lachance." Brick
1:32-7, 1977.

Crawford, Terry. Quarry 23(1):74, 1974.

Tes rivières t'attendent
Amprimoz, Alexandre. Q&Q 42(12):13, 1976.

LACKS, John

The ties of time
Scobie, Stephen. "Poet en masse." CanL 50:75-8, 1971.

LACROIX, Benoît

Les cloches
Blais, Jacques. UTQ 44:338-9, 1975.

LACROIX, Georgette

Entre nous... ce pays
Dionne, René. "Sur les voies de notre poésie--II." Relations 368:56-9, 1972.

LAFOND, Guy

Bibliography
"Oeuvres de Guy Lafond." V&I 4:187-8, 1978.

General
Audet, Noel. "Guy Lafond ou le recours à l'être." V&I 4:193-204, 1978.

Renaud, Thérèse. "La poésie est mon athanor: entretien avec Guy Lafond." V&I 4:179-86, 1978.

Rivard, Yvon. "La poésie de Guy Lafond." Liberté 112-113:343-51, 1977.

Les cloches d'autres mondes
Engel, Christiane. LAQ 1977:119-22.

Recurt, Myriam. "L'âme et l'absolu." CanL 80:98-100, 1979.

Renaud, Thérèse. V&I 4(2):205-16, 1978.

L'eau ronde
Engel, Christiane. LAQ 1977:119-22.

Hébert, François. "Robert Marteau, Guy Lafond, Jean-Marc Fréchette (et Paul Chamberland?)." Liberté 110:70-6, 1977.

LAFOREST, Jean-Richard

Le divan des alternances
Hébert, François. "Deux poètes: Mélançon et Laforest." Liberté
20(6):115-9, 1978.

Lemaire, Michel. LAQ 1978:133-4.

LALONDE, Michèle

General
Jones, D.G. "An interview with Michèle Lalonde." Ellipse 3:33-41,
1970.

Mezei, Kathy. "Interview with Michèle Lalonde." Room of one's own
4(1&2):19-29, 1978.

Moisan, Clément. "Poésie de la libération." Moisan 1979:167-218.

Defense et illustration de la langue québécoise
Bonenfant, Joseph. LAQ 1979:132-5.

Prose et poémes
Bonenfant, Joseph. LAQ 1979:132-5.

LALONDE, Robert

Charivari des rues
Parmentier, Francis. LAQ 1970:149.

LAMARCHE, Gustave

General
Pageau, René. Gustave Lamarche: poète dramatique. Quebec: Garneau,
1976.

Pageau, René. "L'ideologie de Gustave Lamarche." ActN 64:758-77,
1975.

Pageau, René. "Un poète qui s'éxprime." Pageau 1976:137-89.

Le conte des sept jours
Pageau, René. ActN 59:491-503, 1970.

LAMARCHE, Gustave

Oeuvres poétiques
Dionne, René. "Poètes d'hier et d'avant-hier--la poésie québécoise en 1972." Relations 381:122-4, 1973.

Marcotte, Gilles. EF 9:80-2, 1973.

Paradis, Suzanne. LAQ 1972:145-7.

Palinods
Blais, Jacques. "Autour des Palinods de Gustave Lamarche." Blais 1975:233-7.

"Vierge noire de Pologne"
Gay, Paul. "'Vierge noire de Pologne': Gustave Lamarche sur l'opus 26, no. 2, de Frédéric Chopin." Savard 1977: 93-102.

LAMPMAN, Archibald

Bibliography
Bentley, D.M.R. "Archibald Lampman(1861-1899): a checklist." ECW 5:36-49, 1976.

General
Bentley, D.M.R. "Archibald Lampman on poets and poetry." ECW 9:12-25, 1977-78.

Connor, Carl Yoder. Archibald Lampman: Canadian poet of nature. Ottawa: Borealis, 1977.

Davies, Barrie. The alien mind: a study of the poetry of Archibald Lampman. Fredericton: Univ. of New Bruswick, 1970, c.1971.

Davies, Barrie. "Lampman and religion." CanL 56:40-60, 1973. (Also Woodcock 1974: 103-23.)

Davies, Barrie. "Lampman could tell his frog from from his toad: a note on art versus nature." SCL 2:129-30, 1977.

Davies, Barrie. "Lampman: radical poet of nature." EngQ 4(1):33-43, 1971.

Davies, Barrie. "The makeshift truce: Lampman and the position of the writer in nineteenth-century Canada." DR 53:121-42, 1973.

Davies, E. Barry. "Answering harmonies." HAB 23(2):57-68, 1972.

Djwa, Sandra. "Lampman's fleeting vision." CanL 56:22-39, 1973. (Also Woodcock 1974: 124-41.)

170

LAMPMAN, Archibald

General (cont'd.)
Dudek, Louis. "Lampman and the death of the sonnet." Dudek
1978:349-361. (Originally published The Lampman Symposium, Ottawa:
Univ. of Ottawa Press, 1976: 39-48.)

Dudek, Louis. "The significance of Lampman." Dudek 1978:65-78.
(Originally published Culture 18: 277-90, 1957.)

Gnarowski, Michael, ed. Archibald Lampman. Toronto: Ryerson, 1970.
(Critical views on Canadian writers, 3.)

Haines, Victor Yelverton. "Archibald Lampman: this or that." RUO
41:455-71, 1971.

Jobin, Madeline Graddon. Archibald Lampman: Canadian nature poet.
Montreal: McGill Univ., 1971. (M.A. thesis.)

Marshall, Tom. "Archibald Lampman: more facts and dreams." Marshall
1979:17-22.

Mezei, Kathy. "Lampman and Nelligan: dream landscapes." CRCL
6:151-65, 1979.

McMullen, Lorraine, ed. The Lampman symposium. Ottawa: Univ. of
Ottawa Press, 1976. (Re-appraisals: Canadian writers.)

Nesbitt, Bruce. "A gift of love: Lampman and life." CanL 50:35-40,
1971. (Also published Woodcock 1974:142-7.)

Sage, G.B. "Archibald Lampman as I knew him at Trinity University
(with a prefatory note by D.M.R. Bentley.)" CN&Q 18:7-8, 1976.

Steele, Charles R. "The isolate 'I' (eye): Lampman's persona." ECW
16:62-9, 1979-80.

Sutherland, John. "Edgar Allan Poe in Canada." Sutherland
1972:153-62.

Lampman's Kate: late love poems of Archibald Lampman
Davies, Barry. "Marginal Lampman." CanL 73:122-3, 1977.

Denham, Paul. "Accounting for the melancholy." CVII 1(2):5, 1975.

Lyrics of earth
Bentley, D.M.R. "The same unnamed delight: Lampman's essay on
'Happiness' and Lyrics of earth." ECW 5:25-35, 1976.

Poems of Archibald Lampman
Richard Birch, "Retrieval for the layman." BIC 3(6): 22-3, 1974.

The poems
Woodcock, George. "Poet and poetaster." CanL 63:85-9, 1975.

LAMPMAN, Archibald

"Alcyone"
Sutherland, John. "Edgar Allan Poe in Canada." Sutherland,
1972:153-62.

"The favorites of Pan"
Bentley, D.M.R. "Pan and the Confederation poets." CanL 81:59-71,
1979.

"Heat"
Haines, Victor Yelverton. "Archibald Lampton: this or that." RUO
41:455-71, 1971.

"The song of Pan"
Bentley, D.M.R. "Pan and the Confederation poets." CanL 81:59-71,
1979.

LANCTÔT, Jacques

Rupture de ban--paroles d'exil et d'amour
Corriveau, Hugues. LAQ 1979:135-7.

LANE, M. Travis

Homecomings: narrative poems
Barbour, Douglas. "Poetry chronicle V." DR 58:149-69, 1978.

Hamel, Guy. Fiddlehead 115:133-6, 1977.

Hornyansky, Michael. UTQ 47:354-5, 1978.

Nelson, Sharon H. Quarry 26(3):81-3, 1977.

An inch or so of garden
Hornyansky, Michael. UTQ 39:333, 1970.

Poems 1968-1972
Hornyansky, Michael. UTQ 43:361-3, 1974.

LANE, Patrick

General
Bowering, Marilyn. "Pine boughs and apple trees: the poetry of
Patrick Lane." MHRev 45:24-34, 1978.

Mahanti, J.C. "The daemon of the mind: the verse of Patrick Lane."
JCP 2(1):57-66, 1979.

LANE, Patrick

Albino peasants

Barbour, Douglas. "Poetry chronicle V." DR 58:149-69, 1978.

Fernstrom, Ken. Q&Q 43(12):12, 1977.

Mallinson, A. Jean. CVII 4(1):53-5, 1979. (Letter to the ed. re Neil Whiteman's article CVII 3(4).)

Mallinson, Jean. "A reading of Pat Lane." Brick 7:5-8, 1979.

Oliver, Michael Brian. "Lost and found." Fiddlehead 119:106-16, 1978.

Turner, Gordon. "Beating nails into the sky." Event 8(1):174-6, 1979.

White, Howard. CVII 4(1):55, 1979. (Letter to the ed. re Neil Whiteman's article CVII 3(4).)

Whiteman, Neil. "A left to the mind: the poems of Patrick Lane." CVII 3(4):49-52, 1978.

Zonailo, Carolyn. CVII 4(1):52-3, 1979. (Letter to the ed. re Neil Whiteman's article CVII 3(4).)

Beware the months of fire

Barbour, Douglas. Q&Q 40(6):12, 1974.

Dragland, Stan. Quarry 23(4):69-71, 1974.

Gasparini, Len. "One plus three." CanL 63:92-5, 1975.

Hicks, Lorne. CF 54(640-1):21-3, 1974.

Ireland, G.W. QQ 82:301-2, 1975.

Mackintosh, Mhari. CVII 1(1):26-7, 1975.

Macskimming, Roy. "A quatrain of contenders." Bic 3(7):5-6, 9, 1974.

Marlatt, Daphne. "On the outside." Open letter 3d ser. 2:109-12, 1975.

Watt, F.W. "Why poetry? Eleven answers." CF 55(651):40-1, 1975.

White, Howard. CVII 4(1):55, 1979. (Letter to the ed. re Neil Whiteman's article CVII 3(4).)

Whiteman, Neil. "A left to the mind: the poems of Patrick Lane." CVII 3(4):49-52, 1978.

LANE, Patrick

No longer two people
  Amprimoz, Alexandre L. Quarry 28(4):75-7, 1979.

  Brown, Allan. "Playing parts: five from Turnstone Press." Waves
  8(1):67-71, 1979.

Passing into storm
  Lillard, Charles. WCR 8(4):8-9, 1974.

Poems new and selected
  Amprimoz, Alexandre L. "Fear and experience: the poems of Patrick
  Lane." Waves 7(3): 68-71, 1979.
Poems new and selected (cont'd.)
  Barbour, Douglas. "Canadian poetry chronicle: VII." DR 59:154-75,
  1979.

  Dragland, Stan. Fiddlehead 122:124-8, 1979.

  Gasparini, Len. "Pain, thunder, and rainbows." BiC 8(2):24, 1979.

  Gatenby, Greg. Q&Q 46(2):46, 1979.

  Hornyansky, Michael. UTQ 48:340-1, 1979.

  Linder, Norma West. "Starkness and sensibility." CA&B 54(3):28-9,
  1979.

  Mallinson, Jean. "A reading of Pat Lane." Brick 7:5-8, 1979.

  Prato, Edward. WCR 14(1):43-6, 1979.

  Sullivan, Rosemary. "Staying power." CF 58(687):34, 1979.

Separations
  Marshall, Tom. "Canpo: a chronicle." Quarry 19(4):50-4, 1970.

The sun has begun to eat the mountain
  Bergé, Carol. New 20:48-50, 1973.

  Fetherling, Doug. "Surefooted poetry from the west coast." SatN
  87(8):35-7, 1972.

  Hosein, Clyde. "Open highways." BiC 1(10):24-5, 1972.

174

LANE, Patrick

Unborn things: South American poems
Gasparini, Len. "Exile and exhumanation." BIC 5(4):21-2, 1976.

Hamilton, Jamie. "The omens." CanR 3(6):52, 1976.

Livesay, Dorothy. "Transmigrations." CVII 2(1):6-7, 1976.

Mallinson, A. Jean. CVII 4(1):53-5, 1979. (Letter to the ed. re Neil Whiteman's article CVII 3(4).)

Mallinson, Jean. "A reading of Pat Lane." Brich 7:5-8, 1979.

Stuewe, Paul. Q&Q 42(4):25, 1976.

White, Howard. CVII 4(1):55, 1979. (Letter to the ed. re Neil Whiteman's article CVII 3(4).)

Whiteman, Neil. "A left to the mind: the poems of Patrick Lane." CVII 3(4):49-52, 1978.

Woodcock, George. "Playing with freezing fire." CanL 70:84-91, 1976.

LANE, Red

Collected poems
Sutherland, Fraser. "The poetry of Red Lane." CanL 49:47-55, 1971.

LANGEVIN, Gilbert

General
Bourassa, André-G. "L'ange noir qu'est Langevin." Lettres qué 3:8-10, 1976.

Nepveu, Pierre. "Gilbert Langevin, l'énergumène." EF 9:337-44, 1973.

Nepveu, Pierre. "The poetic frenzies of Gilbert Langevin." Ellipse 13:32-41, 1973. (Tr. Jean Vigneault.)

Nepveu, Pierre. "La poétique de Gilbert Langevin." LAQ 1973:312-24.

L'avion rose
Pontbriand, Jean-Noel. LAQ 1976:129-30.

Chansons et poèmes
Blais, Jacques. UTQ 44:339-40, 1975.

Chansons et poèmes 2
Brochu, André. LAQ 1974:129-30.

LANGEVIN, Gilbert

> La douche ou la seringue.
> > Brochu, André. LAQ 1974:129-30.

> Griefs
> > Pontbriand, Jean-Noel.   LAQ 1976:129-30.

> Mon refuge est un volcan
> > Nepveu, Pierre.   LAQ 1978:134-6.

> Novembre
> > Blais, Jacques. UTQ 43:367, 1974.

> Origines 1959-1967
> > Dionne, René. "Gilbert Langevin: sur les voies de notre poésie--IV."
> > Relations 371:157-8, 1972.

> > Mailhot, Laurent. LAQ 1971:137-9.

> Origines 1959-1967 (cont'd.)
> > Marcotte, Gilles. EF 9:80, 1973.

> Ouvrir le feu
> > Mailhot, Laurent.   LAQ 1971:137-9.

> > Marcotte, Gilles. EF 8:94-5, 1972.

> Stress
> > Mailhot, Laurent.   LAQ 1971:137-9.

> > Marcotte, Gilles. EF 8:94-5, 1972.

> La vue du sang
> > Blais, Jacques. UTQ 43:367, 1974.

LAPOINTE, Gatien

> General
> > Bonenfant, Joseph. "La passion des mots chez Gatien Lapointe." LAQ
> > 1970:248-54.

> > Laroche, Maximilien. "L'américanité ou l'ambiguité du je." Laroche
> > 1975:1-17 (Also published ELit 8:103-28, 1975.)

> Ode au Saint-Laurent
> > Maugey, Axel. "Gatien Lapointe." Maugey 1972: 191-200.

> Le premier mot
> > Giroux, Robert. "Le premier mot de Gatien Lapointe." Deuxième
> > mouvement 1(1):13-4, 1974.

LAPOINTE, Paul-Marie

General

Bourassa, André-G. "Paul-Marie Lapointe." Bourassa 1977:159-64.

Dionne, René. "Sur les voies de notre poésie (1)." Relations 366:340-1, 1971.

Dostie, Gaetan. "Paul-Marie Lapointe: le sismographe du Québec." PFr 7:102-16, 1973.

Dostie, Gaetan. "Paul-Marie Lapointe: the seimosgraph of Québec." Ellipse 11:54-65, 1972. (Tr. Susan Copeland.)

Jones, D.G. "A post card from Chicoutimi." SCL 1:170-82, 1976.

Moisan, Clément. "Poésie de la résistance." Moisan 1979:129-66.

Nepveu, Pierre. "L'évidence de la poésie; l'oeuvre de Paul-Marie Lapointe." Nepveu 1979: 195-273.

Nuit du 15 au 26 novembre 1948

Bourassa, André-G. "A special night." ECW 15:120-38, 1979. (Tr. Mark Czarnecki.)

Major, Jean-Louis. Paul-Marie Lapointe: la nuit incendiée. Montréal: Presses de l'Univ. de Montréal, 1978.

Le réel absolu: poèmes 1948-1965

Ferron, Jacques. "Paul-Marie Lapointe: un grand poète." Le maclean 11(11):63, 1971.

Major, Jean-Louis. UTQ 41:346, 1972.

Marcotte, Gilles. EF 8:91-2, 1972.

Paradis, Suzanne. LAQ 1971:122-5.

Tableaux de l'amoureuse,

Bélanger, Marcel. LAQ 1975:102-4.

Bourassa, André-G. "D'après peinture: Bélanger, Leblanc, Marteau, Ouellette, Girardin et Lapointe." Lettres qué 6:10-3, 1977.

Vachon, G-André. "Note sur Réjean Ducharme et Paul-Marie Lapointe: fragment d'un traité du vide." EF 11:355-87, 1975.

LAPOINTE, Paul-Marie

Une unique, Art égyptien, Voyage et autres poèmes

Bélanger, Marcel.   LAQ 1975:102-4.

Bourassa, André-G. "D'après peinture: Bélanger, Leblanc, Marteau, Ouellette, Girardin et Lapointe." Lettres qué 6:10-3, 1977.

Vachon, G-André. "Note sur Réjean Ducharme et Paul-Marie Lapointe: fragment d'un traité du vide." EF 11:355-87, 1975.

Le vierge incendié
Arcand, Pierre-André.   VIP 8:11-38, 1974.

Fisette, Jean. "Le vierge incendié--pour une typologie des énoncés." Fisette 1977:27-75. (Also published Breches 4-5:12-68, 1975.)

Laflèche, Guy. "Écart, violence et révolte chez Paul-Marie Lapointe." EF 6:395-419, 1970.

Major, Jean-Louis. Paul-Marie Lapointe: la nuit incendié. Montréal: Presses de l'Univ. de Montréal, 1978.

Maugey, Axel. "Paul-Marie Lapointe." Maugey 1972, 133-45.

Paradis, Suzanne.   LAQ 1971:122-5.

"Arbres"
Major, Robert. "En marge de 'Arbres' de Paul-Marie Lapointe." Inc 1(1-3):121-9, 1977.

Pélosse, Cécile. "La recherche du pays chez Paul-Marie Lapointe et Gérald Godin--concerto pour arbres." V&I 1:80-8, 1975.

Richard, Robert. "'J'écris arbre': système fractal." Inc. 2-3(1):59-75, 1979.

"En coup de foudre..."
Haeck, Philippe. "Naissance de la poésie moderne au Québec." EF 9:95-113, 1973.

"Je suis une main..."
Fisette, Jean. "Essai de structuration d'un poème de Paul-Marie Lapointe." BdJ 39-40-41:124-53, 1973.

LAPP, Claudia

Honey
Barbour, Douglas. "Canadian poetry chronicle: VI." DR 58:555-78, 1978.

Davies, Gwendolyn. "Something's happening in Montreal." ECW 10:82-7, 1978.

Stange, Ken. "Honey and light." CVII 3(3):5-7, 1978.

LARIVIÈRE, Jean

Innocence
Laflèche, Guy. LAQ 1973:118.

Sauvage
Thério, Adrien. LAQ 1972:173.

LASNIER, Rina

Bibliography
Lajoie, Yvan. "Essai de bibliographie des oeuvres de Rina Lasnier." Liberté 108:143-54, 1976.

General
Bélanger, Marcel. "La genèse d'une thématique." Liberté 108:34-48, 1976.

Bonenfant, Joseph. "Dimensions iconiques de la poésie de Rina Lasnier." Liberté 108:85-101, 1976.

Bonenfant, Joseph et Giguère, Richard "Conversation with Rina Lasnier." Ellipse 22:32-61, 1978. (Tr. by M.L. Taylor.)

Bonenfant, Joseph et Giguère, Richard. "Est-il chose plus belle qu'un orange? Rencontre avec Rina Lasnier." V&I 4:3-32, 1978.

Bourassa, André-G. "Chaîne et trame: Rina Lasnier, Denis Vanier et Josée Yvon." Lettres qué 5:11-3, 1977.

Liberté 108:1976 Whole issue.

Melançon, Joseph. "Une rhétorique de l'ombre." Liberté 108:102-13, 1976.

LASNIER, Rina

General (cont'd.)
Moisan, Clément. "Poésie de la clandestinité." Moisan 1979:91-127.

Moisan, Clément. "Rina Lasnier et Margaret Avison." Liberté 108:21-33, 1976.

Sicotte, Sylvie. L'Arbre dans la poésie de Rina Lasnier. Sherbrooke: Cosmos, 1977. (Profils, 11.)

Vaillancourt, Pierre-Louis. "La poésie est un temple... le thème des oiseaux des Rina Lasnier." Inc. 2-3(1):37-53, 1979.

Le chant de la montée
Lamarche, Gustave. "Rina Lasnier, poète de l'essentiel." Liberté 108:127-32, 1976.

Paradis, Suzanne. "Eloge de Rachel." Liberté 108:12-20, 1976.

L'échelle des anges
Lamarche, Gustave. CC-R 4(2):43-9, 1976.

Escales
Malenfant, Chanel. Étude des thèmes et des images dans Escales de Rina Lasnier. Montreal: Univ. de Montréal, 1974. (M.A. thesis.)

Madones canadiennes
Blais, Jacques. "La poésie du pays: Félix-Antoine Savard et Rina Lasnier." Blais 1975:269-94.

Matins d'oiseaux
Bonenfant, Joseph. LAQ 1978:136-8.

Paliers de paroles
Bonenfant, Joseph. " LAQ 1978:136-8.

La part du feu
Dionne, René. "Où va notre poésie?" Relations 357:55-7, 1971.

Marcotte, Gilles. EF 7:106-7, 1971.

Poèmes
Dionne, René. "Poètes d'hier et d'avant-hier (2): Rina Lasnier." Relations 382:158, 1973.

Marcotte, Gilles. EF 9:77-8, 1973.

Nepveu, Pierre. "Rina Lasnier: poète de l'Informel." LAQ 1972:141-4.

180

LASNIER, Rina

Présence de l'absence
    Lizé, Émile. "Les motifs qui soutiennent les thèmes de Présence de
l'absence de Rina Lasnier." Co-incidences 1 (3):26-39, 1971.

La Salle des rêves
    Dionne, René. "Sur les voies de notre poésie--III." Relations
370:122-4, 1972.

    Kushner, Eva. LAQ 1971:132-6.

    Lamarche, Gustave. ActN 61:161-71, 1971.

    Major, Jean-Louis. UTQ 41:342-3, 1972.

    Major, Jean-Louis. "Rina Lasnier et la connivence des signes." CanL
55: 41-9, 1973.

    Marcotte, Gilles. EF 8:90-91, 1972.

Les signes
    Bourassa, André-G. "Châine et trame: Rina Lasnier, Denis Vanier et
Josée Yvon." Lettres qué 5:11-3, 1977.

    Dionne, René. UTQ 46:377-8, 1977.

    Fisette, Jean. "Poésie récente, poésie diverse." V&I 2:440-3, 1977.

    Labelle, Jean-Paul. "Poésie: Les signes de Rina Lasnier." Relations
37(423):58-9, 1977.

    Melançon, Joseph. LAQ 1976: 139-41.

    Sicotte, Sylvie. V&I 4:33-8, 1978.

"Ensemble"
    Cotnoir, Louise and Malenfant, Chanel. BdJ 39-40-41:86-103, 1973.

"Escales"
    Malenfant, Chanel. Étude des thèmes et des images dans Escales de
Rina Lasnier. Montreal Univ. de Montréal, 1974. (M.A. thesis.)

    Malenfant, Chanel. Liberté 108:49-75, 1976.

"Eve"
    Malenfant, Chanel. Étude des thèmes et des images dans Escales de
Rina Lasnier. Montreal Univ. de Montréal, 1974. (M.A. thesis.)

LASNIER, Rina

"Le figuier maudit"
Malenfant, Chanel. Étude des thèmes et des images dans Escales de Rina Lasnier. Montreal Univ. de Montréal, 1974. (M.A. thesis)

Malenfant, Chanel. "'Le figuier maudit' Escales: l'arbre dans le paysage thématique de Rina Lasnier." VIP 9:113-38, 1975.

"L'iris sauvage"
Major, Jean-Louis. "Rina Lasnier et la connivence des signes." CanL, 55: 41-9, 1973.

"Jungle de feuilles"
Brochu, André. "Absence de Rina Lasnier." V&I 173-81, 1975.

"Le malemer"
Audet, Noël. "Le procès du sens dans un poème de Rina Lasnier." Liberté 108:76-83, 1976.

Lamarche, Gustave. "Rina Lasnier, poète de l'essentiel." Liberté 108:127-32, 1976.

"Psyché"
Malenfant, Chanel. Étude des thèmes et des images dans Escales de Rina Lasnier. Montreal: Univ. de Montréal, 1974. (M.A. thesis.)

"La salle des rêves"
Bonenfant, Joseph. "Dimensions iconiques de la poésie de Rina Lasnier." Liberté 108:85-101, 1976.

LATTA, William

Drifting into grey
Cameron, Michael. "Muddy waters." CVII 4(2):34-5, 1979.

Summer's bright blood
Morton, Colin. "Examining the individual(s)." CVII 3(1):42-3, 1977.

LATTER, Michael E.

Lizard on the scalding stone
de Santana, Hubert. "Poetic torrents, erotic jewels." BiC 5(2):36-8, 1976.

F., M.K. CA&B 51(4):25, 1976.

LAUZON, Dominique

Artères
Fisette, Jean. "Poésie récente, poésie diverse." V&I 2:440-3, 1977.

Poulin, Gabrielle. LAQ 1976:127-9.

La vie simple
Poulin, Gabrielle. LAQ 1976:127-9.

LAVERDIÈRE, Camille

Glaciel
Hamelin, Louis-Edmond. "Vent soutenu chez un poète engagé." Liberté 93:92-3, 1974.

Wyczynski, Paul. "Voix québécoises: Camille Laverdière: Glaciel, Marcel Sabella: Le jour incendié." LAQ 1974:136-8.

Québec nord/américain
Dionne, René. "Sur les voies de notre poésie--II." Relations 368:56-9, 1972.

Fournier, Gérard-Claude. LAQ 1971:173.

LAWRANCE, Scott

Names of thunder
Barbour, Douglas. "Canadian poetry chronicle: VII." DR 59:154-75, 1979.

David, Jack. Q&Q 44(16):9-10, 1978.

Gasparini, Len. "Pain, thunder, and rainbows." BiC 8(2):24, 1979.

Trethewey, Eric. Fiddlehead 123:109-10, 1979.

LAYTON, Irving

Bibliography
Burgess, G.C. Ian. Irving Layton's poetry: a catalogue and a chronology. Montreal: McGill University, 1973, c1974.(M.A. thesis.)

Mayne, Seymour. "Irving Layton: a bibiliography in progress 1931-1971." WCR 7(3):23-32, 1973.

LAYTON, Irving

General

Adams, Richard. The poetic theories of Irving Layton: a study in polarities. Fredericton: Univ. of New Brunswick, 1971. (M.A. thesis.)

Allard, Kerry. "Conversation: Jewish Layton Catholic Hood Protestant Bowering." Open letter 2d ser, 5:30-9, 1973.

Baker, Howard. "Jewish themes in the works of Irving Layton." ECW 10:43-54, 1978.

Buckowski, Denise. "Shakespeare and I..." BiC 7(7):7-9, 1978.

Doyle, Mike. "The occasions of Irving Layton." CanL 54:70-83, 1972.

Dudek, Louis. "Layton now and then: our critical assumptions." Dudek 1978:52-8.

Ferrari, Jean Dominique. The poet and the cokebottle: a study of Irving Layton's poetic vision of common life. Winnipeg: Univ. of Manitoba, 1973. (M.A. thesis.)

Francis, Wynne. "Layton and Nietzsche." CanL 67:39-52, 1976.

Hoadley, Jocelyn M. Free imagery in the poetry of Irving Layton. Montreal: Concordia University, 1975. (M.A. thesis.)

Mantz, Douglas. "An interview with Irving Layton; an example of overcoming distance and restricted budgets." EngQ 10(2):1-12, 1977.

Marshall, Tom. "The swimmer's moment: Irving Layton." Marshall 1979:67-75.

Mayne, Seymour, ed. Irving Layton: the poet and his critics. Toronto: McGraw-Hill Ryerson, 1978.

Mayne, Seymour. A study of the poetry of Irving Layton. Vancouver: Univ. of British Columbia, 1972. (Ph.D. thesis.)

Moisan, Clément. "Poésie de la résistance." Moisan 1979:129-66.

Purdy, Al. "The ego has it both ways: poets in Montreal." Nj 7&8:127-47, 1976.

Osterlund, Steven. Fumigator: an outsider's view of Irving Layton. Cleveland, Ohio: Rumple Studios, 1975.

Pomeroy, Graham. "Latent Layton: a male chauvinist." CanR 1(2)3-5, 1974.

Rowe, Margaret Lillian. Art and life: a study of the poetry of Irving Layton. Halifax: Dalhousie Univ., 1972. (M.A. thesis.)

184

LAYTON, Irving

General (cont'd.)
Reznitsky, Lawrence, J. "Interview with Irving Layton." Le chien d'or 1:n.p., 1972. (13 p.)

Sherman, Ken. "An interview with Irving Layton." ECW 10:7-18, 1978.

Smith, A.J.M. "A salute to Layton: in praise of his earliest masterpieces: 1956." Smith 1977:70-5. (Originally published QQ 62:587-91, 1955-6, under title "The recent poetry of Irving Layton: a major voice.")

Smith, Patricia, Joan Keeney. The theme of death in Irving Layton's poetry. Montreal: Sir George Williams Univ., 1970. (M.A. thesis.)

Smith, Patricia Keeney. "Irving Layton and the theme of death." CanL 48:6-15, 1971.

Stevens, Peter. "The fiery eye: the poetry of Irving Layton." OntR 4:51-8, 1976.

Thomas, Clara. "A conversation about literature: an interivew with Margaret Laurence and Irving Layton." JCF 1(1)65-9, 1972.

Van Wilt, Kurt. "Layton, Nietzsche and overcoming." ECW 10:19-42, 1978.

Waterston, Elizabeth. "Irving Layton: apocalypse in Montreal." CanL 48:16-24, 1971.

Woodcock, George. "Poursuite de Protée: à propos d'Irving Layton." Ellipse 11:96-115, 1972. (Tr. Rodolphe Lacasse.)

The cold green element
Smith, A.J.M. "A salute to Layton: in praise of his earliest masterpieces: 1956." Smith 1977:70-5. (Originally published QQ 62:587-91, 1955-6, under title "The recent poetry of Irving Layton: a major voice.")

The collected poems of Irving Layton
Almon, Bert. New 20:57-8, 1973.

Callaghan, Barry. "A poet in his pride: Layton as messiah." SatN 87(3):31-8, 1972.

Davey, Frank. Open letter 2d ser, 2:50-2, 1972.

Fritch, James E. CA&B 48(2):24, 1972.

Gibbs, Robert. Fiddlehead 94:129-30, 1972.

Levenson, Christopher. QQ 79:272-4, 1972.

LAYTON, Irving

The Collected poems of Irving Layton (cont'd.)
Mayne, Seymour. WCR 7(2):59-60, 1972.

Mezei, Kathy. Quarry 21(4):64-6, 1972.

Watt, F.W. CF 52(620):38, 1972.

Weaver, Robert. "Sum total." BiC 1(7):1-2.

Wilson, Milton. "Notebook on Layton." TamR 61:56-73, 1973.

Woodcock, George. "A grab at Proteus: notes on Irving Layton."
Woodcock 1974b:53-70. (Originally published CanL 28:5-21, 1966.)

The covenant
Barbour, Douglas. "Canadian poetry chronicle: VI." DR 58:555-78, 1978.

Billings, Robert. UWR 13(2):98-100, 1978.

Brown, Russell. "Layton's quarrel." CanL 80:90-2, 1979.

Francis, Wynne. "The farting Jesus: Layton and the heroic vitalists."
CVII 3(3):46-51, 1978.

Gatenby, Greg. Q&Q 43(16):9, 1977.

Geddes, Gary. "Our most erotic puritan." BiC 6(10)12,14, 1977.

Hatfield, Stephen. "The sword sleeps in the hand: lazy aim with the
long pea-shooter." Waves 6(2):72-6, 1978.

Lecker, Robert. Fiddlehead 117:122-4, 1978.

Lemm, Richard. Quarry 27(4):76-9, 1978.

Linder, Norma West. "Strong words indeed." CA&B 53(2):41, 1978.

Van Wilt, Kurt. "Layton's covenant with art." ECW 9:62-5, 1977-78.

The darkening fire: selected poems 1945-1968
Barbour, Douglas. "Canadian poetry chronicle: III." DR 56:560-73,
1976.

CanR 2(4):55, 1975.

Hosek, Chaviva. Q&Q 41(11):6, 1975.

Stevens, Peter. "The fiery eye: the poetry of Irving Layton."
OntarioR 4:51-8, 1976.

LAYTON, Irving

The darkening fire: selected poems 1945-1968 (cont'd.)
Such, Peter. "Three grand old parties." BiC 5(2):9-11, 1976.

Droppings from heaven
Abley, Mark. "Poetry that fell from the sky." Maclean's 93(41):54-8, 1979.

Aubert, Rosemary. Q&Q 45(13):33, 1979.

Smith, Patricia Keeney. "A wild peculiar joy." CF 59(695):32, 1979-80.

Engagements
Gerus, Claire. Q&Q 38(12):8, 1972.

For my brother Jesus
Barbour, Douglas. "Poetry chronicle IV." DR 57:355-71, 1977.

Francis, Wynne. "The farting Jesus: Layton and the heroic vitalists." CVII 3(3):46-51, 1978.

Harrison, Ernest. "The church morbid." BiC 5(5):12-4, 1976.

Hatfield, Stephen. "The sword sleeps in the hand: lazy aim with the long pea-shooter." Waves 6(2):72-6, 1978.

Hornyansky, Michael. UTQ 46:367-8, 1977.

Jonas, George. "Irving Layton on the cross." SatN 91(4):69-70, 1976.

McNamara, Eugene. "In a high clean style." CanL 78:88-90, 1978.

O'Flaherty, Patrick. "Nothing stands." CF 56(665):30, 1976.

Walker, Susan. Q&Q 42(7):40, 1976.

Lovers and lesser men
Dragland, Stan. Fiddlehead 99:99-102, 1973.

Haas, Maara. CA&B 48(4):24, 1973.

Hosein, Clyde. "Kicking against the pricks." BiC 2(2):5-6, 1973.

Lacey, Edward. "Canadian bards and South American reviewers." Nj 4:82-120, 1974.

Ringrose, Christopher Xerxes. DR 53:160-3, 1973.

Stevens, Peter. "The perils of majority." UWR 9(2):100-9, 1974.

Sutherland, Fraser. Q&Q 39(3):8, 1973.

Warkentin, Germaine. "Layton's world." LURev 7:149-53, 1974.

LAYTON, Irving

Nail polish
Cogswell, Fred. QQ 78:3256, 1971.

Gifford, Tony. Quarry 20(4):76-80, 1971.

Hornyansky, Michael. UTQ 41:330-1, 1972.

Hunt, Russell A. Fiddlehead 91:102-4, 1971.

Lochhead, Douglas. DR 51:280-2, 1971.

Wainwright, Andy. "Two hoary old poets." SatN 86(5):25-8, 1971.

Waterston, Elizabeth. "New-found eyes." CanL 52:102-5, 1972.

Now is the place
Sutherland, John. "Mr. Layton's talents." Sutherland 1972:112-4.

The poems of Irving Layton
Barbour, Douglas. "Poetry chronicle V." DR 58:149-69, 1978.

Smith, A.J.M. "Wandering gentile, homebody Jew." BiC 6(6):18-9, 1977.

The pole-vaulter
Bagchee, Shyamal. "Two poets and a half." ECW 3:65-9, 1975.

Baglow, John. "The day is too ordinary." CanR 2(1):28-30, 1975.

Fraser, Keath. "Creative juices swift and slow." BIC 3(7): 16, 1974.

Gibbs, Robert. "Presiding voices: Purdy, Layton and Gustafson." DR 56:356-65, 1976.

Long, Tanya. Q&Q 40(10):24-5, 1974.

Marshall, Tom. "Pole-vaulting over the grave." CVII 1(1):4, 1975.

Monk, Patricia. Quarry 24(2):53-4, 1975.

Mundwiler, Leslie. "Layton and Wayman: poets and the history of Joe Blow." CanD 10(7):60-2, 1975.

Musgrave, Susan. "Layton." Open letter 3d ser, 2:102-3, 1975.

Namjoshi, Suniti. "A would-be pole vaulter." CF 54(646):19, 1974.

Sandler, Linda. "Gustafson & others." TamR 64:89-94, 1974.

Watt, F.W. "Why poetry? Eleven answers." CF 55(651):40-1, 1975.

LAYTON, Irving

A red carpet for the sun
Dudek, Louis. "Layton on the carpet." Dudek 1978:136-40. (Originally published Delta 9:17-9, 1959.)

The shattered plinths
Scott, Peter Dale. "A Canadian chronicle." Poetry 115:353-64, 1970.

The swinging flesh
Dudek, Louis. "Three major Canadian poets--three major forms of archaism." Dudek 1978:153-6. (Originally published Delta 16:23-5 1961.)

The tightrope dancer
Barbour, Douglas. "Canadian poetry chronicle: VII." DR 59:154-75, 1979.

Gasparini, Len. "Of imagination all compact." BiC 7(10):36-7, 1978.

Gatenby, Greg. "Poetry chronicle." TamR 77&78:77-94, 1979.

Nicoll, Sharon. Fiddlehead 123:103-6, 1979.

Pyke, Linda. "New works from three seasoned poets." Q&Q 44(13):8, 1978.

The unwavering eye: selected poems 1969-1975
Adamson, Arthur. "The poet as split infinity." CVII 2(1):47-9, 1976.

Barbour, Douglas. "Canadian poetry chronicle: III." DR 56:560-73, 1976.

Evans, J.A.S. "Undertows and Ovid tones." BiC 4(8):19, 1975.

Oliver, Michael Brian. "Dionysos the Jew." AntigR 24:91-3, 1975.

Stevens, Peter. "The fiery eye: the poetry of Irving Layton." OntR 4:51-8, 1976.

The whole bloody bird
Dowden, Graham. Quarry 20(1):45-8, 1971.

Hornyansky, Michael. UTQ 39:328-9, 1970.

"The birth of tragedy"
Francis, Wynne. "'The birth of tragedy': a Nietzschean reading." Waves 3(3):5-8, 1975.

"For Mao Tse-Tung: a meditation on flies and kings"
Francis, Wynne. "Layton's red carpet: a reading of 'For Mao Tse-Tung: a meditation on flies and kings.'" Inscape 12(1):50-6, 1975.

LAYTON, Irving

"Poetry as the fine art of pugilism"
Layton, Irving. "Open letter to A.J.M. Smith." Nj 7&8:104, 1976.

"A tall man executes a jig"
Thompson, Lee Briscoe and Black, Deborah. "The dance of a pot-bellied poet: explorations into 'A tall man executes a jig.'" Cp 12(2):33-43, 1979.

LEBLANC, Madeleine

J'habite une planète
Bourassa, André-G. "D'après peinture: Bélanger, Leblanc, Marteau, Ouellette, Girardin et Lapointe." Lettres qué 6:10-3, 1977.

LEBLANC, Raymond

General
Arcand, Pierre André; Leblanc, Gérard; Roy, Pierre. "Entrevue avec Raymond Leblanc." RUM 5(1):96-8, 1972.

Arcand, Pierre André; Leblanc Gérard; et Roy, Pierre. "Une poésie militante." RUM 5(1):115-8, 1972.

"Entrevue avec Raymond Leblanc" RUM 5(1): 97-8, 1972.

Cri de terre: poèmes 1969-1971
Arcand, Pierre-André. "Poets from the end of the earth." Ellipse, 16:76-82, 1973. (Tr. Barbara Kuritzky.)

Duguay, Calixte. RUM 8(1):107-11, 1975.

Duclos, Jocelyn-Robert. LAQ 1973:130-1.

Mitcham, Allison. HAB 25:91-2, 1974.

Masson, Alain. "Étranglement étalement." RUM 7(2):165-95, 1974.

Poulin, Gabrielle. "L'Acadie et ses poètes." Relations 36(411):29-31, 1976.

LECKNER, Carol N.

Daisies on a whale's back
Allison, Diane. "Kitsch and Kin." BiC 5(5):16, 1976.

Gasparini, Len. "Handsprings and flops." BiC 4(8):21-2, 1975.

LECLERC, André

Poussières-Taillibert
Giguère, Richard. "Trois tendances de la poésie québécoise." LAQ
1976: 114-6.

LECLERC, Félix

Bibliography
Boivin, Aurélien. "Bibliographie." QuéFr. 33:44, 1979.

General
Boivin, Aurélien, et al. "Félix Leclerc: entrevue." QuéFr. 33:37-40,
1979.

Gaulin, André. "Il faut imaginer Félix heureux." QuéFr. 33:43-4,
1979.

Royer, Jean. "L'alouette en colère." Presqu'amérique 1(11):23-4,
1972.

Cent chansons
Lacroix, Pierre. LAQ 1970:125-6.

LECLERC, Michel

Dorénavant la poésie
Bourassa, André-G. "L'Hexagone au quart de tour." Lettres qué
9:11-4, 1978.

Delisle, Claude. LAQ 1977:164-6.

Nepveu, Pierre. "La jeune poésie, la critique peut-être..." Lettres
qué 6:13-5, 1977.

Odes pour un matin public
Gallays, François. LAQ 1972:174.

Le traversée du réel précédé
Bourassa, André-G. "L'Hexagone au quart de tour." Lettres qué
9:11-4, 1978.

Delisle, Claude. LAQ 1977:164-6.

Nepveu, Pierre. "La jeune poésie, la critique peut-être..." Lettres
qué 6:13-5, 1977.

LEE, Dennis

General
Pearce, Jon. "Enacting a meditation: Dennis Lee." JCP 2(1):5-23, 1979. (Interview.)

Witten, Mark. "The case of the midwife lode." BiC 6(10):6-8, 1977.

Civil elegies and other poems
Fetherling, Doug. "A poet-publisher with a voice like no one else's." SatN 87(6):37, 1972.

Helwig, David. Quarry 21(3):66-7, 1972.

Lee, Dennis. Quarry 21(3):67-70, 1972. (Response to review by David Helwig.)

Newman, Christina. "A feeling for the nation that made him." Maclean's 85(6):88, 1972.

Schroeder, Andreas. "Difficult sanities." CanL 55:102-5, 1973.

Swann, Susan. "From minding to feeling." BiC 1(10):21-2, 1972.

The death of Harold Ladoo
Helwig, David. "From Ondaatje to Lee: words that live as poetry." SatN 94(9):58-9, 1979.

MacEwen, Gwendolyn. Q&Q 42(12):13, 1976.

McNamara, Eugene. "In a high clean style." CanL 78:88-90, 1978.

Such, Peter. "Requiem for the way it was." BiC 5(11):34-6, 1976.

Garbage delight
Newson, Bryan. "Let's ear it for aural Lee." BiC 6(9):11, 1977.

The gods
Abley, Mark. "Poetry that fell from the sky." Maclean's 93(41):54-8, 1979.

Pearson, Ian. Q&Q 45(13):33-4, 1979.

LEE, John B.

Poems only a dog could love
Barbour, Douglas. "Canadian poetry chronicle: VI." DR 58:555-78, 1978.

Lane, M. Travis. "Cat and dog." Fiddlehead 111:139-42, 1976.

LEFRANÇOIS, Alexis

General
Lefrançois, Alexis. "Mais que dire, sinon..." NBdJ 70:30-49, 1978.

La belle été
Bourneuf, Roland. LAQ 1977:171-4.

Nepveu, Pierre. "Alexis Lefrançois: les 'mots éblouis de silence.'"
Lettres qué 8:15-6, 1977.

Calcaires
Bonenfant, Joseph. LAQ 1971:155-6.

Marcotte, Gilles. EF 8:99, 1972.

Sanderson, Gertrude Kearns. AntigR 10:111-3, 1972.

Rémanences
Bourneuf, Roland. LAQ 1977:171-4.

Hébert, François. "Lefrançois, Beaulieu, Nepveu, Vanier." Liberté
114:93-9, 1977.

Nepveu, Pierre. "Alexis Lefrançois: les 'mots éblouis de silence.'"
Lettres qué 8:15-6, 1977.

La tête
Bourneuf, Roland. LAQ 1977:171-4.

Nepveu, Pierre. "Alexis Lefrançois: les 'mots éblouis de silence'."
Lettres qué 8:15-6, 1977.

36 petites choses pour la 51
Bélanger, Yrénée. LAQ 1972:160.

Ferron, Jacques. "Dussault: l'intelligence du monde et de la vie."
Le maclean 12(5):65, 1972.

Marcotte, Gilles. EF 9:85-6, 1973.

LEGAGNEUR, Serge

Textes on croix
Bourassa, André-G. LAQ 1978:138-9.

Hébert, François. Liberté 118-119: 246-7, 1978.

LEGAULT, Leonard

Gravelburg and other places
Billings, R. Quarry 23(3):76, 1974.

LÉGER, Pierrot

Le show d'Évariste le Nabord-à-Bab
Corriveau, Hugues. LAQ 1977:143-4.

LEGRIS, Isabelle

Le sceau de l'ellipse
Major, Robert. LAQ 1979:137-41.

LEIGH, Simon

Dying flowers
Hornyansky, Michael. UTQ 43:361, 1974.

LEIGHTON, Alasdair

Shapeless flame
Sutherland, Fraser. "Group groping and singular sensing." BiC
1(10):30, 1972.

LELIÈVRE, Sylvain

General
Bourassa, André-G. "Les poètes de la musique." Lettres qué 11:32-7,
1978.

LEMAIRE, Michel

L'enver des choses
Dionne, René. UTQ 46:379-81, 1977.

Fisette, Jean. "Poésie récente, poésie diverse." V&I 2:440-3, 1977.

Melançon, Robert. LAQ 1976:125-7.

Nepveu, Pierre. Lettres qué 5:13-5, 1977.

Poulin, Gabrielle. "En robe 'demi-deuil': la poésie de Michel
Lemaire." Relations 37(427):190-1, 1977.

194

LEMIEUX, Gilles

L'
Laflèche, Guy.   LAQ 1973:118-9.

LEMIEUX-LÉVESQUE, Alice

Vers la joie
VieFr 30:190-1, 1976.

LEMIRE, Gilles

Code d'oubli
Corriveau, Hugues.   LAQ 1978: 94-6.

LENOIR, Joseph

General
Lortie, Jeanne d'Arc.   "Nationalisme humanitaire: Joseph Lenoir."
Lortie 1975:276-90.

LE PAN, Douglas

General
Hamilton, S.C.   "European emblem and Canadian image: a study of
Douglas Le Pan's poetry." Mosaic 3(2): 62-73, 1970.

Marshall, Tom. "The lake of darkness: Douglas Le Pan's roving
picket." Marshall 1979: 132-34.

The wounded prince and other poems
Priestman, Donald G. "Man in the maze." CanL 64:52-66, 1975.

The net and the sword
Priestman, Donald G. "Man in the maze." CanL 64:52-66, 1975.

"Canoe trip"
Stewart, Hugh. "Literary mining in the Canadian shield." Copperfield
3:57-64, 1970.

"A country without a mythology"
Stewart, Hugh. "Literary mining in the Canadian shield." Copperfield
3:57-64, 1970.

LEROUX, Jean-Pierre

Dans l'intervalle
Corriveau, Hugues. LAQ 1979:141-3.

LE SANN, Jacqueline

The invisible ladder/L'échelle invisible
Farmiloe, Dorothy. Q&Q 42(9):36, 1976.

LESCARBOT, Marc

General
Emont, Bernard. "Marc Lescarbot, premier poète de l'Acadie et de la Nouvelle-France." RUM 7(2):93-117, 1974.

LESLIE, Kenneth

General
Perly, Susan. "We bury our poets. Kenneth Leslie: a homesick bluenoser." CF 55(651)31-3, 1975.

The poems of Kenneth Leslie
Shucard, Alan R. "Kenneth Leslie." CanL 55:115-7, 1973.

Shucard, Alan R. WLWe 11(2):105-6, 1972.

Sutherland, Fraser. "Promises, promises." Bic 1(7):22, 1972.

LÉVEILLÉ, J.R.L.

Ouvrière de la première mort
Bouvier, Luc. LAQ 1978:139-41.

LÉVEILLÉE, Claude

L'étoile d'Amérique
Fournier, Gérard-Claude. LAQ 1972:178.

196

LEVENSON, Christopher

Into the open
Barbour, Douglas. "Canadian poetry chronicle: VI." DR 58:555-78, 1978.

Barlow, Garnet. Quarry 27(4):83-6, 1978.

Toth, Nancy. "Organized decays." CVII 4(3):38-41,43, 1979.

The journey back and other poems
Macfarlane, David. "To fall is not to finish." BiC 8(2):25, 1979.

McNally, Paul. Fiddlehead 121:154-5, 1979.

Stills
Barbour, Douglas. QQ 79:571-2, 1972.

Stevens, Peter. Quarry 21(4):66-9, 1972.

LÉVESQUE, Charles

General
Lortie, Jeanne d'Arc. "Voix du peuple: Charles Lévesque." Lortie 1975:291-302.

LÉVESQUE, Raymond

Au fond du chaos
Dionne, René. "Sur les voies de notre poésie--II." Relations 368:56-9, 1972.

Gallays, François. LAQ 1971:171.

Le temps de parler
Major, Robert. LAQ 1978:141-2.

LILLARD, Charles

Cultus coulee
Gibbs, Robert. Fiddlehead 90:115-6, 1971.

LILLARD, Charles

Drunk on wood, & other poems
Barbour, Douglas. "Canadian poetry chronicle: VI." DR 58:555-78, 1978.

Beardsley, Doug. "A trial of immortality: recent Canadian poetry." Nj 6:118-27, 1976.

Ramsey, Jarold. "Shades of regionalism: three northwest poets." WCR 9(2):48-51, 1974.

Ricou, Laurie. Q&Q 40(7):20, 1974.

Wynand, Derk. MHRev 31:165-6, 1974.

Voice, my shaman
Barbour, Douglas. "Canadian poetry chronicle: VI." DR 58:555-78, 1978.

Hedin, Robert. WCR 12(3):62-4, 1978.

LIMAN, Claude

Landing
Brown, Russell M. "Northern journey." CanL 76:119-20, 1978.

Lauder, Scott. "Finding a place." CF 58(685):49-50, 1978.

Milner, Phil. AntigR 28:112-4, 1977.

Oliver, Michael Brian. "Raising Canada." Fiddlehead 114:141-5, 1977.

Peterson, Brad. UWR 13(1):95-7, 1977.

Wagner, Linda W. "The most contemporary of poetics." OntR 7:88-95, 1977-78.

Wallace, Bronwen. Quarry 26(1):69-70, 1977.

LINDER, Norma West

On the side of the angels
Harper, A.W.J. "Four reviews." OV 8(2):n.p., 1972.

Ring around the sun
Boland, Viga. CA&B 52(1):28, 1976.

Jewinski, Ed. Q&Q 42(10):44-5, 1976.

LIVESAY, Dorothy

General
Dorothy Livesay issue. Room of one's own 5(1/2), 1979. (Whole issue.)

Foulks, Debbie. "Livesay's two seasons of love." CanL 74:63-73.

Gibbs, Jean. "Dorothy Livesay and the transcendentalist tradition." HAB 21(2)24-39, 1970.

Leland, Doris. "Dorothy Livesay: poet of nature." DR 51:404-12, 1971.

Lever, Bernice. "An interview with Dorothy Livesay." CF 55(654) 45-52, 1975.

Livesay, Dorothy. "A Prairie sampler." Mosaic 3(3):85-92, 1970.

Livesay, Dorothy. "Song and dance." CanL 41:40-8, 1969.

Marshall, Tom. "Major Canadian poets III: the modernists." CF 58(686):13-7, 1979.

O'Donnell, Kathleen. "Dorothy Livesay and Simone Routier: a parallel study." HAB 23(4):28-37, 1972.

Stevens, Peter. "Dorothy Livesay: the love poetry." CanL 47:26-43, 1971. (Also Woodcock 1974b:33-52.)

Stevens, Peter. "Out of the silence and across the distance: the poetry of Dorothy Livesay." QQ 78:579-91, 1971.

Walker, Susan. "Livesay: turning back the ice age." Q&Q 42(5):38, 1976.

Zimmerman, Susan. "Livesay's houses." CanL 61:32-45, 1974.

Collected poems: the two seasons
Almon, Bert. "Triumphs of the sun: 3 seasoned poets--Dorothy Livesay, Miriam Waddington, & Phyllis Webb." New 24:106-8, 1974.

Baugh, Edward. Quarry 22(4):72-4, 1973.

Fetherling, Doug. "Canada, country you love to hate..." SatN 88(3):37, 1973.

Marshall, Tom. QQ 80:655-6, 1973.

Mitchell, Beverley. Fiddlehead 99:96-9, 1973.

LIVESAY, Dorothy

Collected poems: the two seasons (cont'd.)
Mitchell, Beverley. "'How silence sings' in the poetry of Dorothy Livesay, 1926-1973." DR 54:510-28, 1974.

Ringrose, Christopher Xerxes. DR 53:171-3, 1973.

Rogers, Linda. "A woman for all seasons." BiC 2(1):50, 1973.

Shelton, Robin. "Livesay's two seasons." CanL 58:77-82, 1973.

Vernon, Lorraine. "Livesay's coming of age." LURev 6:246-50, 1973.

Disasters of the sun
Gibbs, Robert. Fiddlehead 94:134-5, 1972.

Ice age
Barbour, Douglas. "Canadian poetry chronicle: III." DR 56:560-73, 1976.

Buri, S.G. "Tackling the world unbalanced." CVII 2(2):9-11, 1976.

Gatenby, Greg. "On Ice age." TamR 70:91-4, 1977.

Gotlieb, Phyllis. QQ 84:331-2, 1977.

Govier, Katherine. "A grande-dame's wide angle vision." CF 56(662):50, 1976.

Hamilton, Jamie. "Marzipan Livesay." CanR 3(5):49, 1976.

Jewinski, Hans. Q&Q 42(1):25-6, 1976.

Jordan, Kimberley. Brick 2:40-1, 1978.

Lever, Bernice. Waves 4(2):10-2, 1976.

Read, Daphne. WLWE 17(1):191-6, 1978.

Such, Peter. "Three grand old parties." BiC 5(2):9-11, 1976.

Woodcock, George. "Playing with freezing fire." CanL 70:84-91, 1976.

Nine poems of farewell
McCarthy, Dermot. "Mosquitoes and mundane heroism." ECW 5:75-9, 1976.

Mitchell, Beverley. Fiddlehead 99:96-9, 1973.

LIVESAY, Dorothy

Plainsongs
   Ditsky, John. CF 49:270-1, 1970.

Plainsongs. Rev. ed.
   Bailey, Don. "A provincial look at ten volumes of Canadian poetry."
   QQ 79:242-54, 1972.

The woman I am
   Aubert, Rosemary. Q&Q 43(17):34, 1977.

   Fletcher, Peggy. "The printed page their classroom." CA&B
   53(4):42-3, 1978.

   Jewinsky, Hans. "... they licked the platter clean." BiC 7(1):26,
   1978.

LOCHHEAD, Douglas

The full furnace: the collected poems.
   Barbour, Douglas. "Canadian poetry chronicle 2." DR 55:748-59,
   1975-76.

   Bishop, A.G. Q&Q 41(6):30, 1975.

   Doyle, Mike. "The limits of the garden." CanL 72:74-77, 1977.

   McCarthy, Dermot. "A pyre engagement." BiC 4(7):17-8, 1975.

   Merrett, Robert James. QQ 83:166, 1976.

   Quickenden, Robert. "A sense of place." CVII 1(2):17-9, 1975.

   Willmot, Rod. "The smoking lamp." Fiddlehead 107:140-2, 1975.

LOISELOT, André

Le diable aux vaches
   Étienne, Gérard. "Littérature joualisante ou le joual en
   littérature?" LAQ 1974:148-50.

LOKIN, Claude P.

   Voir/see PÉLOQUIN, Claude.

LO MONACO, Dan

    The world is drawn by your senses
      Bowering, Marilyn. Q&Q 42(10):45, 1976.

LONGCHAMPS, Renaud

    General
      Longchamps, Renaud. "L'entropie du désir." NBdJ 66:20-30, 1978.

    Anticorps
      Kushner, Éva. "Vers une poésie de la poésie?" LAQ 1974:115-8.

    Charpente charnelle
      Kushner, Éva. "Vers une poésie de la poésie?" LAQ 1974:115-8.

    Comme d'hasard ouvrable
      Giroux, Robert. LAQ 1977:181-2.

    Didactiques, une sémiotique de l'espèce
      Nepveu, Pierre. "Sens interdit: poèmes de Normand de Bellefeuille,
      Renaud Longchamps et Roger Magini." Lettres qué 3:11-3, 1976.

    L'état de matière
      Corriveau, Hugues. LAQ 1977:152-3.

    Sur l'air du lire
      Giguère, Richard. "Les herbes rouges: une grande 'petite revue.'"
      LAQ 1975:118-21.

LORANGER, Jean-Aubert

    General
      Giroux, Robert. "Patterns in Jean-Aubert Loranger." Ellipse
      20:49-65, 1977. (Tr. Valerie Vanstone.)

      Giroux, Robert. "Va-et-vient et circularité de la reverie chez
      Jean-Aubert Loranger." V&I 2:71-91, 1976.

      Guilmette, Bernadette. "Jean-Aubert Loranger: du Nigog à l'École
      littéraire de Montréal." Ottawa 1972:280-97.

LORANGER, Jean-Aubert

Les atmosphères
Wyczynski, Paul. "Jean-Aubert Loranger, cet inconnu." LAQ 1970:123-5.

Poèmes
Wyczynski, Paul. "Jean-Aubert Loranger, cet inconnu." LAQ 1970: 123-5.

Terra-nova
Bourassa, André-G. "Entre l'espace et le temps: ou le lieu de rencontre de Pierre Morency, Jean-Aubert Loranger, Denis Vanier et Michel Van Schendel." Lettres qué 14:18-21, 1979.

"L'invitation au retour"
Bélanger, Claude. "De quelques aspects d'un poème." BdJ 39-41:36-47, 1973.

LORD, René

Élégie à la reine de coeur
Gallays, François. LAQ 1972:174-5.

LOWTHER, Pat

General
Hayes, Diana. "'Genius loci' in the poetry of Pat Lowther." Event 8(1):162-73, 1979.

Ryan, Sean. "Florence McNeil and Pat Lowther." CanL 74:21-9, 1977.

"Pat Lowther: a tribute." CVII 2(1):15-7, 1976.

The age of the bird
Woodcock, George. "Purdy's prelude and other poems." CanL 64:92-8, 1975.

Milk stone
Abley, Mark. "Between the banal and the beautiful." CVII 1(2):35-6, 1975.

Barbour, Douglas. "The poets and presses revisited: circa 1974." DR 55:338-60, 1975.

Bessai, Diane. "Poetry from Ottawa." CF 55(652):36-8, 1975.

Gasparini, Len. "Fluid gig for McNamara's band." BiC 4(3):24-6, 1975.

Ravel, Aviva. Fiddlehead 105:118-20, 1975.

LOWTHER, Pat

A stone diary
Fulford, Robert. "The death-haunted poetry of Pat Lowther." SatN 92(4):71, 1977.

Gotlieb, Phyllis. Quarry 26(3):86-8, 1977.

Hosek, Chaviva. Fiddlehead 118:164-5, 1978.

Levenson, Christopher. QQ 85:352-4, 1978.

MacEwen, Gwendolyn. Q&Q 43(6):44, 1977.

Namjoshi, Suniti. "Inscribed on stone." CF 57(672):51, 1977.

Quickenden, Robert. "Language in the hiss of blood." CVII 3(2):3-5, 1977.

Safarik, Allan. "A final tribute." CanR 4(5):31, 1977.

This difficult flowering
Oates, Joyce Carol. "Three poets." FPt 4:77-81, 1970.

MACCULLOCH, Clare

From Manido, the windmaker
Bailey, Don. Quarry 20(3):47-9, 1971.

Lobsticks
McFadgen, Lynn. Q&Q 40(8):24, 1974.

MACDONALD, Bernell

I can really draw eagles
Cameron, Allen Barry. CF 50:310, 1970.

MacSween, R.J. AntigR 1(2):103-4, 1970.

Parentheses
Gasparini, Len. "Mythopoeic hits and Ms." BiC 4(1):21-2, 1975.

MACDONALD, Goodridge

Selected poems
MacSween, R.J. AntigR 1(2):104-5, 1970.

MACEWEN, Gwendolyn

General

Atwood, Margaret, "MacEwen's muse." CanL 45:24-32, 1970. (Also Woodcock 1974b: 215-24.)

Atwood, Margaret. "La muse de MacEwen." Ellipse 7:83-93, 1971. (Tr. Rodolphe Lacasse.)

Bartley, Jan. The marriage of parts: Gwendolyn MacEwen's sources and their applications. Downsview, Ontario: York Univ., 1975.(M.A. thesis.)

Davey, Frank. "Gwendolyn MacEwen: the secret of alchemy." Open letter 2d ser, 4:5-23, 1973.

"Gwendolyn MacEwen." Ellipse 7:51-3, 1971. (Tr. Daniel Racine.)

MacEwen, Gwendolyn. Colombo 1971:65-72.

Marshall, Tom. "Arcana Canadiana: Gwendolyn MacEwen." Marshall 1979:150-3.

Moisan, Clément. "La 'nouvelle culture,' la contre-culture ou the brilliant minority." Moisan 1979:218-68.

Sandler, Linda. "Gwendolyn MacEwen: the poet as healer." Q&Q 41(5):28, 1975.

Slonim, Leon. "Exoticism in modern Canadian poetry." ECW 1:21-6, 1974.

Warwick, Ellen D. "To seek a single symmetry." CanL 71:21-34, 1976.

The armies of the moon

Booth, Luella Kerr. "Five book reviews." OV 8(3):n.p., 1972.

Davey, Frank. "Gwendolyn MacEwen: the secret of alchemy." Open letter 2d ser, 4:5-23, 1973.

Dragland, Stan. Quarry 21(4):57-62, 1972.

Gustafson, Ralph. "Circumventing dragons." CanL 55:105-8, 1973.

Hosein, Clyde. "Psalms of existence." BiC 1(10):5-6, 1972.

Rockett, W.H. "Despite the careful structure, it misses." SatN 87(7)45-6, 1972.

Sherman, Joseph. Fiddlehead 94:119-20, 1972.

MACEWEN, Gwendolyn

Breakfast for barbarians
Fox, Gail. Quarry 19(2):57-9, 1970.

Moisan, Clément. "Ecriture et errance dans les poésies de Gwendolyn MacEwen et Nicole Brossard." CRCL 2:72-92, 1975.

The fire eaters
Alberti, A.J. "Note book." ECW 5:83-5, 1976.

Barbour, Douglas. "Poetry chronicle IV." DR 57:355-71, 1977.

Bartley, Jan. "Into the fire." Open letter 3d ser, 5:85-7, 1976.

Doan, Judy. "In the beginning was the word." CVII 2(3):20-1, 1976.

Geddes, Gary. "Now you see it..." BiC 5(7):4-6, 1976.

Hosek, Chaviva. "Powerful images in two new collections." Q&Q 42(9):36, 1976.

Marshall, Tom. "The mythmakers." CanL 73:100-3, 1977.

Oliver, Michael Brian. Fiddlehead 111:124-6, 1976.

Spettigue, D.O. Quarry 26(1):72-4, 1977.

Magic animals: selected poems old and new
Barbour, Douglas. "Canadian poetry chronicle 2." DR 55:748-59, 1975-76.

Dault, Gary Michael. "Chewing the lips of Pan." BiC 4(5):16, 1975.

Elson, Brigid. QQ 82:474-5, 1975.

Lane, M. Travis. Fiddlehead 105:127, 1975.

Namjoshi, Suniti. "Oracles and metrics." CF 55(650):62-3, 1975.

The shadow maker
Barbour, Douglas. "The young poets and the little presses, 1969." DR 50:112-26, 1970.

Fox, Gail. Quarry 19(2):57-9, 1970.

Hornyansky, Michael. UTQ 39:333, 1970.

Moisan, Clément. "Ecriture et errance dans les poésies de Gwendolyn MacEwen et Nicole Brossard." CRCL 2:72-92, 1975.

MACKAY, Louis Alexander

The ill-tempered lover and other poems
Sutherland, John. "Louis MacKay: the critic is to blame." Sutherland 1972:114-9.

MACKINNON, Stuart

The intervals
Barbour, Douglas. "The poets and presses revisited: circa 1974." DR 55:338-60, 1975.

Baxter, M.D. Quarry 23(4):68-9, 1974.

Brown, Doug. Alive 36:10, 1974.

Doyle, Mike. "Animate imaginings." CanL 66:94-7, 1975.

Ireland, G.W. QQ 82:302-3, 1975.

Solecki, Sam. "Political poetry." CF 54(647):46-7, 1975.

The lost surveyor
Barbour, Douglas. "Canadian poetry chronicle: III." DR 56:560-73 1976.

Cowan, Doris. "Theodo lights." BiC 5(8):8, 9, 1976.

Gervais, C.H. Quarry 26(1):65-6, 1977.

Hornyansky, Michael. UTQ 46:369, 1977.

Skydeck
Colwell, Fred. Quarry 21(1):67-9, 1972.

Helwig, David. "Four poets." QQ 79:404-7, 1972.

Marshall, Tom. CF 52(616):69-70, 1972.

Sutherland, Fraser. "Tradesmen's entrance." BiC 1(4):14, 1971.

The welder's arc
Barbour, Douglas. "The young poets and the little presses, 1969." DR 50:112-26, 1970.

Lane, M. Travis. "In a glass darkly but face to face." Fiddlehead 83:71-3, 1970.

Zitner, S.P. CF 49:299, 1970.

MACLEAN, Sunyata

Poems to define the corona of silence
Lane, M. Travis. Fiddlehead 90:120-5, 1971.

MACPHEE, Rosalind

Scarecrow
Gilhuley, Gordon. JCP 2(1):102-3, 1979.

MACPHERSON, Jay

The boatman
Dudek, Louis. "The eye of the needle - of no use to camels." in
Dudek 1978:79-82.(Originally published Delta 1:1957.)

Marshall, Tom. QQ 77:294-5, 1970.

Namjoshi, Suniti. "In the whale's belly: Jay Macpherson's poetry."
CanL 79:54-9, 1978.

Welcoming disaster
Bromwich, David. "Engulfing darkness, penetrating light." Poetry
127:234-9, 1976.

Charlton, Brian. Brick 1:27, 1977.

Downes, G.V. "Along the pilgrim's way." CVII 1(2):12-3, 1975.

Gasparini, Len. "Some ghosts are clearer than others." BiC
4(7):18-9, 1975.

Hornyansky, Michael. UTQ 44:335-6, 1975.

Namjoshi, Suniti. "In the whale's belly: Jay Macpherson's poetry."
CanL 79:54-9, 1978.

MADOFF, Mark

Histories of our Lady of Burrard
Browne, Colin. "Deliberately deceptive." CVII 4(3):36-7, 1979.

The patient Renfield
Henderson, Brian. "Warning! On the death of the avant garde." ECW 5:103-5, 1976.

MAGARAC, Joseph Henry

Wind, water, and earth
Lanczos, Elmar. WCR 9(3):50-1, 1975.

MAGINI, Roger

L'ABCD'ELLES
Nepveu, Pierre. "Sans interdit: poèmes de Normand de Bellefeuille, Renaud Longchamps et Roger Magini." Lettres qué 3:11-3, 1976.

MAILLET, Roger

General
Chevalier, Willie. "Roger Maillet." Académie 14:44-55, 1972.

MAIR, Charles

Dreamland and other poems
Woodcock, George. "Poet and poetaster." CanL 63:85-9, 1975.

MAJOR, André

    General
      Pelletier, Jacques. "André Major, écrivain et Québécois." VIP
      3:27-62, 1970.

    Poèmes pour durer
      Major, Jean-Louis. UTQ 39:429, 1970.

    The scarecrows of Saint Emmanuel (Tr. Sheila Fischman.)
      Godard, Barbara. "Why things happen." Waves 6(3):77-9, 1978.

MAJOR, Jean-René

    Toundras, chronique d'une errance
      Breton, Jean. MLit 61:37, 1972.

      Vigneault, Robert. LAQ 1972:169-70.

MALENFANT, Paul Chanel

    Forges Froides
      Bouvier, Luc. LAQ 1977:134-6.

      Nepveu, Pierre. "Le poème : du fait divers à l'évènement." Lettres
      qué 10:16-8, 1978.

    Poèmes de la mer pays
      Amprimoz, Alexandre. "Quebec writers: the anatomy of solitude." TamR
      72:79-87, 1977.

      Moisan, Clément. LAQ 1976:123-5.

MALOUIN, Reine

    Amour-feu
      VieFr. 30:190-1, 1976.

    Sphère armillaire
      Dionne, René. "Sur les voies de notre poésie--III." Relations
      370:122-4, 1972.

MALTMAN, Kim

The country of the mapmakers
Jenoff, Marvyne. "Seven books from two small presses." CVII 3(4):40-5, 1978.

Heckman, Grant. Quarry 27(3):80-1, 1978.

MANDEL, Eli

General
Fee, Margery. "An interview with Eli Mandel." ECW 1:2-13, 1974.

Ower, John. "Black and secret poet: notes on Eli Mandel." Woodcock 1974b:138-50. (Originally published CanL 42:14-25, 1969.)

Another time
Bouraoui, H.A. Waves 6(2):76-8, 1978.

Cooley, Dennis. "Double or nothing: Eli Mandel's Out of place and Another time." ECW 10:73-81, 1978.

Staines, David. "Eli Mandel's investigations." BForum 4:139-43, 1978.

Crusoe: poems selected and new
André, Michael. QQ 80:659, 1973.

Bennett, Donna A. "A formal madness." LURev 7(1):119-23, 1974.

Bishop, A.G. Q&Q 39(5):27, 1973.

Cameron, A. Barry. CF 53(634-5):34-5, 1973.

Fetherling, Doug. "A poet for all traditions." SatN 88(7):40, 1973.

Hornyansky, Michael. UTQ 43:355-6, 1974.

Levenson, Christopher. "Magpies and nightingales." CanL 62:91-3, 1974.

Stevens, Peter. "The perils of majority." UWR 9(2):100-9, 1974.

Verbicky-Park, Elaine. White pelican 4(1):53-5, 1974.

Vernon, Lorraine. "An exact madness." BiC 2(3):45, 47, 1973.

Woodcock, George. WLWE 13(2):283-7, 1974.

MANDEL, Eli

Out of place

Barbour, Douglas. "Poetry chronicle V." DR 58:149-69, 1978.

Bessai, Diane. "Interior travels." CF 57(679):33, 1978.

Cooley, Dennis. "Double or nothing: Eli Mandel's Out of place and Another Time." ECW 10:73-81, 1978.

Daniel, Lorne. Q&Q 43(12):13, 1977.

Lecker, Robert. Fiddlehead 117:120-2, 1978.

New, W.H. "This year country." CanL 77:2-3, 1978.

Plantos, Ted. "Mandel's past, Colombo's candy, Purdy's earth." BiC 7(2)16-7, 1978.

Sherman, Kenneth. Waves. 6(2):79-81, 1978.

Stony plain

Bennett, Donna A. "A formal madness." LURev 7(1):119-23, 1974.

Cameron, A. Barry. CF 53(634-5):34-5, 1973.

Fetherling, Doug. "A poet for all traditions." SatN 88(7):40, 1973.

Levenson, Christopher. "Magpies and nightingales." CanL 62:91-3, 1974.

Stevens, Peter. "The perils of majority." UWR 9(2):100-9, 1974.

Woodcock, George. WLWE 13(2):283-7, 1974.

MANDEL, Miriam

Lions at her face

Lawrence, Karen. White pelican. 4(1):48-51, 1974.

Grant, Judith. Q&Q 39(6):13, 1973.

Mallinson, Jean. "Words for the unspeakable." CF 56(661):27-30, 1976.

Woodcock, George. "Purdy's prelude and other poems." CanL 64:92-8, 1975.

MANDEL, Miriam

    Station 14
      Aubert, Rosemary. Q&Q 44(8):47, 1978.

MARCHAND, Clément

    General
      Royer, Jean. "Les poètes de 1930: entretiens avec Alfred DesRochers
    et Clément Marchand." Estuaire 5:88-102, 1977.

MARCHAND, Olivier

    General
      Dionne, René. "Sur les voies de notre poésie (1)." Relations
    366:340-1, 1971.

    Par détresse et tendresse
      Marcotte, Gilles. EF 95-6, 1972.

      Renaud, André. LAQ 1971:140-2.

MARLATT, Daphne

    General
      Arnason, David; Cooley, Dennis and Enright, Robert. "There's this and
    this connexion." CVII 3(1):28-33, 1977.

      Bowering, George. "Given this body: an interview with Daphne
    Marlatt." Open letter 4th ser, 3:32-88, 1979.

      Lecker, Robert. "Daphne Marlatt's poetry." CanL 76:56-67, 1978.

    Frames
      Marshall, Tom. QQ 77:294-5, 1970.

    Our lives
      Dawson, Fielding. "A psychic hammer." Open letter 3d ser, 7:108-10,
    1977.

      Shames, P'nina. "Our lives." Open letter 3d ser, 4:87-8, 1976.

    Rings
      Coleman, Victor. Open letter 2d ser, 1:78-80, 1971-72.

      Garnet, Eldon. "Five poets on the brink of our consciousness." SatN
    87(6):38-42, 1972.

MARLATT, Daphne

Steveston

Barbour, Douglas. "The phenomenological I: Daphne Marlatt's Steveston." Bessai 1977:174-88.

Barbour, Douglas. "The poets and presses revisited: circa 1974." DR 55:338-60, 1975.

Bowering, George and Marlatt, Daphne. "Keep witnessing: a review/interview." Open letter 3d ser, 2:26-38, 1975.

Charlton, Brian. "Selvedge: where nature and imagination meet." Brick 1:47-51, 1977.

Lecker, Robert A. Q&Q 41(4):39, 1975.

Lillard, Charles. MHRev 38:148-50, 1976.

Mays, John Bentley. " Ariadne: prolegomenon to the poetry of Daphne Marlatt." Open letter 3d ser, 3:5-33, 1975.

Newton, Stuart. WCR 10(2):66-8, 1975.

Vancouver poems

Bagchee, Shyamal. Q&Q 39(2):13-4, 1973.

Barbour, Douglas. "Three west coast poets and one from the east." LURev 6:240-5, 1973.

Bowering, George. Open letter 2d ser, 8:96-7, 1974.

Helwig, David. "Opacities."CanL 60:118-9, 1974.

Mays, John Bentley. "Ariadne: prolegomenon to the poetry of Daphne Marlatt." Open letter 3d ser, 3:5-33, 1975.

Varney, Edwin. WCR 10(2):72-3, 1975.

Zócalo

Levy, Eric P. "Strategies." CanL 82:89-91, 1979.

MARRIOTT, Anne

Countries

Barbour, Douglas. DR 52:167-9, 1972.

Sandstone and other poems

Sutherland, John. "Anne Marriott's native realism." Sutherland 1972:100-1.

MARSAIS, Adolphe

General
Lortie, Jeanne d'Arc. "Campagne canadienne: Adolphe Marsais." Lortie 1975:319-37.

MARSHALL, J.

The west coast trail poems
Barbour, Douglas. "Canadian poetry chronicle: VI." DR 58:555-78, 1978.

MARSHALL, Tom

General
Marshall, Tom. Colombo 1971:73-83.

Pearce, Jon. "Filling up the whole round: an interview with Tom Marshall." QQ 83:413-23, 1976.

The earth book
Barbour, Douglas. "The poets and presses revisited: circa 1974." DR 55:338-60, 1975.

Dragland, Stan. Quarry 24(2):48-51, 1975.

Gasparini, Len. "Fluid gig for McNamara's band." BiC 4(3):24-6, 1975.

Hicks, Lorne. "Conscious paranoia." CF 55(650):62, 1975.

McFadgen, Lynn. Q&Q 41(2):27, 1975.

McWhirter, George. Fiddlehead 105:132-3, 1975.

Solecki, Sam. QQ 82:298-300, 1975.

Magic water
Dagg, Mel. Fiddlehead 93:112-3, 1972.

Dragland, Stan. Quarry 24(2):48-51, 1975.

Fox, Gail. Quarry 21(1):57-60, 1972.

Helwig, David. CF 51(612-3):82, 1972.

Stevens, Peter. QQ 78:627-8, 1971.

MARSHALL, Tom

The silences of fire
Barbour, Douglas. "The young poets and the little presses, 1969." DR 50:112-26, 1970.

Dragland, Stan. Quarry 24(2):48-51, 1975.

Gervais, G.H. Quarry 19(2):60-1, 1970.

Lee, Dennis. "Poet or man?" TamR 54:81-4, 1970.

The white city
Amprimoz, Alexandre L. Brick 2:41-2, 1978.

Amprimoz, Alexandre. "A note on Tom Marshall's The white city." ECW 6:82-5, 1977.

Barbour, Douglas. Fiddlehead 113:146-7, 1977.

Barbour, Douglas. "Poetry chronicle IV." DR 57:355-71, 1977.

Dragland, Stan. ECW 12:192-203, 1978.

Gasparini, Len. "Gail and Anne, Tom and Gary, Brenda and Erica." BiC 6(2):24-6, 1977.

Hickmore, G.L. Quarry 26(1):63-5. 1977.

Kent, David. "A garden in the bush." ECW 6:77-81, 1977.

MacKendrick, Louis K. Q&Q 42(15):38, 1976.

O'Flaherty, Patrick. "Book of wind." CF 56(667):63, 1976-7.

Ricou, Laurie. "Another world." CanL 77:120-2, 1978.

Stevens, Peter. "The elements of Tom Marshall." OntR 6:102-5, 1977.

MARSOLAIS, Gilles

La caravelle incendiée
Pageau, René. "Préfontaine--Marsolais--Dumont." ActN 60:865-71, 1971.

Les matins saillants
Pageau, René. "Préfontaine--Marsolais--Dumont." ActN 60:865-71, 1971.

Saint-Amour, Robert. LAQ 1970:148.

MARTEAU, Robert

General
Hébert, Francois. "The angel within." Ellipse 19:31-7, 1976. (Tr. Ann and Andrée Labbée.)

Ouellette, Fernand. "Robert Marteau and light." Ellipse 19:42-3, 1976. (Tr. Sheila Fischman.)

Page, Richard. "Alchemy: a key to Robert Marteau's works." Ellipse 19:38-41, 1976. (Tr. Mary Ricard (text) and G.M. Lang (poetry).)

Atlante
Bourassa, André-G. "D'après peinture: Bélanger, Leblanc, Marteau, Ouellette, Girardin et Lapointe." Lettres qué 6:10-3, 1977.

Delisle, Claude. LAQ 1976:119-23.

Hébert, François. "Robert Marteau, Guy Lafond, Jean-Marc Fréchette (et Paul Chamberland?)." Liberté 110:70-6, 1977.

MARTEL, François

De la contradiction de deux étreintes
Nepveu, Pierre. "Du corps et de quelques poètes." Lettres qué 16:21-3, 1979-80.

Roussan, Wanda de. LAQ 1979: 143-4.

MARTIN, Danielle

À perce-poche
Chamberland, Roger. LAQ 1979:144.

MARTY, Sid

Headwaters
Crawford, Terry. Quarry 23(2):72, 1974.

Copperfield. 5:148-52, 1974.

Fine, F.L. "Headwaters." CanR 1(1):15, 1974.

Gutteridge, Don. QQ 81:148-9, 1974.

Hicks, Lorne. CF 54(640-1):21, 1974.

Hosein, Clyde. "Seeker on the mountain." BiC 3(4):31-2, 1974.

MARTY, Sid

> Headwaters (cont'd.)
> Lacey, Edward. "Canadian bards and South American reviewers." Nj
> 4:82-120, 1974.
>
> Lane, M. Travis. "'Siwashing that all consuming art': Sid Marty's
> Headwaters." Fiddlehead 102:125-33, 1974.
>
> Lee, Dennis. "The new poets: fresh voices in the land." SatN
> 88(12):33-5, 1973.
>
> Lillard, Charles. WCR 8(4):8-9, 1974.
>
> Purdy, Al. WascanaR 8(2):73-5, 1973.
>
> Ricou, Laurie. Q&Q 39(8):12, 1973.
>
> Safarik, Allan. "Marty and Wayman." TamR 62:86-9, 1974.

MASON, Robert Greg

> Magicturnings
> Woodruff, Sandra. HAB 25:81-2, 1974.

MASSICOTTE, Edouard-Zotique

> General
> Sainte-Berthe, Soeur. "Edouard-Zotique Massicotte, poète." Ottawa
> 1972:66-84.

MATHEWS, Robin

> The geography of revolution
> Watt, F.W. "Why poetry? Eleven answers." CF 55(651):40-1, 1975.
>
> Language of fire: poems of love and struggle
> Burgess, G.C. Ian. Fiddlehead 112:147-8, 1977.
>
> Gervais, Marty. Q&Q 42(14):9, 1976.
>
> Goldie, Terry. Quarry 26(2):66-7, 1977.
>
> Granatstein, J.L. "Whack on the head." CF 56(668):56, 1977.
>
> Lorimer, James. "Robin's egging us on again." BiC 6(1):23, 1977.
>
> Mallinson, Jean. "Poetry miscellany." ECW 7/8:151-8, 1977.
>
> Tefs, Wayne. "Conflagration and poetry." Sphinx 7(v.2(3)):74-7,
> 1977.

MATHEWS, Robin

This cold fist
Buri, S.G. "The armory of love." AspG 1:31-3, 1972.

Ditsky, John. CF 50:190, 1970.

MATHIEU, Pierre

General
Pageau, René. "Pierre Mathieu à la recherche de l'absolu." AcN 60:507-14, 1971.

Interlune
Henchiri, Sliman. LAQ 1970:127.

Mots dits québécois
Henchiri, Sliman. LAQ 1971:165.

MATTEAU, Robert

Un cri de loin
Bélanger, Christian. LAQ 1979:146.

MAURICE, Mireille

Longue-haleine
Henchiri, Michelle. LAQ 1970:145.

MAYNE, Seymour

Diasporas
Linder, Norma West. "There for the digging." CA&B 53(4):41, 1978.

McNally, Paul. Fiddlehead 120:129-31, 1979.

Sherman, Kenneth. "Bravado & wit." CanL 80:96-7, 1979.

For stems of light
Powell, D. Reid. "3 books from Valley Editions." Alive 35:12, 1974.

Rogers, Linda. "Handful of dust." CanL 65:119-20, 1975.

Manimals
Bowering, George. Quarry 19(3):64, 1970.

MAYNE, Seymour

Mouth
Barbour, Douglas. DR 51:139-41, 1971.

Cameron, Allen Barry. CF 50:311, 1970.

Pivato, Joseph. "Mouth exhausted silence." CanL 52:106-8, 1972.

Mutetations
Sullivan, D.H. WCR 5(2):71, 1970.

Name
Atherton, Stan. "Echoes from within." CF 56(667):62, 1976-7.

Barbour, Douglas. "Canadian poetry chronicle 2." DR 55:748-59, 1975-76.

Fletcher, Peggy. CA&B 51(1):28, 1975.

Gasparini, Len. "Handsprings and flops." BiC 4(8):21-2, 1975.

Gatenby, Greg. EngQ 8(4):86-7, 1975-76.

Greenglass, E.E. "1's and eyes." CanL 71:92-5, 1976.

McFadgen, Lynn. Q&Q 41(5):44, 1975.

Newton, Stuart. WCR 11(3):46-8, 1977.

Solecki, Sam. Fiddlehead 112:151-5, 1977.

MCAULEY, John

Nothing ever happens in Pointe-Claire
David, Jack. "Three from Montreal." CVII 3(3):23-4, 1978.

MCCAFFERY, Steve

General
McCaffery, Steve. "Poetics: a statement." PTor 38:n.p., 1979.

Carnival
Alpert, Barry. "Reading concrete." Open letter 3d ser, 3:93-4, 1975.

Douglas, Charles. "Poetry: presence and presentation." LURev 7-8:74-85, 1975.

Dr. Sadhu's muffins: a book of written readings
Alpert, Barry. "Written on the wind (of Lake Ontario)." Open letter 3d ser, 2:5-25, 1975.

MCCAFFREY, Steve

Dr. Sadhu's muffins: a book of written readings (cont'd.)
Arnason, David. Q&Q 40(12):26, 1974.

Barbour, Douglas. "The poets and presses revisited: circa 1974." DR 55:338-60, 1975.

McNamara, Eugene. "Scream of speech?" CanL 70:100-1, 1976.

Silliman, Ron. "Locus (i) of McCaffery's work(s)(ing)." CVII 3(2):22-3, 1977.

Watt, F.W., "Why poetry? Eleven answers." CF 55(651):40-1, 1975.

Ow's waif
Barbour, Douglas. "Canadian poetry chronicle: III." DR 56:560-73, 1976.

Shikatani, Gerry. Q&Q 42(9):36, 1976.

Silliman, Ron. "Locus(i) of McCaffery's work(s)(ing). CVII 3(2):22-3, 1977.

MCCARTHY, Dermot

North shore: a book of poems
Dempster, Barry. Q&Q 45(8):51, 1979.

Fletcher, Peggy. "Vision and the personal dark." CA&B 54(4):26-7, 1979.

MCCLUNG, Nellie

Baraka
Schoemperlen, Diane. Event 8(1):186-7, 1979

MCCRACKEN, Kathleen

Reflections
Stevenson, Warren. "Move over Musgrave." CanL 80:103-4, 1979.

Zonailo, Carolyn. Room of one's own 3(4):42-3, 1978.

MCCRAE, John

General
Brodie, A.H. "John McCrae--A centenary reassessment." HAB 23(1):12-22, 1972.

MCFADDEN, David

  General

    Bowering, George. "It's a funny thing: an interview of David McFadden." Copperfield 3:77-82, 1970.

    Kiverago, Ronald. "'Local poet deserves attention': the poetics of David McFadden." Open letter 3d ser, 5:16-26, 1976.

    Norris, Ken and Farkas, André. "David McFadden in Hamilton." CVII 3(2):42-9, 1977.

  I don't know

    King-Edwards, L. "A man alone." CVII 4(1):16-7, 1979.

  Intense pleasure

    Bell, John. Quarry 21(4):62-3, 1972.

    Currie, Sheldon. AntigR 11:110-1, 1972.

    Gustafson, Ralph. "Circumventing dragons." CanL 55:105-8, 1973.

    Helwig, David. "Four poets." QQ 79:404-7, 1972.

    Howell, Bill. "That's my boy?" BiC 1(10):27-8, 1972.

    Sherman, Joseph. Fiddlehead 94:118-9, 1972.

  A knight in dried plums

    Barbour, Douglas. "Canadian poetry chronicle 2." DR 55:748-59, 1975-76.

    Fletcher, Peggy. CA&B 51(1):26, 1975.

    Gasparini, Len. "Handsprings and flops." BiC 4(8):21-2, 1975.

    Greenglass, E.E. "I's and eyes." CanL 71:92-5, 1976.

    Lund, Mary. Fiddlehead 108:108-11, 1976.

    Mundwiler, Leslie. "After realism: McFadden and Wayman." CVII 3(2):36-40, 1977.

    Sarna, Lazar. "Aims apart." ECW 3:63-5, 1975.

  Letters from the earth to the earth

    Barbour, Douglas. "The young poets and the little presses, 1969." DR 50:112-26, 1970.

    Helwig, David. Quarry 19(2):59-60, 1970.

    Sullivan, D.H. WCR 5(2):71, 1970.

MCFADDEN, David

On the road again
  Barbour, Douglas. "Canadian poetry chronicle: VII." DR 59:154-75, 1979.

  Bell, John. Quarry 28(2):76-8, 1979,

  Daniel, Lorne. Q&Q 44(7):44, 1978.

  Gatenby, Greg. "Poetry chronicle." TamR 77&78:77-94, 1979.

  King-Edwards, L. "A man alone." CVII 4(1):16-7, 1979.

  Linder, Norma West. "There for the digging." CA&B 53(4):41, 1978.

  Mullins, Stanley G. UWR 14(1):75-6, 1978.

The poet's progress
  Barbour, Douglas. "Canadian poetry chronicle: VI." DR 58:555-78, 1978.

  David, Jack. Fiddlehead 118:169-70, 1978.

  King-Edwards, L. "A man alone." CVII 4(1):16-7, 1979.

  Kiverago, Ron. "The poet's pilgrimage." Open letter 3d ser, 9:151-3, 1978.

The saladmaker
  Amprimoz, Alexandre. "Dusted inside." CanL 82:99-101, 1979.

  Davies, Gwendolyn. "Something's happening in Montreal." ECW 10:82-7, 1978.

  Gervais, Marty. Q&Q 43(14):10, 1977.

  King-Edwards, L. "A man alone." CVII 4(1):16-7, 1979.

  Oliver, Michael Brian. "Lost and found." Fiddlehead 119:106-16, 1978.

  Varney, Edwin. "Vintage McFadden." CVII 4(3):20-1, 1979.

  Wood, Mary. "Saladmaker." Brick 4:45-6, 1978.

MCFARLANE, Myra

The fat executioner
  Gasparini, Len. "Mythopoeic hits and Ms." BiC 4(1):21-2, 1975.

  Livesay, Dorothy. CVII 1(2):37, 1975.

MCFARLANE, Myra

> The fat executioner (cont'd.)
> Powell, D. Reid. "3 books from Valley Editions." Alive 35:12, 1974.

MCGEE, Bob

> The shanty-horses
> Linder, Norma West. "Tales well told." CA&B 54(1):34, 1978.
>
> Miles, Ron. "Boxed set." CanL 81:138-9, 1979.

MCGEE, Thomas D'Arcy

> General
> O'Donnell, Kathleen. "D'Arcy McGee's Canadian ballads." RUO
> 41:314-21, 1971.

MCILWAIN, Sandy

> And between us, the night
> Hamel, Guy. "Recent Fiddlehead poetry books." Fiddlehead 118:137-45,
> 1978.

MCINNIS, R.F.M.

> The renegade's lament
> Denham, Paul. HAB 25:367, 1974.

MCINTYRE, James

> General
> Elliott, Gordon. "James McIntyre: neglected emigré." DR 52:553-71,
> 1972-73.

MCKAY, Don

> Air occupies space
> Billings, R. Quarry 23(3):75, 1974.
>
> Dragland, Stan. "Who is Don McKay?" ApF 2:r2-8, 1975.

MCKAY, Don

Air occupies space (cont'd.)
Hornyansky, Michael. UTQ 44:329, 1975.

Liman, Claude. "Open sesame." CVII 3(4):25-8, 1978.

Lependu
Barbour, Douglas. "Canadian poetry chronicle: VII." DR 59:154-75, 1979.

Geiger, Roy. Fiddlehead 122:128-31, 1979.

Kleinzahler, August. "The world well limned." BiC 8(9):14, 1979.

Long Sault
Charlton, Brian. "Selvedge: where nature and imagination meet." Brick 1:47-51, 1977.

Dragland, Stan. "A Long Sault reader." Brick 3:28-31, 1978.

McCarthy, Dermot. "Ancestors, real or imaginative." ECW 4:73-5, 1976.

MCKINNON, Barry

The carcasses of spring
Barbour, Douglas. "Play in the western world." CanL 52:77-81, 1972.

The death of a lyric poet: poems & drafts
Wynand, Derk. "Of death and typography." CVII 2(1):44-5, 1976.

I wanted to say something
Wynand, Derk. "Of death and typography." CVII 2(1):44-5, 1976.

Songs & speeches
Wah, Fred. "To locate." Open letter 3d ser, 7:110-1, 1977.

MCLACHLAN, Alexander

General
Hughes, Ken. "Poet laureate of labour." CanD 11(4):33-40, 1976.

The poetical works of Alexander McLachlan
Sorfleet, John R. Q&Q 41(11):7, 1975.

"The emigrant"
Hughes, Kenneth J. "The completeness of McLachlan's 'The emigrant'." ESC 1:172-87, 1975.

Hughes, Kenneth J. "McLachlan's style." JCP 1(2):1-4, 1978.

MCLACHLAN, Alexander

"The emigrant" (cont'd.)
Hughes, Kenneth James and Spraxton, Birk. "Crawford's 'Malcolm's Katie' and MacLachlan's 'The emigrant.'" CN&Q 19:10-1, 1977.

Kuroptawa, Joy. "McLachlan's 'The emigrant' and 'Rule Britannia.'" CN&Q 17:14-5, 1976.

MCLEAN, Anne

Lil
Linder, Norma West. "There for the digging." CA&B 53(4):41, 1978.

Miles, Ron. "Boxed set." CanL 81:138-9, 1979.

Rogers, Janet and Warland-Van Horne, Betsy. "Mandrake gestures hypnotically..." CVII 4(2):42-5, 1979.

Whiteman, Bruce. Quarry 27(4):87, 1978.

MCLEOD, J.B. Thornton

Voir/see THORNTON-MCLEOD, Joan B.

MCLEOD, Joseph

Cleaning the bones
Barbour, Douglas. "Canadian poetry chronicle: VI." DR 58:555-78, 1978.

Whiteman, Bruce. "Big seeing & necessary as breath." ECW 10:57-60, 1978.

Conversations with Maria
Lever, Bernice. "Seven nearly alive books." Alive 40:18, 1974.

MCLUHAN, Elizabeth

Routes/Roots
Barbour, Douglas. "Canadian poetry chronicle 2." DR 55:748-59, 1975-76.

Bishop, A.G. Q&Q 40(12):26, 1974.

David, Jack. Alive 40:13, 1974.

Gasparini, Len. "Mythopoeic hits and Ms." BiC 4(1):21-2, 1975.

MCNAMARA, Eugene

Dillinger poems
  Bailey, Don. "A provincial look at ten volumes of Canadian poetry."
QQ 79:242-54, 1972.

Diving for the body: poems
  Barbour, Douglas. "The poets and presses revisited: circa 1974." DR
55:338-60, 1975.

  Gasparini, Len. "Fluid gig for McNamara's band." BiC 4(3):24-6,
1975.

  Liman, Claude G. "Finding the body." Fiddlehead 107:143-9, 1975.

  McKay, Don. Brick 2:16-7, 1978.

  Pyke, Linda Annesley. Q&Q 41(4):38, 1975.

  Scobie, Stephen. Fiddlehead 106:108-9, 1975.

  Tefs, Wayne. "Re-awakening the dark gods." CVII 2(1):24-5, 1976.

  Wallace, Bronwen. Quarry 24(2):56, 1975.

  Watt, F.W. "Why poetry? Eleven answers." CF 55(651):40-1, 1975.

Hard words: poems 1971
  Barbour, Douglas. QQ 80:142, 1973.

In transit
  Barbour, Douglas. "Canadian poetry chronicle: III." DR 56:560-73,
1976.

  McKay, Don. Brick 2:16-7, 1978.

  McNally, Paul. Fiddlehead 118:165-7, 1978.

  Merrett, Robert James. "Winning a reader." CanL 79:96-8, 1978.

  Oughton, John. "Simple songs, tricky cycles." BiC 5(4):20-1, 1976.

Outerings
  Brewster, Elizabeth. CF 51(606-7):37, 1971.

Passages and other poems
  Ditsky, John. CF 53(631):35, 1973.

  Liman, Claude G. "Finding the body." Fiddlehead 107:143-9, 1975.

  McWhirter, George. MHRev 26:236-7, 1973.

  Woodcock, George. "Purdy's prelude and other poems." CanL 64:92-8,
1975.

MACNAMARA, Eugene

Screens
Barbour, Douglas. "Canadian poetry chronicle: VI." DR 58:555-78, 1978.

Billings, Robert. UWR 13(2):102-3, 1978.

Daniel, Lorne. "From screen gems to animal acts." BiC 8(4):11-2, 1979.

McNally, Paul. Fiddlehead 118:165-7, 1978.

MCNEIL, Florence

General
Ryan, Sean. "Florence McNeil and Pat Lowther." CanL 74:21-9, 1977.

Wiseman, Christopher. "Reticence and emergence: the poetry of Florence McNeil." CVII 4(2);36-40, 1979.

A balancing act
Abley, Mark. "Poetry that fell from the sky." Maclean's 93(41):54-8, 1979.

Emily
Lillard, Charles. MHRev 38:144-7, 1976.

Long, Tanya. Q&Q 41(10):18, 1975.

Marshall, Tom. "Dorothy's daughters: three more Emilys." CVII 2(2):29, 1976.

Mezei, Kathy. Quarry 25(2):65-7, 1976.

Milner, Phil. AntigR 27:89-90, 1976.

Rogers, Linda. "The old Carr smell." BiC 4(12):27-8, 1975.

Thompson, Shawn. Brick 2:39-40, 1978.

Wilson, Jean. "Life and Claustrophobia." CanL 75:88-90, 1977.

Ghost towns
Downes, G.V. MHRev 39:134-5, 1976.

Fletcher, Peggy. CA&B 51(1):26, 1975.

Gasparini, Len. "Some ghosts are clearer than others." BiC 4(7):18-9, 1975.

Gutteridge, Don. QQ 84:129-30, 1977.

MCNEIL, Florence

Ghost towns (cont'd.)
Livesay, Dorothy. "Grit in the oyster." CanL 67:107-9, 1976.

Marken, Ronald. "Watering the dry roots." CVII 1(2):20-1, 1975.

Pyke, Linda Annesley. Q&Q 41(4):38, 1975.

The rim of the park
Bessai, Diane. "Simple complexities." CanL 60:124-6, 1974,

MCPHEE, Wallace

Snow in April
Power, Nick. Q&Q 41(13):33-4, 1975.

MCROBBIE, Kenneth

First ghost to Canada
Brown, Allan. "Playing parts: five from Turnstone Press." Waves 8(1):67-71, 1979.

What is on fire is happening
Almon, Bert. WCR 11(2):41, 1976.

Barbour, Douglas. "The poets and presses revisited: circa 1974." DR 55:338-60, 1975.

Gasparini, Leonard. "Flat, muddled, and egotistical." BiC 4(10):27,29, 1975.

Shapiro, Daniel. "On fire." CVII 1(1):19, 1975.

MCWHIRTER, George

Catalan poems
Bailey, Don. "A provincial look at ten volumes of Canadian poetry." QQ 79:242-54, 1972.

Marshall, Tom. CF 52(616):70, 1972.

Sutherland, Fraser. "Tradesmen's entrance." BiC 1(4):14, 1971.

MCWHIRTER, George

   Queen of the sea
     Hosek, Chaviva. Q&Q 43(9):8, 1977.

     Scherzer, D.K. Quarry 26(2):59-61, 1977.

     Stedingh, R.W. MHRev 43:140-1, 1977.

     Trethewey, Eric. Fiddlehead 119:134-5, 1978.

   Twenty-five
     Trethewey, Eric. Fiddlehead 119:135-6, 1978.

MELANÇON, Joseph-Marie

   General
     Legare, Romain. "Lucien Rainier, poète de l'art pur et de l'âme chrétienne." Ottawa 1972:85-109.

     Pageau, René. "Lucien Rainier (1877-1956)." Académie 14:108-19, 1972.

MÉLANÇON, Robert

   Peinture aveugle
     Hébert, François. "Deux poètes: Mélançon et Laforest." Liberté 120:115-9, 1978.

     Marchand, Jacques. LAQ 1979:147.

     Nepveu, Pierre. "Robert Mélançon. Gilles Cyr. Jean Charlebois. Jean-Yves Théberge." Lettres qué 14:22-5, 1979.

MELFI, Mary

   The dance, the cage and the horse
     Bolick, Merle Wallis. Quarry 25(4):73, 1976.

     Linder, Norma West. CA&B 52(2):36, 1976.

     Milner, Phil. AntigR 27:91-2, 1976.

MÉNARD, Guy

   Fragments
     Rancourt, Guy. LAQ 1979:148-50.

MÉNARD, Lucie

L'outre-mesure
    Cotnoir, Louise. LAQ 1979:99-100.

MICHAUD, Jacques

Vingt fois cinq
    Bouvier, Luc. LAQ 1979:117.

MILLER, George

General
    Johnson, Sam F. "George Miller: a critique of his poetry." Old nun
    1:23-6, 1975.

    Plantos, Ted. "The George Miller revival." Old nun 1:43-7, 1975.

MILLER, Malcolm

The kings have donned their final mask
    Cogswell, Fred. Fiddlehead 83:77-8, 1970

MILLER, Peter

A shifting pattern
    Dudek, Louis. "A load of new books: Smith, Webb, Miller/Souster,
    Purdy, Nowlan." Dudek 1978:168-74. (Originally published Delta
    10:27-32, 1963.)

MILLS, Sparling

Falling in love again
    OV 10(2):n.p., 1975.

Woman, be honest: poems and graphics
    Gasparini, Len. "Six poets who found a critic." BiC 3(7):20-2, 1974.

    Linder, Norma West. "Some better than others." CA&B 52(4):44, 1977.

MILOT, Pierre

   Mathématique brisée
   Carrière, André. "Trois auteurs en quête d'un langage." LAQ
   1973:100-1.

MIRON, Gaston

   Bibliography
   Cimon, Renée. "Bibliographie sommaire." Miron 1970:157-67.

   General
   Beaulieu, Michel. "Gaston Miron, poète, éveilleur de conscience."
   Forces 39:51-6, 1977.(English version: 69-70. Tr. Geneviève Cabana.)

   Beaulieu, Victor-Lévy. "Gaston Miron: vivre dans la vigilance de
   notre dignité réalisée." Maintenant 102:13-5, 1971.

   Brault, Jacques. "Gaston Miron, politics or poetry." Ellipse 6:54-8,
   1971. (Tr. Barbara Belyea.)

   Cloutier, Cecile. "Gaston Miron: pivot de la poésie québéçoise."
   CMLR 32:6-9, 1975.

   Dallard, Sylvie. "Gaston Miron ou les 'Signes de notre vie.'"
   Dallard 1977:193-267.

   Gaulin. "Miron, le poète qui vit 'sans relâch à bout portant.'"
   QuéFr 14:18-20, 1974.

   Jones, D.G. "Gaston Miron: a testimony." Ellipse 5:55-7, 1970.

   Major, André. "Pourquoi pas, un jour, le prix Nobel de littérature à
   Gaston Miron?" Forces 39:50, 1977.

   Maugey, Axel. "Gaston Miron et Aimé Césaire poètes de la liberté
   humaine." Littératures 1971:235-47.

   "Miron." BdJ 26(10) 1970 (Whole issue.)

   Moisan, Clément. "Poésie de la résistance." Moisan 1979:129-66.

   Pépin, Jean-Marie. "Miron: l'écrivain en quête de signes." QuéFr
   14:13-8, 1974.

   Rancourt, Jacques. "Langage de l'identité québécoise: Gaston Miron."
   Brindeau 1973:562-70.

   Rosadon, Danièle. La forcené magnifique: Gaston Miron, poète
   québecois." Actes du 5ème Congrès des romanistes scandinaves, Turku,
   1973: 161-76.

   Royer, Jean. "Témoignage Gaston Miron: N.D.L.R." LAQ 1970:119-22.

232

MIRON, Gaston

    General (cont'd.)
    Vachon, G-André. "Gaston Miron, or the invention of substance."
    Ellipse 5:38-54, 1970. (Tr. Cormac Gerrard Cappon.)

    Vachon, G-André. "Gaston Miron ou l'invention de la substance."
    Miron 1970:133-49.

    Courtepointes
    Malenfant, Paul Chanel. LAQ 1976:156-61.

    Roberto, Eugène. "Courtepointes." Inc 2-3(1):55-7, 1979.

    Roberto, Eugène. "Miron poète classique." Lettres qué 1(2):43-5,
    1976.

    L'homme rapaillé
    Audet, Noël. "Langage poétique: écart ou errance du sens." V&I
    3:459-66, 1978.

    Bélanger, Georges. "L'homme repaillé: thème du pays." LauURev
    5(2):103-12, 1973.

    Bonenfant, Joseph. "L'ombre de Mallarmé sur la poésie de Saint-Denys
    Garneau et de Miron." VIP 6:51-63, 1973.

    Brault, Jacques. "Sur la langue des poètes: Villon et Miron."
    Liberté 115:23-44, 1978.

    Hesbois, Laure. "Gaston Miron: à bout portant." V&I 4:39-49, 1978.

    Major, Jean-Louis. UTQ 40:436-7, 1971.

    Marcotte, Gilles. EF 7:103-6, 1971.

    Maugey, Axel. "Gaston Miron." Maugey 1972:171-83.

    Mounin, Georges. "Gaston Miron vu de loin." Liberté 116:79-87, 1978.

    Nepveu, Pierre. "Miron dépaysé; lecture de L'homme rapaillé."
    Nepveu 1979: 111-194.

    Pelosse, Cécile. LAQ 1970:102-18.

    Sanderson, Gertrude. AntigR 1(3):126-9, 1970.

    La vie agonique
    Fabi, Thérèse. "Miron le libérateur: étude lexicale de trois poèmes
    de La vie agonique." ActN 64:179-92, 1974.

    "La batèche"
    Boucher, Jean-Pierre. "Libre, comme... Québec: 'Le Damned Canuck' de
    Gaston Miron." Boucher 1977:123-38.(Extrait de 'La batéche'.)

MIRON, Gaston

"Courtepointe 5"
Roberto, Eugène. "Le couple dans la 'Courtepointe 5' de Gaston Miron." Inc 1(1-3):100-5, 1977.

"Le damned Canuck"
Boucher, Jean-Pierre. "Libre, comme... Québec: 'Le Damned Canuck' de Gaston Miron." Boucher 1977:123-38. (Extrait de 'La batéche'.)

"L'octobre"
Larocque, Hubert. "'L'octobre' de Gaston Miron." Inc 1(1-3):106-20, 1977.

Mailhot, Laurent. "L'octobre du québécanthrope." BdJ 26:27-32, 1970.

"Premiers poèmes"
Bolduc, Yves. "Lecture des 'Premiers poèmes' de Gaston Miron." Co-incidences 4(1):5-22, 1974.

"Les siècles de l'hiver"
Bonenfant, Pierre. "Théorie des générateurs de Jean Ricardou: essai d'application au poème 'Les siècles de l'hiver' de Gaston Miron." BdJ 39-41:26-35, 1973.

MOINEAU, Guy

La fuite et la conversation
Corriveau, Hugues. LAQ 1978:93-4.

Nepveu, Pierre. "Le poème: du fait divers à l'événement." Lettres qué 10:16-8, 1978.

MOIR, James M.

Family chronicle: poems and photographs of the Canadian West
Linder, Norma West. "Voices of character." CA&B 54(4):30-1, 1979.

MONETTE, Pierre

Temps supplémentaire
Giguère, Richard. LAQ 1979:106.

Traduit du jour le jour
Corriveau, Hugues. LAQ 1978:93-4.

234

MORENCY, Pierre

Bibliography
"Bibliographie." Nord 3:127-8, 1972.

General
Bernier, Yvon. "Pierre Morency et les intermittences de la poésie."
CC-R 2(3):43-53, 1974.

Châtillon, Pierre. " Les femmes-châteaux. " Nord 3:49-64, 1972.

Cloutier, Rachel; Fosty, Andrée; Gignac, Rodrigue. "Entrevue avec
Pierre Morency." Nord 3:9-27, 1972.

Morency, Pierre. "Poésie sur le toit." Estuaire 1:21-5, 1976.

Nord 3, 1972. (Whole issue.)

Rancourt, Jacques. "Vérité de la poitrine: Pierre Morency." Brindeau
1973:601-4.

Smith, Donald. "Entrevue: Pierre Morency, poète et dramaturge."
Lettres qué 12:39-47, 1978.

Au nord constamment de l'amour
Arcand, André. "Pierre Morency: une difficile naissance au monde."
Nord 3:91-114, 1972.

Bellemare, Gaston. "La parole dans l'oeuvre de Pierre Morency."
Nord 3:65-73, 1972.

Châtillon, Pierre. LAQ 1970:132-3.

Paradis, Suzanne. "Au nord constamment de l'amour." Nord 3:81-9,
1972.

Lieu de naissance
Bernier, Yvon. LAQ 1973:97.

Blais, Jacques. UTQ 43:369, 1974.

Poèmes de la froide merveille de vivre
Arcand, André. "Pierre Morency: une dificile naissance au monde."
Nord 3:91-114, 1972.

Bellemare, Gaston. "La parole dans l'oeuvre de Pierre Morency." Nord
3:65-73, 1972.

Cloutier, Cécile. "Pierre Morency ou la poésie en mode majeur." Nord
3:115-25, 1972.

Laberge, Marie. "L'essentiel ne se dit qu'avec le coeur." Nord
3:75-80, 1972.

MORENCY, Pierre

Poèmes de la vie déliée
Arcand, André. "Pierre Morency: une difficile naissance au monde." Nord 3:91-114, 1972.

Bellemare, Gaston. "La parole dans l'oeuvre de Pierre Morency." Nord 3:65-73, 1972.

Cloutier, Cécile. "Pierre Morency ou la poésie en mode majeur." Nord 3:115-25, 1972.

Torrentiel
Bourassa, André G. "Entre l'espace et le temps: ou le lieu de rencontre de Pierre Morency, Jean-Aubert Loranger, Denis Vanier et Michel Van Schendel." Letters qué 14:18-21, 1979.

Michaud, Ginette. LAQ 1978:142-3.

"Les femmes chateaux"
Châtillon, Pierre. "Les femmes châteaux." Nord 3:49-64, 1972.

"Le temps des oiseaux"
Bourque, Paul-André. "Poètes et artistes du Québec: L'Amour. Textes de Raoul Duguay... (etc.)." LAQ 1975: 139-45.

MORIN, Lorenzo

Le gage
Giroux, Robert. LAQ 1976:144-6.

MORRISSEY, Stephen Edgar

The trees of unknowing
Fletcher, Peggy. "Vehicles of expression." CA&B 55(1):24, 1979.

MOUAT, Kit

Time smoulders and other poems
Chope, Gordon. "A humanist's poems." HiC 4(4):22, 1971.

MOURÉ, Erin

Empire, York Street
Aubert, Rosemary. Q&Q 45(7):39, 1979.

Moritz, A.F. "Lines from the junction." BiC 8(3):16-7, 1979.

MRKICH, Dan

The white spectre
Fletcher, Peggy. "Good things come in small packages." CA&B
54(3):31-2, 1979.

MULLER, Hugo

Waswanipi: Songs of a scattered people
Luste, George. Q&Q 43(3):12, 1977.

MUNDWILER, Leslie

Double feature
Gasparini, Len. Alive 35:10, 1974.

Melnick, P. "Breathers." BiC 3(3):5-6, 1974.

MURRAY, Rona

Ootischenie
Lloyd, Marie Myers. Quarry 24(1):75-6, 1975.

McCarthy, Dermot. Brick 1:30-1, 1977.

Rogers, Linda. "Handful of dust." CanL 65:119-20, 1975.

The power of the dog
Cogswell, Fred. "Lonely runners." CanL 44:86-8, 1969.

Oates, Joyce Carol. "Three poets." FPt 4:77-81, 1970.

Selected poems
Alderson, Sue Ann. WCR 9(2):45-7, 1975.

Barbour, Douglas. "Canadian poetry chronicle 2." DR 55:748-59,
1975-76.

Brown, Allan. "Two Sono Nis poets." Brick 3:35-6, 1978.

Gasparini, Len. "Some ghosts are clearer than others." BiC
4(7):18-9, 1975.

Novik, Mary. "The trials of apprenticeship." CVII 2(3):51, 1976.

Skelton, Robin. MHRev 36:144, 1975.

Smith, Patricia Keeney. "Ice and fire." CanL 74:107-10, 1977.

MUSGRAVE, Susan

General
  Brown, Dennis. "Susan Musgrave: the self and the other." CanL 79:60-73.

  Grady, Wayne. "Susan Musgrave comes to grips with the mystical world of West Coast mythology." BiC 8(4):32, 1979.

  McMillan, Sharon. "Susan Musgrave: hinging the blind memory." MHRev 45:73-81, 1978.

  Rossiter, Sean. "The darkness inside Susan." SatN 90(6):35-8, 1975.

  Sullivan, Rosemary. "The white goddess: poetry of Susan Musgrave." CVII 1(2):14-5, 1975.

  Zilm, Glennis. "Poetry should have some mystery." Q&Q 41(1):6, 1975.

Becky Swan's book
  Barbour, Douglas. "Canadian poetry chronicle: VI." DR 58:555-78, 1978.

  Bayard, Caroline. Q&Q 44(8):46, 1978.

  Brennan, Pegeen. "Striking imagery." CanL 82:113-5, 1979.

  Levenson, Christopher. Quarry 27(4):80-1, 1978.

  MacMillan, Carrie. Fiddlehead 119:132-4, 1978.

  Madoff, Mark. "Secret evil and liaisons." CVII 4(3):21-2, 1979.

Entrance of the celebrant
  Fox, Gail. CF 53(632):43, 1973.

  Helwig, David. "Opacities." CanL 60:118-9,1974.

  Solecki, Sam. QQ 80:311-2, 1973.

  Walker, Susan. Q&Q 39(3):8, 1973.

Grave dirt and selected strawberries
  Balsevich, Mary. "A primer of mythology." Open letter 2d ser, 7:120-3, 1974.

  Bishop, A.G. Q&Q 40(1):13, 1974.

  Edwards, Mary Jane. CF 54(643):43, 1974.

  Fetherling, Doug. "Think hard, relax, think again." SatN 89(1):33-4, 1974.

  Novak, Barbara. NL 3:50-2, 1976.

  Rogers, Linda. "Magical music." CanL 61:121-2, 1974.

MUSGRAVE, Susan

Gullband: thought measles was a happy ending

Long, Tanya. Q&Q 41(3):24, 1975.

Thompson, Eric. "Plain and fantasy." CanL 65:101-4, 1975.

The impstone

Alderson, Steve. WCR 11(3):53-4, 1977.

Barbour, Douglas. "Poetry chronicle IV." DR 57:355-71, 1977.

Bolick, Merle Wallis. Quarry 25(4):72-3, 1976.

Downes, G.V. MHRev 39:134, 1976.

Harvey, Roderick W. "Views of reality." ECW 5:86-9, 1976.

Martineau, Stephen. "Catching sharp moments." CF 56(665):30, 1976.

MacEwen, Gwendolyn. Q&Q 4294):24, 1976.

Skelton, Robin. "Chime of symbols, tingle of greatness." BiC 5(4):17, 1976.

Smith, Patricia Keeney. "A variety of voices." CanL 78:91-4, 1978.

Steele, Charles R. "The imprint of memory." CVII 3(2):50, 1977.

A man to marry, a man to bury

Aubert, Rosemary. Q&Q 45(5):33, 1979.

Barbour, Douglas. Quarry 28(4):84-7, 1979.

Collins, Anne. "Like a shotgun to the heart." Maclean's 92(9):55, 1979.

Fletcher, Peggy. "Vision and the personal dark." CA&B 54(4):26-7, 1979.

Monk, Patricia. DR 59:570-2, 1979.

Moritz, A.F. "Bone hurt and battle-weary." BiC 8(4):10-1, 1979.

Sherman, Kenneth. "Tasteful necrophilia." CF 59(690):42-3, 1979.

Selected poems

Lane, M. Travis. "Be bold, be bold, be not too bold: the subject in poetry." Fiddlehead 106:121-7, 1975.

MUSGRAVE, Susan

> Selected strawberries and other poems
>> Barbour, Douglas. "Canadian poetry chronicle: VI." DR 58:555-78, 1978.
>>
>> Billings, Robert. UWR 13(2):100-1, 1978.
>>
>> Isaacs, Fran. Room of one's own 3(4):45-6, 1978.
>>
>> Levenson, Christopher. Quarry 27(4):80-1, 1978.
>>
>> MacMillan, Carrie. Fiddlehead 119:131-2, 1978.
>>
>> Woodcock, George. "Sibyls and other Greeks." CVII 3(4):6-7, 1978.

> Songs of the sea-witch
>> Barbour, Douglas. DR 50:431-3, 1970.
>>
>> Ditsky, John. CF 50:406, 1971.
>>
>> Fiamengo, Marya. "Careful and careless." CanL 53:104-5, 1972.
>>
>> Helwig, David. Quarry 20(1):49-50, 1971.
>>
>> Hornyansky, Michael. UTQ 40:376, 1971.
>>
>> Hornyansky, Michael. UTQ 42:371-2, 1973.
>>
>> Woods, Elizabeth. "Out of context." TamR 55:79-84, 1970.

NARRACHE, Jean

> General
>> Choquette, Robert. "Émile Coderre." Académie 14:56-70, 1972.
>>
>> Fournier-Ouellet, A. Emile Coderre, Raymond Souster: two poets, two cultures: similarities and contrasts. Montreal: McGill Univ., 1973, c1974. (M.A. thesis.)

NARVEY, Bernard

Of glorious Leos
Cameron, Michael. "Muddy waters." CVII 4(2):34-5, 1979.

Fletcher, Peggy. "Poetic travelling: some true/some new." CA&B 53(3):40-1, 1978.

NATIONS, Opal L.

Sitting on a lawn with a lady twice my size
Broten, Delores. "Inter medias res." ECW 9:94-6, 1977/78.

NAUSE, John

The valley and other poems
Heenan, J.M.H. "Two from Borealis." CVII 3(4):15-7, 1978.

NELLIGAN, Émile

Bibliography
Wyczynski, Paul. Bibliographie descriptive et critique d'Emile Nelligan. Ottawa, Eds. de l'Univ. d'Ottawa, 1973. (Bibliographies du Canada francais, 1.)

General
Bessette, Gerard. "Nelligan et les remous de son subconscient." Ottawa, 1972:131-49.

Boulanger, Daniel. "Lettre à Émile Nelligan." QuéFr. 34:50-1, 1979.

Dostie, Gaëtan. "Emile Nelligan: poète du désir." QuéFr 25:21-3, 1977.

Fabi, Thérèse. "L'effritement de Nelligan." ActN 65:425-37, 1976.

Mezei, Kathy. "Lampman and Nelligan: dream landscapes." CRCL 6:151-65, 1979.

Smith, Donald. "Nelligan et le feu." VIP 7:113-9, 1973.

Wyczynski, Paul. " Nelligan devant la critique." QuéFr 25:24-8, 1977.

Wyczynski, Paul. Nelligan et la musique. Ottawa, Ed. de l'Univ. d'Ottawa, 1971. (Cahiers du Centre de recherche en civilisation canadienne-français, 3.)

NELLIGAN, Émile

"Les chats"
Laflèche, Guy. "Sémiotique et poétique: 'Les chats' d'Émile
Nelligan." V&I 4:50-76, 1978.

"Clavier d'Antan"
Bissonnette, Pierrette et Bouchard, Jean-Pierre. "Analyse de 'Clavier
d'Antan,' poème d'Émile Nelligan." RUO 40:597-604, 1970.

"Rêve de Watteau"
Boucher, Jean-Pierre. "Par le gros bout de la lorgnette...'Reve de
Watteau' d'Émile Nelligan." Boucher 1977:7-23.

"Soir d'hiver"
Masson, Alain. "Discordia concors: analyse d'un poème de Nelligan."
RUM 6(3):95-117, 1973.

NELSON, Sharon

A broken vessel
MacKendrick, L.K. Q&Q 39(2):12, 1973.

NEPVEU , Pierre

Épisodes
Hébert, François. "Lefrançois, Beaulieu, Nepveu, Vanier." Liberté
114:93-9, 1977.

Poulin, Gabrielle. "Voies rapides et Épisodes de Pierre Nepveu, poète
du macadam." Relations 37(428):222-3, 1977.

Voies rapides
Gervais, Marielle. LAQ 1971:142-4.

Marcotte, Gilles. EF 8:99-100, 1972.

Poulin, Gabrielle. "Voies rapides et Épisodes de Pierre Nepveu, poète
du macadam." Relations 37(428):222-3, 1977.

NÉRON, Denys

L'équation sensible
Bourneuf, Roland. LAQ 1979:150-2.

NEUFELDT, Leonard

A way of walking
Lanczos, Elmar. WCR 8(2):61-3, 1973.

Madigan, Michael. "Root and flower: eleven books of poems." MQR 14:220-8, 1975.

NEWCOMBE, Rosemary

Dear John
Bailey, Don. "A provincial look at ten volumes of Canadian poetry." QQ 79:242-54, 1972.

NEWLOVE, John

Bibliography
Lecker, Robert A. "An annotated bibliography of works by and about John Newlove." ECW 2:28-53, 1975.

General
Atwood, Margaret. "Comment est-ce que je vais m'en sortir: la poésie de John Newlove." Ellipse 10:102-16, 1972. (Tr. Rodolphe Lacasse.)

Atwood, Margaret. "How do I get out of here: the poetry of John Newlove." Open letter, 2d ser, 4:59-70, 1973.

Bartley, Jan. "Something in which to believe for once: the poetry of John Newlove." Open letter 2d ser, 9:19-48, 1974.

Gervais, C.H. "Alienation in John Newlove's poetry." Alive 41:28, 12, 1975.(Paging due to typographical error)

Gould, Mary Rebecca. The several masks of John Newlove: a study of the confessional and non-confessional poetic stances of John Newlove. Kingston, Ontario: Queen's Univ., 1975. (M.A. thesis.)

Henderson, Brian. "Newlove: poet of appearance." ECW 2:9-27, 1975.

Moisan, Clément. "Poésie de la libération." Moisan 1979:167-218.

Moritz, A.F. "The man from Vaudeville, Sask." BiC 7(1):9-12, 1978.

Newlove, John. Columbo 1971:84-96.

Black night window
Barbour, Douglas. "The search for roots: a meditative sermon of sorts." LHY 13(2):1-14, 1972.

Hunt, Russell A. Fiddlehead 85:98-101, 1970.

NEWLOVE, John

The cave
  Gustafson, Ralph. QQ 78:140-2, 1971.

  Hunt, Russell A. Fiddlehead 85:98-101, 1970.

  Marshall, Tom. "Canpo: a chronicle." Quarry 19(4):50-4, 1970.

  Pacey, Desmond. CF 50:309-10, 1970.

  Purdy, A.W. "Calm surfaces destroyed." CanL 48:91-2, 1971.

Elephants, mothers and others
  Dudek, Louis. "The new Vancouver poetry." Dudek 1978:186-92.
  (Originally published in Culture 25;323-30, 1964.)

The fat man: selected poems 1962-1972
  Casto, Robert C. "Savaging the image: the poetry of John Newlove."
  Waves 6(1):72-4, 1977.

  Fletcher, Peggy. "No two alike." Ca&B 53(2):43-4, 1978.

  Hornyansky, Michael. UTQ 47:348, 1978.

  Jewinski, Hans. "... they licked the platter clean." BiC 7(1):26,
  1978.

  Jewinski, Ed. Q&Q 43(15):36, 1977.

  Safarik, Allen. Quarry 27(2):82-4, 1978.

  Skelton, Robin. "Newlove's power." CanL 79:101-3, 1978.

  Solecki, Sam. "Birney and Newlove selected." Fiddlehead 118:146-52,
  1978.

  Steele, Charles R. UWR 13(2):111-2, 1978.

Lies
  Bennett, Donna A. "Reunion: contemporary Canadian poetry." LURev
  6:236-9, 1973.

  Bowering, George. "Where does the truth lie?" Open letter 2d ser,
  4:71-4, 1973.

  Estok, Michael. "All in the family: the metaphysics of domesticity."
  DR 52:653-67, 1973.

  Fetherling, Doug. "Implosion exposed." BiC 2(1):38, 1973.

  Friesen, Ronald. Q&Q 39(1):11, 1973.

  Haas, Maara. CA&B 49(1):24, 1973.

244

NEWLOVE, John

Lies (cont'd.)
Johnson, Rick.   Quarry 22(2):64-6, 1973.

Lane, Patrick.   "Inner landscape as despair." CapR 2:59-63, 1972.

Purdy, Al.   WascanaR 8(2):70-2, 1973.

Ryan, Tom.   WLWE 13(2):293-5, 1974.

Solecki, Sam.   QQ 80:312, 1973.

Warkentin, Germaine.   "Drifting to oblivion." CanL 56:121-2, 1973.

Samuel Hearne in wintertime
Davey, Frank.   "The explorer in Western Canadian literature." SCL 4(2):91-100, 1979.

NICHOL,bp

Bibliography
David, Jack, comp.   "Published autopography." ECW 1:39-46, 1974.

General
Bayard, Caroline and David, Jack.   "bpNichol." Bayard 1978:15-49.

David, Jack.   "Visual poetry in Canada: Birney, Bissett, and bp." SCL 2:252-66, 1977.

David, Jack.   "Writing writing: bpNichol at 30." ECW 1:27-38, 1974.

Harvey, Roderick W.   "bpNichol: the repositioning of language." ECW 4:19-33, 1976.

"Interview/bp Nichol." CapR 8/9:313-46, 1975/76.

Moisan, Clément.   "La 'nouvelle culture', la contre-culture ou the brilliant minority." Moisan 1979:219-68.

Norris, Ken.   "Interview with bpNichol: Feb. 13, 1978." ECW 12:243-50, 1978.

Phillips, Ben T.   "A b.p. Nichol craft morsel: excerpt from interview... 1st of August 1978." PTor 48:n.p., 1979.

NICHOL, bp

General (cont'd.)
Scobie, Stephen. "Vingt ans de poésie concrète,: Ellipse 17:180-8, 1975. (Tr. Lyse Rouillard-Valence.)

ABC
Davey, Frank. "At a dead end." CanL 55:118-9, 1973.

Garnet, Eldon. "Killing the poem to make it new." SatN 88(3):40, 1973.

Aleph unit
David, Jack. "A friendly poem." Open letter 2d ser, 9:109-10, 1974.

Beach head
Barbour, Douglas. Quarry 20(4):62, 1971.

Borders (phono record)
Scobie, Stephen. "I dreamed I saw Hugo Ball: bpNichol, dada and sound poetry," Boundary 2, 3:213-25, 1974.

Journal
Scobie, Stephen. Fiddlehead 121:136-8, 1979.

Konfessions of an Elizabethan fan dancer
McNamara, Eugene. "Scream or speech?" CanL 70:100-1, 1976.

Love: a book of remembrances
Alpert, Barry. "Written on the wind (of Lake Ontario)." Open letter 3d ser, 2:5-25, 1975.

Barbour, Douglas. Fiddlehead 105:121-2, 1975.

Barbour, Douglas. "The poets and presses revisited: circa 1974." DR 55:338-60, 1975.

Dault, Gary Michael. "Garnet and other glows." BiC 4(2):24-5, 1975.

David, Jack. Q&Q 41(1):26, 1975.

Griggs, Terry. Brick 1:10-5, 1977.

McNamara, Eugene. "Scream or speech?" CanL 70:100-1, 1976.

246

NICHOL, bp

The martyrology books I & II

Barbour, Douglas. "Journey in a mythic landscape." CanL 56:93-7, 1973.

Garnet, Eldon. "Killing the poem to make it new." SatN 88(3):40, 1973.

Orr, George B. Q&Q 38(9):8, 1972.

Scobie, Stephen. "In search of new myths." LURev 6:232-6, 1973.

Scobie, Stephen. WLWE 13(2):288-92, 1974.

Scobie, Stephen. "Look out, the saints are comin' through..." Fiddlehead 120:115-22, 1979.

Sutherland, Fraser. "The effigies and the agonies." BiC 2(3):44-5, 1973.

The martyrology: books III & IV

Barbour, Douglas. "bpNichol: the life of letters & the letters of life." ECW 7/8:179-90, 1977. (apparently incorrectly collated; reprinted with slightly different collation ECW 9:97-108, 1977-78)

Barbour, Douglas. "Poetry chronicle V." DR 58:149-69, 1978.

Fernstrom, Ken. Q&Q 43(6):44, 1977.

Scobie, Stephen. "Look out, the saints are comin' through..." Fiddlehead 120:115-22, 1979.

Scobie, Stephen. "The mythology of language." CVII 3(2):52-3, 1977.

Steele, Charles R. UWR 13(2):110-1, 1978.

Monotones

Bowering, George. Open letter 2d ser, 2:82-4, 1972.

Garnet, Eldon. "Killing the poem to make it new." SatN 88(3):40, 1973.

Scobie, Stephen. "A dash for the border." CanL 56:89-92, 1973.

Starkman, Harvey. Q&Q 38(7):11, 1972.

Still water

Barbour, Douglas. Quarry 20(4):62-3.

NOBLE, Charles

Haywire rainbow
  Di Cicco, Pier Giorgio. "No man is an island, true, but there can be a circean catch to regionalism." BiC 8(1):21-2, 1979.

  Hall, Phil. "Haywire rainbow--the whole damn country's haywire." UWR 14(2):108-9, 1979.

  Barbour, Douglas. "Canadian poetry chronicle: VII." DR 59:154-75, 1979.

Three
  Gervais, C.H. "Staying true." CanL 76:104-7, 1978.

  Klepac, Walter. Q&Q 39(12):12, 1973.

NOLAN, Gladys

Ghosts in the garden
  Booth, Luella Kerr. "Five book reviews." OV 8(3):n.p., 1972.

  Harper, A.W.J. "Four reviews." OV 8(2):n.p., 1972.

NORMAN, Colin

Predictable conditions
  Amprimoz, Alexandre L. Q&Q 42(7):42, 1976.

  Gatenby, Greg. "Sur realism rampant." BiC 5(8):21-2, 1976.

  Hornyansky, Michael. UTQ 46:375-7, 1977.

NORRIS, Ken

The perfect accident
  Fletcher, Peggy. "Vision and the personal dark." CA&B 54(4):26-7, 1979.

Report on the second half of the twentieth century
  Davies, Gwendolyn. "Something's happening in Montreal." ECW 10:82-7, 1978.

  Hamilton, Jamie. "Work in progress." CVII 3(3):52-3, 1978.

  Wood, Mary. "Quiet rage." Brick 4:26, 1978.

NORRIS, Ken

Under the skin
Gatenby, Greg. "Sur realism rampant." BiC 5(8):21-2, 1976.

Hamilton, Jamie. "Work in progress." CVII 3(3):52-3, 1978.

Vegetables
Barbour, Douglas. "Canadian poetry chronicle: VI." DR 58:555-78, 1978.

Hamilton, Jamie. "Work in progress." CVII 3(3):52-3, 1978.

NOWLAN, Alden

General
Baxter, Marilyn. "Wholly drunk or wholly sober?" CanL 68-9:106-11, 1976.

Bly, Robert. "For Alden Nowlan, with admiration." TamR 54:32-8, 1970.

Cameron, Donald. "The poet from Desolation Creek." SatN 88(5):28-32, 1973.

Fraser, Keath. "Notes on Alden Nowlan." CanL 45:41-51, 1970.

Metcalf, John. "Alden Nowlan." CanL 63:8-17, 1975.

Nowlan, Alden. Colombo 1971:97-105.

Nowlan, Alden. "Something to write about." CanL 68-9:7-12, 1976.

Oliver, Michael Brian. "Dread of the self: escape and reconciliation in the poetry of Alden Nowlan." ECW 5:50-66, 1976.

Oliver, Michael Brian. Poet's progress: the development of Alden Nowlan's poetry. Fredericton, N.B: Fiddlehead Poetry Books, 1978. (Fiddlehead poetry book, 248)

Oliver, Michael Brian. "The presence of ice: the early poetry of Alden Nowlan." SCL 1:210-22, 1976.

Russell, Kenneth C. "Naming the darkness: a note on Alden Nowlan's poetry." Inscape 13(1):65-72, 1976.

Ustick, Michael. "Repression: the poetry of Alden Nowlan." CanL 60:43-50, 1974.

NOWLAN, Alden

Between tears and laughter
Almon, Bert.   New 20:59-60, 1973.

Gold, H.   New 18:42-3, 1972.

Hornyansky, Michael.   UTQ 41:336, 1972.

Howell, Bill.   "Mise en scene."   BiC 1(6):20-1, 1971.

Lacey, Edward.   "Canadian bards and South American reviewers."   Nj 4:82-120, 1974.

MacSween, R.J.   AntigR 9:103, 1972.

Pacey, Peter.   Fiddlehead 93:114-6, 1972.

Shucard, Alan.   "Meeting midway."   CanL 56:126-7, 1973.

Solecki, Sam.   QQ 80:312-3, 1973.

Double exposure
Gibbs, Robert.   Fiddlehead 122:111-5, 1979.

I'm a stranger here myself
Barbour, Douglas.   "Canadian poetry chronicle: III."   DR 56:560-73, 1976.

Charlton, Aydon.   Sphinx 4:75-6, 1975.

Lauder, Scott.   "Decency of feeling."   CF 55(650):61-2, 1975.

McFadden, David.   QQ 82:645-6, 1975.

Rapoport, Janis.   TamR 66:106, 1975.

Ricou, Laurie.   Q&Q 41(4):38-9, 1975.

Scobie, Steven.   Fiddlehead 106:106-8, 1975.

Tefs, Wayne.   "The familiar afflictions of being human--more journeys into Nowland."   CVII 1(1):20-1, 1975.

Wilson, Betty.   CA&B 50(4):26, 1975.

Wolfe, Monia.   "Verbal magic realism."   BiC 4(6):21, 1975.

NOWLAN, Alden

The mysterious naked man
    Ballstadt, Carl. CF 50:224-5, 1970.

    Barbour, Douglas. DR 50:425-7, 1970.

    Chevraux, Sharleen M. CA&B 50(1):28, 1974.

    Fraser, Keath. "Existence and sonorous art." CanL 45:87-8, 1970.

    Garnet, Eldon. "For the poets, the landscape is the great Canadian myth." SatN 85(2):31-3, 1970.

    Livingstone, Donald. "In his own image." FPt 5:67-9, 1970.

    Purdy, Al. WascanaR 5(2)58-60, 1970.

Playing the Jesus game: selected poems
    Doyle, Mike. "Made in Canada ?" Poetry 119:356-62, 1972.

    Marshall, Tom. "Canpo: a chronicle." Quarry 19(4):50-4, 1970.

Shaped by this land
    Cameron, Barry. "Artistic schizophrenia." CanL 68-9:150-2, 1976.

    Clermont, Ghislain and Mitcham, Allison.   RUM 10(3):145-7, 1977.

    Wolfe, Monia. "Verbal magic realism." BiC 4(6):21, 1975.

Smoked glass
    Barbour, Douglas. "Canadian poetry chronicle: VI." DR 58:555-78, 1978.

    Daniel, Lorne. Q&Q 44(2):44, 1978.

    Drew, John. "Eastern exposure." CF 57(679):39-40, 1978.

    Gibbs, Robert. Fiddlehead 122:111-5, 1979.

    Gibson, Kenneth. "A poetry chronicle." Waves 7(2):57-60, 1979.

    Lazonick, Bayla. Quarry 27(2):76-8, 1978.

    Mandel, Eli. "Three modernists in perspective." BiC 7(10):35-6, 1978.

    Roberts, Kevin. "Conversational craftsman." CanL 76:108-10, 1978.

The things which are
    Dudek, Louis. "A load of new books: Smith, Webb, Miller/Souster, Purdy, Nowlan." Dudek 1978:168-74. (Originally published Delta 20:27-32, 1963.)

NOWLAN, Alden

"The execution"
Dudek, Louis, "A reading of two poems by Alden Nowlan." Dudek 1978:282-9. (Originally published Fiddlehead 81:51-2, 1969.)

"The bull moose"
Dudek, Louis. "A reading of two poems by Alden Nowlan." Dudek 1978:29-9. (Originally published Fiddlehead 81:51-2, 1969.)

NYNYCH, Stephanie J.

General
Basmajian, Shant. Old nun 1:59-60, 1975.

...and like i see it
Saunders, Brenda. Old nun 1:15, 1975.

By death never leave me
Gervais, C.H. "Staying true." CanL 76:104-7, 1978.

Hamilton, Jamie. "Visual filters, pyrex forms." BiC 4(11):18-9, 1975.

OAKLEY, Wayne

Sucking the breath of texts, wooing the sky
Wyrcoff, Daniel. Quarry 28(1):95-6, 1979.

OATES, Joyce Carol

Angel fire
Mazzaro, Jerome. "A poet of being." MPS 4:228-30, 1973.

Anonymous sins & other poems
French, Roberts W. "The novelist-poet." PrS 44:177-8, 1970.

Mazzaro, Jerome. "Oh women, oh men!" MPS 1:39-41, 1970.

McGann, Jerome. "Poetry and truth." Poetry 117:195-203, 1970.

Skelton, Robin. MHRev 13:110-1, 1970.

Stevens, Peter. CF 49:243-4, 1970.

Thomas, Peter. Fiddlehead 84:112-3, 1970.

OATES, Joyce Carol

The fabulous beasts
Mazzaro, Jerome. "Two poets." MPS 7:244 -7, 1976.

Love and its derangements
Gregory, Hilda. "Love's country." PrS 45:78-80, 1971.

Mazzaro, Jerome. "Feeling one's Oates." MPS 2:133-7, 1971.

O'HUIGIN, Sean

The inks and the pencils and the looking back
Barbour, Douglas. "Aural possibilities." ECW 16:147-52, 1979-80.

ONDAATJE, Michael

General
Abley, Mark. "Home is where the hurt is." Maclean's 92(17):62, 1979.

Hunter, Lynette. "Form and energy in the poetry of Michael Ondaatje." JCP 1(1):49-70, 1978.

Marshall, Tom. "Deeper darkness, after choreography: Michael Ondaatje." Marshall 1979:144-9.

Scobie, Stephen. "His legend a jungle sleep: Michael Ondaatje and Henri Rousseau." CanL 76:6-21.

Scobie, Stephen and Barbour, Douglas. "A conversation with Michael Ondaatje." White pelican 1(2):6-15, 1971.

Solecki, Sam. "Nets and chaos: the poetry of Michael Ondaatje." SCL 2:36-48.

Watson, Sheila. "Michael Ondaatje: the mechanization of death." White pelican 2(4):56-64, 1972.

Witten, Mark. "Billy, Buddy, and Michael." BiC 6(6):9-13, 1977.

The collected works of Billy the kid
Blott, Anne. "Stories to finish: The collected works of Billy the kid." SCL 2:188-202, 1977.

Cogswell, Fred. Fiddlehead 88:105-6, 1971.

David, Jack. "Michael Ondaatje's The collected works of Billy the kid." CN&Q 13:11-2, 1974.

ONDAATJE, Michael

The collected works of Billy the Kid (cont'd.)
Davis, Marilyn. CF 51(606-7):34-5, 1971.

Dragland, Stan. Quarry 20(3):61-9, 1971.

Duckles, Richard. "A quick draw." Open letter 2d ser, 1:73, 1971-72.

Fetherling, Doug. "A new way to do it." SatN 86(2):29-39, 1971.

Fetherling, Doug. "Poetic journal." TamR 57:80-4, 1971.

Healey, James. PrS 49:88, 1975.

Hornyansky, Michael. UTQ 40:377-8, 1971.

Hunter, Lynette. "Form and energy in the poetry of Michael Ondaatje."
JCP 1(1):49-70, 1978.

Hutcheon, Linda. "Snow storm of paper: the act of reading in
self-reflexive Canadian verse." DR 59:114-26, 1979.

Kertzer, J.M. "On death and dying: The collected works of Billy the
kid." ESC 1:86-96, 1975.

Lee, Dennis. "Part two: The collected works of Billy the Kid; part
three: Interlude." Lee 1977:13-60.

New 17:53, 1971.

Sarkar, Eileen. "Michael Ondaatje's Billy the kid: the esthetics of
violence." WLWE 12(2):230-9, 1973.

Schroeder, Andreas. "The poet as gunman." CanL 51:80-2, 1972.

Scobie, Stephen. "Two authors in search of a character." CanL
54:37-55, 1972.

Skelton, Robin. MHRev 18:127, 1971.

Stevens, Peter. QQ 78:326-7, 1971.

Watson, Sheila. "Michael Ondaatje: the mechanization of death." Open
letter 3d ser, 1:158-66, 1975.

The dainty monsters
Barbour, Douglas. "The young poets and the little presses, 1969." DR
50:112-26, 1970.

Schreiber, Ron. New 12:43-6, 1970.

Scott, Peter Dale. "A Canadian chronicle." Poetry 115:353-64, 1970.

ONDAATJE, Michael

The man with seven toes
Barbour, Douglas. "The young poets and the little presses, 1969." DR 50:112-26, 1970.

Marshall, Tom. "Canpo: a chronicle." Quarry 19(4):50-4, 1970.

Rat jelly
Almon, Bert. "A bitter aspic." BiC 2(2):17, 1973.

Barbour, Douglas. "Three west coast poets and one from the east." LURev 6:240-5, 1973.

Barbour, Douglas. Q&Q 39(3):9, 1973.

Barrie, B.D. Fiddlehead 98:119-20, 1973.

Bowering, George. Open letter 2d ser, 8:97-9, 1974.

McKinnon, David. Open letter 2d ser, 5:122-3, 1973.

McWhirter, George. Quarry 23(1):75-6, 1974.

Musgrave, Susan. MHRev 31:161-2, 1974.

Scobie, Stephen. WLWE 13(2):279-82, 1974.

Stevens, Peter. QQ 80:656-7, 1973.

Wagner, Linda W. "Four young poets." OntR 1:89-97, 1974.

There's a trick with a knife I'm learning to do: poems 1963-1978
Abley, Mark. "Bone beneath skin." Maclean's 92(17):62-3, 1979.

Barbour, Douglas. "All that poetry should be." CF 59(690):34-5, 1979.

Hicks, Lorne. Q&Q 45(6):47, 1979.

Linder, Norma West. "Voices of character." CA&B 54(4):30-1, 1979.

McNally, Paul. QQ 86:720-1, 1979.

Solecki, Sam. "Sharpening his act." BiC 8(6):11, 1979.

O'GRADY, Standish

The emigrant, a poem, in four cantos
O'Donnell, Kathleen. "Standish O'Grady." Le chien d'or 3: n.p., 1974.

O'REILLY, Yvan

> Symbiose de flashes
>> Corriveau, Hugues. LAQ 1977:143-4.

OUELLETTE, Fernand

> General
>> Audet, Noel. "Structures poétiques dans l'oeuvre de Fernand Ouellette." VIP 3:103-24, 1970.
>>
>> Bonenfant, Joseph. "Fernand Ouellette, or poetry as a search for wholeness." Ellipse 10:62-9, 1972. (Tr. Jay Bochner.)
>>
>> Bonenfant, Joseph. "Principes d'unité dans l'oeuvre de Fernand Ouellette." ELit 5:447-61, 1972.
>>
>> Cloutier, Cécile. "L'influence de quelques poètes français sur quelques poètes québécois." PFr 9:44-51, 1974.
>>
>> Nepveu, Pierre. "Une poétique de la tension; l'oeuvre de Fernand Ouellette." Nepveu 1979:21-110.
>>
>> Ouellette, Fernand. Journal dénoué Montréal, Presses de l'Univ. de Montréal, 1974.
>>
>> Ouellette, Fernand. "Poetry in my life." Ellipse 10:46-58, 1972. (Tr. C.R.P. May.)
>>
>> Rancourt, Jacques. "Montée mystique des corps: Fernand Ouellette." Brindeau 1973:584-8.

> À découvert
>> Roy, Max. LAQ 1979:153-6.

> Ces anges de sang
>> Poulin, Gabrielle. "Cet autre visage de Fernand Ouellette." Relations 387:313-4, 1973.

> Errances
>> Bourque, Paul-André. "Poètes et artistes du Québec: L'Amour. Textes de Raoul Duguay... (etc.)" LAQ 1975:139-45.

> Ici, ailleurs, la lumière
>> Bourassa, André-G. "D'après peinture: Bélanger, Leblanc, Marteau, Ouellette, Girardin et Lapointe." Lettres qué 6:10-3, 1977.
>>
>> Bourassa, André-G. "L'Hexagone au quart de tour." Lettres qué 9:11-4, 1978.
>>
>> Brochu, André. LAQ 1977:127-30.

OUELLETTE, Fernand

Poésie: poèmes 1953-1971
Mailhot, Laurent. LAQ 1972:130-5.

Marcotte, Gilles. EF 9:75-7, 1973.

Marteau, Robert. "Un poète du Québec, Fernand Ouellette." Esprit 425:1286-94.

Poulin, Gabrielle. "Cet autre visage de Fernand Ouellette." Relations 387:313-4, 1973.

Le soleil sous la mort
Lepage, Yvan G. "La proprioception dans Le soleil sous la mort de Fernand Ouellette." Eigeldinger 1978, 247-56.

Maugey, Axel. "Fernand Ouellette." Maugey 1972, 220-6.

"Doigts fusées"
Bonenfant, Joseph. "Lecture structurale d'un poème de F. Ouellette. BdJ 39-41:4-25, 1973.

"Les fougères"
Bonenfant, Joseph. "Principes d'unité dans l'oeuvre de Fernand Ouellette." ELit 5: 447-61, 1972.

OUTRAM Richard

General
de Santana, Hubert. "Monarch in Mufti." BiC 5(9):6,8-9, 1976.

Turns and other poems
Barbour, Douglas. "Canadian poetry chronicle:III." DR 56:560-73, 1976.

Bishop, A.G. Q&Q 42(4):25, 1976.

de Santana, Hubert. "A freak of genius." BiC 5(3):19-20, 1976.

Ellenwood, Ray. Brick 2:57, 1978.

Heinzelman, Kurt. "Five poets of the Commonwealth." Poetry 131:225-35, 1978.

Hornyansky, Michael. UTQ 45:343-4, 1976.

MacKendrick, Louis K. "Small press review." OntR 8:106-12, 1978.

Woodcock, George. "Playing with freezing fire." CanL 70:84-91, 1976.

OWER, John

Legendary acts
Fletcher, Peggy. "Poetic travelling: some true/some new." CA&B
53(3):40-1, 1978.

West, David S. "Old wine, broken bottles, cut glass." CanL
80:109-12, 1979.

PADGETT, Wayne

Horse's nose poems
Gazan, Jack. HiC 7(3):23, 1974.

Hoekema, Henry. WCR 9(1):48-9, 1974.

PAGE, P.K.

Bibliography
Preston, Michele. "The poetry of P.K. Page: a checklist." WCR
13(3):12-7, 1979.

General
Keeler, Judy. "An interview with P.K. Page." CF 55(654):33-5, 1975.

Mallinson, Jean. "Retrospect and prospect." WCR 13(3):8-11, 1979.

Marshall, Tom. "Facts and dreams again." Marshall 1979:107-11.

Moisan, Clément. "Poésie de la clandestinité." Moisan 1979:91-127.

Namjoshi, S. "Double landscape." CanL 67:21-30, 1976.

Pearce, Jon. "Fried eggs and the workings of the Right Lobe:
interview with P.K. Page." Quarry 28(4):30-42, 1979.

Rooke, Constance. "P.K. Page: the chameleon and the centre." MHRev
45:169-95, 1978.

Smith, A.J.M. "La poésie de P.K. Page." Ellipse 18:126-38, 1976.
(Adapté de A.J.M. Smith par G. Ceschi.)

Smith, A.J.M. "The poetry of P.K. Page." CanL 50:17-27, 1971.
(Also Smith 1973: 146-55; Woodcock 1974b:80-91.)

Sullivan, Rosemary. "A size larger than seeing: the poetry of P.K.
Page." CanL 79:32-42, 1978

Sutherland, John. "P.K. Page and Preview." Sutherland 1972:96-7.

Sutherland, John. "The poetry of P.K. Page." Sutherland 1972:101-12.

PAGE, P.K.

    Cry Ararat
      Jones, D.G.   "Cold eye and optic heart: Marshall McLuhan and some
      Canadian poets."   MPS 5:170-87, 1974.

    Poems selected and new, 1942-1973
      Adamson, Arthur.   CVII 1(1):9-10, 1975.

      Barnes, Elizabeth A.   Quarry 24(1):70-1, 1975.

      Beardsley, Doug.   "A trial of immortality: recent Canadian poetry."
      Nj 6:118-27, 1976.

      Hornyansky, Michael.   UTQ 44:331-2, 1975.

      Inkster, Tim.   TamR 63:83-4, 1974.

      Marshall, Tom.   "Inferno, Paradise and Slapstick."   CanL 64:104-7,
      1975.

      Pearson, Alan.   CF 54(640-1):17-8, 1974.

      Scobie, Stephen.   QQ 81:645-7, 1974.

      Safarik, Allan.   "Eyes behind the page."   CanR 1(4):23-4, 1974.

      Wieland, Sarah.   Q&Q 40(7):21, 1974.

PAGEAU, René

    L'ombre de l'hiver
      Métivier, Henri.   ActN 59:605-7, 1970.

    Que tourne le soleil
      Bisson-Henchiri, Michelle.   LAQ 1972:166.

    Rumeurs de la nuit
      Henchiri, Sliman.   LAQ 1970:144.

      Lamarche, Gustave.   ActN 60:687-90, 1971.

    Vienne l'été
      Benoît, Monique.   LAQ 1974:138-9.

PALLASCIO-MORIN, Ernest

Les amants ne meurent pas
Henchiri, Sliman. LAQ 1971:162-3.

PARADIS, Suzanne

General
Bourque, Paul-André. "Suzanne Paradis: poète, romancier et critique: vingt années d'écriture." Lettres qué, 16:59-65, 1979-80.

Paradis, Suzanne. "Quelques observations sur le métier d'écrivain." Protée 2(3):65-7, 1973.

Rancourt, Jacques. "De l'enfance à l'âge adulte: Suzanne Paradis." Brindeau 1973:589-96.

Les chevaux de verre
Guévremont, Lise. LAQ 1979:157-8.

Il y eut un matin
Le Grand, Éva. LAQ 1972:168.

Noir sur sang
Pontbriand, Jean Noel. LAQ 1976:155-6.

Poèmes
Bouvier, Luc. LAQ 1978:145-6.

Pour voir les plectrophanes naître
Dallard, Sylvie. LAQ 1970:141.

Marcotte, Gilles. EF 8:96-7, 1972.

La voie sauvage
Barry, Catherine A. "Suzanne Paradis, 'Mara', and the Voie Sauvage." FR 51:696-9, 1978.

Moisan, Clément. LAQ 1973:127-8.

"Mara"
Barry, Catherine A. "Suzanne Paradis, 'Mara', and the Voie Sauvage." FR 51:696-9, 1978.

PARÉ, Yvon

L'octobre des Indiens
Le Grand, Éva. LAQ 1971:169

PASS, John

John Pass: poems (Air, 18)
Billings, R.   Quarry 23(2):74, 1974.

Lacey, Edward. "Canadian bards and South American reviewers." Nj 4:82-120, 1974.

Port of entry
Davis, Frances. "Hermetic journies and reductions." CVII 3(1):4-5, 1977.

PATTON, Andrew

Poems and quotations
Power, Nick. Q&Q 41(13):33-4, 1975.

PEARSON, Alan

Freewheeling through gossamer dragstrips
Barbour, Douglas. "Canadian poetry chronicle:III." DR 56:560-73, 1976.

Billings, Robert. Quarry 25(3):73-4, 1976.

Engel, Howard. "Pleasing voices." CF 56(662):54, 1976.

Hamilton, Jamie. Q&Q 42(4):24, 1976.

Hornyansky, Michael. UTQ 45:344, 1976.

MacKendrick, Louis K. "Small press review." OntR 8:106-12, 1978.

Merrett, Robert James. "Winning a reader." CanL 79:96-8, 1978.

Oughton, John. "Simple songs, tricky cycles." BiC 5(4):20-1, 1976.

PELLETIER, Pierre

Temps de vies
Plamondon, Gaétan. LAQ 1979:158-9.

PELLETIERE, Cathie

Widow's walk
Amprimoz, Alexandre L. Quarry 26(4):69-70, 1977.

Hamel, Guy. "Recent Fiddlehead poetry books." Fiddlehead 118:137-45, 1978.

PÉLOQUIN, Claude

General
Bayard, Caroline and David, Jack. "Claude P. Lokin." Bayard 1978 37-56.

Bonenfant, Joseph. "Péloquin: l'oeuvre." Lettres qué 7:42-6, 1977.

Bourassa, André-G. "Les poètes de la musique." Lettres qué 11:32-7, 1978.

Rancourt, Jacques. "Impulsion cosmique: Claude Péloquin." Brindeau 1973:605-7.

Robert, Guy. "Péli-Pélo." Le maclean 14(12):70, 1974.

Warden, kathy. "'Pelo' joins Calgary Canadian collection." Q&Q 42(17):13, 1976.

L'autopsie merveilleuse
De Bellefeuille, Normand. LAQ 1979:159-60.

Un grand amour
Bélanger, Yrénée. LAQ 1972:170.

Inoxydables
Bourassa, André-G. "Poésie et communication--en forme de journal et d'examen de (...) science." Lettres qué 8:12-4, 1977.

Pour la grandeur de l'homme
Saint-Amour, Robert. LAQ 1971:154.

Le premier tiers
Bourassa, André-G. LAQ 1976:130-4.

Le répas est servi
Robert, Guy. LAQ 1970:143-4.

PERREAULT, Ginette

Un monde bien ordinaire
Blais, Jacques.   UTQ 43:369-70, 1974.

Blais, Jacques.   UTQ 44:341-2, 1975.

Étienne, Gérard.   "Littérature joualisante ou le joual en
littérature?" LAQ 1974:148-50.

PERRAULT, Pierre

Bibliographie
Cormier, François & Yves Lacroix.   "Oeuvres de Pierre Perrault." V&I
3:371-8, 1978.

General
Dubruc, Yvon and Lacroix, Yves.   "Pierre Perrault, l'envie de se
taire." V&I 3:353-69, 1978.

Royer, Jean.   "Entretien avec Pierre Perrault." Estuaire 3:77-90,
1977.

Tessier, Jocelyne.   "Pierre Perrault, l'homme et sa parole." V&I
3:379-95, 1978.

Chouennes
Bourassa, André-G.   "Un Perrault ancien et un Chamberland nouveau."
Lettres qué 1(1):10-2, 1976.

Melançon, Robert.   LAQ 1975:97-100.

Tessier, Jocelyne.   "Pierre Perrault, l'homme et sa parole." V&I
3:379-95, 1978.

En désespoir de cause
Gallays, Francois.   LAQ 1971:168-9.

Marcotte, Gilles.   EF 8:96-7, 1972.

Gélivures
Bourassa, André-G.   "L'hexagone au quart de tour." Lettres qué
9:11-4, 1978.

Bouvier, Luc.   LAQ 1977:174-8.

Dubuc, Yvon & Yves Lacroix.   "Pierre Perrault, l'envie de se taire."
V&I 3:353-69.

Giguère, Richard.   UTQ 47:360-1, 1978.

Tessier, Jocelyne.   "Pierre Perrault, l'homme et sa parole." V&I
3:379-94, 1978.

PERSKY, Stan

The day
Varney, Ed. WCR 10(2):50-1, 1975.

Slaves
Giangrande, Carole. "Poetry of bondage." Open letter 3d ser, 2:98-9, 1975.

Wrestling the angel
David, Jack. Fiddlehead 118:169, 1978.

Fraser, Keath. "The pain of its own rejection." ECW 11:284-8, 1978.

PHILLIPS, Bluebell S.

The plate glass sky
Booth, Luella Kerr. "Five book reviews." OV 8(3):n.p., 1972.

Selected poems
Linder, Norma West. "Some better than others." CA&B 52(4):44, 1977.

PHILLIPS, David

The coherence
Barbour, Douglas. CanL 52:77-81.

Wave
Barbour, Douglas. DR 50:435, 1970.

Barbour, Douglas. "Play in the western world." CanL 52:77-81, 1972.

PICHÉ, Alphonse

General
Smith, Donald. "Alphonse Piché. Un poète qui nous est rendu." Lettres qué 2:34-7, 1976.

Poèmes (1946-1968)
Dionne, René. UTQ 46:382, 1977.

Gaulin, André. LAQ 1976:151-3.

PILON, Jean-Guy

   General
      Bonenfant, Joseph. "Lumière et violence dans la poésie de Jean-Guy
      Pilon." EF 6:79-90. 1970.

      Cloutier, Cécile. "L'influence de quelques poètes français sur
      quelques poètes québécois." PFr 9:44-51, 1974.

      Marcotte, Gilles. EF 6:228-30, 1970.

      Marcotte, Gilles. "Jean-Guy Pilon, poète." Liberté 95-6:54-5, 1974.

      Rancourt, Jacques. "Comme eau retenue: Jean-Guy Pilon." Brindeau
      1973:577-84.

   Cloîtres de l'été
      Maugey, Axel. "Jean-Guy Pilon." Maugey 1972:164-71.

   Saisons pour la continuelle
      Major, Jean-Louis. UTQ 39:426-7, 1970.

   Silences pour une souveraine
      Mailhot, Laurent. LAQ 1972:164.

      Marcotte, Gilles. EF 9:84-5, 1973.

PITTMAN, Al

   Once when I was drowning
      Gatenby, Greg. "Poetry chronicle." TamR 77&78:77-94, 1979.

      Linder, Norma West. "Tales well told." CA&B 54(1):34, 1978.

      Moritz, A.F. "Lost glories, found clichés." BiC 8(1):14, 1979.

      Trethewey, Eric. Fiddlehead 123:111-2, 1979.

   Seaweed and rosaries
      Ditsky, John. CF 49:270-1, 1970.

PLAMONDON, Luc

   General
      Ducharme, André. "Mosaique express--Luc Plamondon ce parolier
      caméléon." Châtelaine 15:16, 1974.

PLANTOS, Ted

    General
      Johnson, Valerie Miner. "Keeping watch on Cabbagetown: poet of the
      street." SatN 87(7):23-6, 1972.

    The light is on my shoulder
      Amprimoz, Alexandre L. Quarry 26(4):70, 1977.

      Barbour, Douglas. "Canadian poetry chronicle: VI." DR 58:555-78,
      1978.

    The universe ends at Sherbourne & Queen: poems and prose
      Dunlop, Donna. Q&Q 44(2):44, 1978.

      Jewinski, Ed. "The poet as locksmith." PTor 28:n.p., 1978.

      Tidler, Charles. "'Ted Plantos' Cabbagetown chaos." CVII 4(2):50-2,
      1979.

PLOURDE, Marc

    The white magnet
      Beardsley, Doug. "A trial of immortality: recent Canadian poetry."
      Nj 6:118-27, 1976.

      Breakey, Al. Alive 34:9, 1974.

      Cameron, A.A. Brick 1:44-5, 1977.

      Crawford, Terry. Quarry 23(1):78-9, 1974.

      Mayne, Seymour. "Other Montrealers." CanL 64:98-101, 1975.

POLSON, Don

    Brief evening in a Catholic hospital and other poems
      Barbour, Douglas. QQ 80:141-2, 1973.

      Marcellin, Philip. Alive 34:22, 1974.

      Ricou, Laurence R. HAB 25:279, 1974.

    Wakening
      Barnes, W.J. Quarry 21(2):67-70, 1972.

      Van den Hoven, A. "Two Windsor poets: Len Gasparini & Don Polson."
      Alive 21:4-5, 1972.

PONTAUT, Alain

Le tour du lac
Lacroix, Pierre. LAQ 1971:158.

PONTBRIAND, Jean-Noël

Les eaux conjuguées
Wyczynski, Paul. LAQ 1974:133-4.

L'envers du cri
Henchiri, Sliman. LAQ 1972:176.

Étreintes
Cloutier, Cécile. LAQ 1976:169-70.

La saison élatée
Wyczynski, Paul. LAQ 1974:133-4.

Transgressions
Gaudet, Gérald. LAQ 1979:160-1.

Nepveu, Pierre. "Du corps et de quelques poètes." Lettres qué 16:21-3, 1979-80.

POOLE, N.

Halfway to the factory
Barbour, Douglas. "Canadian poetry chronicle:III." DR 56:560-73, 1976.

Jewinski, Ed. Q&Q 42(1):25, 1976.

POWELL, Craig

General
Stephen, Sid. "An overheard conversation." CVII 2(4):40-1, 1976.

Rehearsal for dancers
Barbour, Douglas. "Canadian poetry chronicle:VI." DR 58:555-78, 1978.

Dempster, Barry. Q&Q 44(13):14, 1978.

Folsom, Eric. Quarry 28(1):81-5, 1979.

Macfarlane, David. "To fall is not to finish." BiC 8(2):25, 1979.

POZIER, Bernard

À l'aube dans l'dos
Roy, Max. LAQ 1977:130-2.

Code d'oubli
Corriveau, Hugues. LAQ 1978:94-6.

Double tram
Haeck, Philippe. LAQ 1979:169.

Manifeste: Jet/Usage/Résidu
Fisette, Jean. "Parutions récentes: de Desrochers aux Écrits des forges." V&I 3:497-500, 1978.

Nepveu, Pierre. "La poésie qui se fait et celle qui ne se fait pas." Lettres qué 9:15-7, 1978.

PRATT, Charles

Day hunt
Rogers, Linda. "Three trails." BiC 1(11):28-9, 1972.

PRATT, E.J.

Bibliography
Laasko, Lila. "E.J. Pratt: a preliminary checklist." CLJ 34(4):273-94, 1977.

General
Birbalsingh, Frank. "The tension of his time." CanL 64:75-82, 1975.

Broad, Margaret. The nature of the evolution of man in relation to the problem of immortality in the poetry of E.J. Pratt. Montréal, McGill Univ., 1975. (M.A. thesis.)

Buitenhuis, Peter. "E.J. Pratt." Staines 1977:46-68.

Clark, James Murray. E.J. Pratt and the will to believe: an examination of his unpublished Clay and his poetry. Fredericton: Univ. of New Brunswick, 1971, c1972. (M.A. thesis.)

Clever, Glenn, ed. The E.J. Pratt symposium. Ottawa, Univ. of Ottawa Press, 1977. (Re-appraisals: Canadian writers.)

268

PRATT, E.J.

General (cont'd.)
Clever, Glenn. On E.J. Pratt. Ottawa: Borealis Press, 1977.

Collins, Robert G. "E.J. Pratt: the Homeric voice." RNL 7:83-109, 1976.

Davey, Frank. "E.J. Pratt: apostle of corporate man." CanL 43:54-66, 1970. (Also Woodcock 1974b:1-13.)

Davey, Frank. "E.J. Pratt: rationalist technician." CanL 61:65-78, 1974.

Djwa, Sandra. "Canadian poets and the great tradition." CanL 65:42-52, 1975.

Djwa, Sandra. "E.J. Pratt and the evolutionary thought: towards an eschatology." DR 52:414-26, 1972.

Djwa, Sandra. E.J. Pratt: the evolutionary vision. Toronto: Copp Clark, 1974. (Studies in Canadian literature.)

Djwa, Sandra. "Litterae ex machina." HAB 25:22-31, 1974.

Dudek, Louis. "E.J. Pratt: poet of the machine age." Dudek 1978:116-21. (Originally published TamR 6:74-80, 1958.)

Gibbs, Robert J. Aspects of irony in the poetry of E.J. Pratt. Fredericton: Univ. of New Brunswick, 1970, c1971. (Ph.D. thesis.)

Marshall, Tom. "The major Canadian poets: E.J. Pratt." CF 57(675):19-21, 1977.

Marshall, Tom. "Weather: E.J. Pratt." Marshall 1979:34-40.

Mensch, Fred. Aspects of heroism and evolution in some poems by E.J. Pratt. Burnaby, B.C.: Simon Fraser Univ., 1972. (M.A. thesis.)

O'Flaherty, Patrick. "E.J. Pratt and Newfoundland/1882-1907." O'Flaherty 1979:111-26.

Pratt, Mildred Claire. The silent ancestors: the forebears of E.J. Pratt. Toronto: McClelland and Stewart, 1971.

Smith, A.J.M. "A garland for E.J. Pratt:1958." Smith 1977:81-5. (Originally published Table ronde 6:66-71, 1958.)

Sproxton, Bird E. "E.J. Pratt as psychologist, 1919-1920." CN&Q 14:7-9, 1974.

Stonehewer, Lila. An interpretation of symbols in the work of E.J. Pratt. Montreal: McGill Univ., 1970. (M.A. thesis.)

PRATT, E.J.

General (cont'd)
Sutherland, John. "E.J. Pratt: application for a grant." Sutherland 1972:172-7.

Thorpe, John B.M. <u>Man and religion in the poetry of E.J. Pratt.</u> Montréal: McGill Univ., 1970. (M.A. thesis.)

Whalley, George. "Birthright to the sea: some poems of E.J. Pratt." QQ 85:578-94, 1978.

Collected poems
Sutherland, John. "Newfoundland attitudes." Sutherland 1972:166-9.

Still life and other verse
Sutherland, John. "E.J. Pratt's right-hand punch." Sutherland 1972:164-5.

The witches' brew
Djwa, Sandra. "Milton and the Canadian folk tradition: some aspects of E.J. Pratt's <u>The witches' brew.</u>" LHY 13(2):56-71, 1972.

Gibbs, Robert. "Poet of apocalypse." CanL 70:32-42, 1976.

"Brébeuf and his brethren"
Djwa, Sandra. "The civil polish of the horn: E.J. Pratt's 'Brébeuf and his brethren'." Ariel 4(3):82-102, 1973.

Hunt, Peter R. <u>Two Catholic epics of the twentieth century: James McAuley's "Captain Quiros" and E.J. Pratt's "Brébeuf and his brethren."</u> Fredericton: Univ. of New Brunsick, 1975, c1976. (M.A. thesis.)

Innis, Kenneth. "'The history of the frontier like a saga': Parkman, Pratt, and the Jesuit enterprise." Lewis 1977:179-88.

"Clay"
Gibbs, Robert. "A knocking in the clay." CanL 55:50-64, 1973.

"The great feud"
Gibbs, Robert. "Poet of apocalypse." CanL 70:32-42, 1976.

"Towards the last spike"
Cole, Wayne. "The railroad in Canadian literature." CanL 77:124-130, 1978.

Middlebro', Tom. "A commentary on the opening lines of E.J. Pratt's 'Towards the last spike.'" SCL 1(1976):242-43.

New, William H. "The identity of articulation: Pratt's 'Towards the last spike'." LHY 13(2);137-48, 1972. (Also New 1972:32-42.)

Sutherland, John. "Ironic balance." Sutherland 1972:169-72.

PRATT, E.J.

"The witches' brew"
Macpherson, Jay. Pratt's romantic mythology: "The witches' brew."
St. John's, Nfld.: Memorial Univ., 1972. (The Pratt Lecture, 1972.)

PRÉFONTAINE, Yves

A l'orée des travaux.
Major, Jean-Louis. "Déclin ou renouveau d'une poésie du pays?"
Savard 1977:205-15.

Sanderson, Gertrude Kearns and Rens, Jean-Guy. AntigR 1(4):104-5,
1971.

Débâcle
Lafleur, Louis. LAQ 1970:138.

Major, Jean-Louis. "Déclin ou renouveau d'une poésie du pays?"
Savard 1977:205-15.

Marcotte, Gilles. EF 8:97-8, 1972.

Pageau, René. "Préfontaine--Marsolais--Dumont." ActN 60:865-71,
1971.

Sanderson, Gertrude Kearns and Rens, Jean-Guy. AntigR 1(4):104-5,
1971.

Pays sans parole
Pageau. René. "Préfontaine--Marsolais--Dumont." ActN 60:865-71,
1971.

Maugey, Axel. "Yves Préfontaine." Maugey 1972:183-91.

PREWETT, Frank

General
Precosky, Donald. "Frank Prewett: a Canadian Georgian poet." SCL
4(2):132-6, 1979.

Thorpe, Michael. "Frank Prewett: a Canadian among the Georgians."
FDP 2:181-94, 1979.

PRICE, E. Carmie

The state of the union
Gow, Patricia. WCR 8(1):59-60, 1973.

PROVENCHER, Jean

Douleur du fragment
Paradis, Suzanne. "Écrits des forges." LAQ 1975:125-6.

Les sangles
Émond, Maurice. LAQ 1974:135-6.

Michon, Jacques. "Surréalisme et modernité." EF 11:121-9, 1975.

PURDY, Al

General
Bowering, George. Al Purdy. Toronto: Copp Clark, 1970. (Studies in Canadian literature, 6.)

Bowering, George. "Purdy: man and poet." CanL 43:24-35, 1970.

Buri, S.G. and Enright, Robert. "Selection from an interview with Al Purdy... on November 11, 1975, in Winnipeg." CVII 2(1):50-8, 1976.

Cohn-Sfetcu, Ofelia. "The privilege of finding an opening in the past: Al Purdy and the tree of experience." QQ 83:262-9, 1976.

Cohn-Sfetcu, Ofelia. "To live in abundance of life: time in Canadian literature." CanL 76:25-36, 1978.

Doyle, Mike. "Proteus at Robin Lake." CanL 61:7-23, 1974. (Also Woodcock 1974b:92-109.)

Lee, Dennis. "Rejoinder." SatN 87(9):30-3, 1972.

Lee, Dennis. "Running and dwelling: homage to Al Purdy." SatN 87(7):14-6, 1972.

Lye, John. "The road to Ameliasburg." DR 57:242-53, 1977.

Marshall, Tom. "Space and ancestors: Al Purdy." Marshall 1979:89-98.

Mathews, Robin. "Rejoinder." SatN 87(9):30-3, 1972.

Miller, Susan Marlis. Myth in the poetry of A.W. Purdy. Kingston, Ont.: Queens Univ., 1971. (M.A. thesis.)

Purdy, Al. "The ego has it both ways: poets in Montreal." Nj 7&8:127-47, 1976.

Reigo, Ants. "The Purdy poem." CanL 79:127-31.

Tihanyi, Eva. "An excerpt from an interview with Al Purdy, Spring, 1976." PTor 25:n.p., 1978.

PURDY, Al

At Marsport drugstore

Brook, David. "Amorous Al on his ambling pad." BiC 7(7):23, 1978.

Dempster, Barry. Q&Q 44(10):12, 1978.

Trethewey, Eric. "Praising water and friendship, praising love." Fiddlehead 121:146-8, 1979.

Being alive: poems 1958-78

Barbour, Douglas. "Canadian poetry chronicle: VII." DR 59:154-75, 1979.

Fetherling, Doug. "Al Purdy's obsessive search for roots." SatN 93(9):68-70, 1978.

Gasparini, Len. "Of imagination all compact." BiC 7(10):36-7, 1978.

Gatenby, Greg. "Poetry chronicle." TamR 77&78:77-94, 1979.

Pyke, Linda. "New works from three seasoned poets." Q&Q 44(13):8, 1978.

Trethewey, Eric. "Praising water and friendship, praising love." Fiddlehead 121:146-8, 1979.

A handful of earth

Barbour, Douglas. "Canadian poetry chronicle: VI." DR 58:555-78, 1978.

Farmiloe, Dorothy. Q&Q 43(16):9-10, 1977.

Lemm, Richard. Quarry 27(2):90-2, 1978.

Plantos, Ted. "Mandel's past, Colombo's candy, Purdy's earth." BiC 7(2):16-7, 1978.

Trethewey, Eric. "Praising water and friendship, praising love." Fiddlehead 121:146-8, 1979.

Woodcock, George. "Sibyls and other Greeks." CVII 3(4):6-7, 1978.

Hiroshima poems

Barbour, Douglas. Q&Q 39(1):11, 1973.

Pokorny, Amy. Quarry 22(2):75-6, 1973.

Warkentin, Germaine. "Drifting to oblivion." CanL 56:121-2, 1973.

PURDY, Al

In search of Owen Roblin

Bagchee, Shyamal. "Two poets and a half." ECW 3:65-9, 1975.

Cameron, Barry. "The motive for fiction." CF 54 (647):47-8, 1975.

David, Jak. Q&Q 49(10)24, 1974.

Dragland, Stan. Fiddlehead 110:138-42, 1976.

Gervais, C.H. "In search of the Canadian documentary." Alive 42:41, 1975.

Gibbs, Robert. "Presiding voices: Purdy, Layton and Gustafson." DR 56:356-65, 1976.

Gutteridge, Don. QQ 82:139-40, 1975.

Hornyansky, Michael. UTQ 44:330, 1975.

Keitner, Wendy. HAB 27:74-5, 1976.

Levenson, Christopher. "Origins and lemons." BiC 3(8):26-7, 1974.

Sandler, Linda. "Purdy on Owen Roblin." TamR 65:98-100, 1975.

Woodcock, George. "Purdy's prelude and other poems." CanL 64:92-8, 1975.

Love in a burning building

Atwood, Margaret. "Love is ambiguous... sex is a bully." CanL 49:71-5, 1971.

Barbour, Douglas. DR 51:289-90, 1971.

Helwig, David. Quarry 20(2):56-7, 1971.

Hornyansky, Michael. UTQ 40:379-80, 1971.

Wainwright, Andy. "Love, flesh and Al Purdy." SatN 85(9):36, 1970.

North of summer

Turner, Gordon P. "The breath of Arctic men: the Eskimo north in poetry from within and without." QQ 83:130-35, 1976.

On the Bearpaw Sea

Woodcock, George. "Purdy's prelude and other poems." CanL 64:92-8, 1975.

Poems for all the Annettes

Dudek, Louis. "A load of new books: Smith, Webb, Miller/Souster, Purdy, Nowlan." Dudek 1978:168-74. (Originally published Delta 20:27-32, 1963.)

PURDY, Al

<u>The poems of Al Purdy</u>
   Harvey, Roderick W. Q&Q 42(7):41, 1976.

<u>Selected poems</u>
   Aide, William. Quarry 22(1):66-70, 1973.

   Almon, Bert. New 24:58-9, 1973.

   Helwig, David. "Four poets." QQ79:404-7, 1972.

   Keyes, Mary. CF 52(617):42-3, 1972.

   Mundwiler, Leslie. Open letter 2d ser, 3:75-8, 1972.

   Sherman, Joseph. Fiddlehead 94:120-2, 1972.

   Shucard, Alan R. WLWE 11(2):106-8, 1972.

   Stevens, Peter. "The Beowulf poet is alive and well." CanL 55:99-102, 1973.

   Weaver, Robert. "A radical romantic." BiC 1(11);16-7, 1972.

<u>Sex and death</u>
   Barbour, Douglas. Q&Q 39(8):12, 1973.

   Bowering, George. "Suitcase poets." CanL 61:95-100, 1974.

   Cameron, Barry. "The motive for fiction." CF 54(647):47-8, 1975.

   Lawrence, Karen. "And so it goes..." White pelican 4(1):51-3, 1974.

   Levenson, Christopher. QQ 81:318-20, 1974.

   Liman, Claude G. "Flight from silence." LURev 7(1):113-9, 1974.

   Musgrave, Susan. MHRev 31:162-3, 1974.

   Stevens, Peter. "The perils of majority." UWR 9(2):100-9, 1974.

   Sutherland, Fraser. "Purdy's wordy." BiC 2(4):4-5, 1973.

   Woodcock, George. "Savoring love and life in sex and death." Maclean's 87(2):80, 1974.

PURDY, Al

Sundance at dusk
Barbour, Douglas. "Poetry chronicle IV." DR 57:355-71, 1977.

Jewinski, Ed. Q&Q 42(17):30, 1976.

McFadden, David. QQ 84:687-8, 1977.

McKay, Don. "Two voices: Purdy and Bowering." UWR 13(1):99-104, 1977.

Scobie, Stephen. Fiddlehead 114:138-40, 1977.

Wayman, Tom. "Let's hear it for the Big P." BiC 5(10):22-4, 1976.

West, David S. "Purdy." Brick 4:52, 1978.

PYKE, Linda

Prisoner
Aubert, Rosemary. Q&Q 44(13):14, 1978.

Barbour, Douglas. "Canadian poetry chronicle: VII." DR 59:154-75, 1979.

Gatenby, Greg. "Poetry chronicle." TamR 77&78:77-94, 1979.

Marshall, Tom. "The lady and the convict." CF 58(686):45, 1979.

McFadden, Dave. "Of newts and natural gold." BiC 8(1):14-5, 1979.

Saunders, Leslie. Quarry 28(1):78-80, 1979.

RACINE, Jean-E.

Poèmes posthumes (1958-1969)
Bouvier, Luc. LAQ 1977:168-70.

Gaulin, André, "Amis d'exil de ce monde caduc." QuéFr 28:58, 1977.

Recurt, Myriam. "L'ame et l'abolu." CanL 80:98-100, 1979.

RACINE, Luc

Les jours de mai
Bélanger, Yrénée. LAQ 1971:153.

Major, Jean-Louis. UTQ 41:347-8, 1972.

RACINE, Luc

    Opus I
      Major, Jean-Louis. UTQ 39:432-3, 1970.

    Villes
      Dionne, René. "Où va notre poésie?" Relations 357:55-7, 1971.

      Lapointe, Gatien. LAQ 1970:134-5.

      Marcotte, Gilles. EF 7:112, 1971.

RAINIER, Lucien

    Voir/see MELANÇON, Joseph-Marie)

RANCOURT, Jacques

    La journée est bien partie pour durer
      Pontbriand, Jean-Noel. "Poètes québécois publiés en France." LAQ
      1975:134-7.

RAPOPORT, Janis

    Jeremy's dream
      Bird, A.L. Q&Q 40(7):20-1, 1974.

      Julian, Marilyn. Quarry 23(4):72-4, 1974.

      Livesay, Dorothy. CVII 1(2):37, 1975.

      Marcellin, Phil. Alive 35:9, 1974.

      Scott, Chris. "Name tactics." BiC 3(3):14,17, 1974.

    Winter flowers
      Aubert, Rosemary. Q&Q 45(11):11, 1979.

      Linder, Norma West. "Voices of character." CA&B 54(4):30-1, 1979.

RAPPAPORT, Henry

    Dream surgeon
      Newton, Stuart. "Review." Event 7(1):139-42, 1978.

RASHLEY, R.E.

Rock painter
Brown, Allan. "Playing poets: five from Turnstone Press." Waves 8(1):67-71, 1979.

Folsom, Eric. Quarry 28(1):81-5, 1979.

REANEY, James

General
Cowan, Doris. "With Reaney eyes." BiC 7(5):18-21, 1978.

Dudek, Louis. "A problem of meaning." CanL 59:16-29, 1974.

Nichol, bp "Letter re James Reaney." Open letter 2d ser, 6:5-7, 1973.

Woodman, Ross. James Reaney. Toronto: McClelland and Stewart, c1971. (Canadian writers, 12.)

Poems
Atwood, Margaret. "Reaney collected." CanL 57:113-7, 1973. (Also Woodcock, 1974b:151-8.)

Bradbury, Maureen. Q&Q 39(2):13, 1973.

Doerksen, Daniel. W. Fiddlehead 94:120-1, 1973.

Estok, Michael. DR 53:383-7, 1973.

Helwig, David. QQ 81:482-3, 1974.

Hornyansky, Michael. UTQ 42:375-6, 1973.

Watt, F.W. CF 53(631):32-3, 1973.

Wolfe, Morris. "Just sigh and turn the pages quickly." SatN 88(3):34-5, 1973.

The red heart and other poems
Blyth, Molly. "James Reaney's poetic in The red heart." ECW 2:2-8, 1975.

Sutherland, John. "James Reaney: pell-mell rhythms and wopsical assonance." Sutherland 1972:147-53.

REANEY, James

   Selected longer poems
      Fletcher, Peggy. "One down, two to go." CA&B 52(4):43, 1977.

      Macpherson, Jay. "A hairy time in old Baldoon." BiC 6(5):19-20, 1977.

      Stuewe, Paul. Q&Q 43(3):12, 1977.

   Selected shorter poems
      Barbour, Douglas. "Canadian poetry chronicle 2." DR 55:748-59, 1975-76.

      Barnes, Elizabeth A. Quarry 24(4):76-7, 1975.

      Dunlop, Donna. QQ 84:127-8, 1977.

      Evans, J.A.S. Q&Q 42(2):44-5, 1976.

      Quickenden, Robert. "Passing into source." CVII 2(1):11-12, 1976.

      Sandler, Linda. "James Reaney's poetic hall of mirrors." SatN 90(6):83-5, 1975.

REED, John R.

   Hercules
      Hornyansky, Michael. UTQ 43:360-1, 1974.

RENAUD-LEDUC, Thérèse

   General
      Renaud, Thérèse. Une mémoire déchirée: récit. Montréal: H.M.H., 1978. (L'arbre.)

   Les sables du rêve
      Bourassa, André-G. "Poésie automatiste: poésie surréaliste." LAQ 1975:104-6.

      Haeck, Philippe et Savary, Claire. "Le rire de la reine." V&I 2:13-9, 1976.

RENY, Roger

   Sous le masque de la vérité
      Gallays, François. LAQ 1972:178-9.

RIDDELL, John

Criss-cross: a textbook of modern composition
Levy, Eric P. "Strategies." CanL 82:89-91, 1979.

RIEL, Louis

Poésies de jeunesse
Bouvier, Luc. LAQ 1978:144-5.

Thério, Adrien. "À retenir pour vos lectures." Lettres qué 12:55, 1978.

"Incendium"
Flanagan, Thomas and Yardley, John. "Louis Riel as a Latin poet." HAB 26:33-45, 1975.

RIKKI (Erica Ducornet)

From the star chamber
Enright, Robert. "Voices from a hungry centre." CVII 1(2);32-3, 1975.

McCarthy, Dermot. Brick 1:28-9, 1977.

Knife notebook
Barbour, Douglas. "Poetry chronicle V." DR 58:149-69, 1978.

Hamel, Guy. "Recent Fiddlehead poetry books." Fiddlehead 118:137-45, 1978.

Weird sisters
Broten, Delores. "Inter medias res." ECW 9:94-6, 1977/78.

RINGROSE, Christopher Xerxes

Western reunion
Struthers, Carolyn. OV 7(2):n.p., 1971.

RIOUX, Hélène

Finitudes
Paradis, Suzanne. LAQ 1972:183.

RIVARD, Yvon

Frayère
Rivard, Yvon. "De l'image au poème." Liberté 110:35-6, 1977.

ROBB, Wallace Havelock

The Tyrian quill
Stanley, George F.G.   QQ 77:296-7, 1970.

ROBERT, Guy

Québec se meurt
Major, Jean-Louis.   UTQ 39:428, 1970.

Textures
Giroux, Robert.   LAQ 1976:143-4.

ROBERTS, Charles G.D.

General
Adams, John Coldwell. "Sir Charles G.D. Roberts' later poetry, 1926-1942." JCP 1(2);43-58, 1978.

Gibbs, Robert. "Voice and persona in Carman and Roberts." MacKinnon 1977:56-76.

Keith, W.J. "A choice of worlds: God, man and nature in Charles G.D. Roberts." Woodcock 1974:87-102.

Mallinson, Jean. "Kingdom of absence." CanL 67:31-8, 1976.

Marshall, Tom. "Mountaineers and swimmers." CanL 72:21-8, 1977. (Also Marshall 1979:9-16.)

Mathews, Robin. "Charles G.D. Roberts and the destruction of Canadian imagination." JCF 1(1);47-56, 1972.

McMullen, Lorraine. "The poetry of earth: a note on Roberts' sonnets." SCL 1:247-53, 1976.

Rogers, A. Robert. "American recognition of Bliss Carman and Sir Charles G.D. Roberts." HAB 22(2);19-25, 1971.

The selected poems of Sir Charles G.D. Roberts (Ed. Desmond Pacey.)
Chalmers, John W.   CA&B 50(2);27, 1974.

MacKendrick, Louis K.   Q&Q 40(6):12, 1974.

Marchand, Blaine. "Landscape of a leader." CanR 1(4);26, 1974.

ROBERTS, Charles G.D.

Selected poetry and critical prose (Ed. W.J. Keith.)
Steele, Charles. Ariel 6(3);101-2, 1975.

Woodcock, George. "A magic house of ice." CanL 61:113-5, 1974.

"The pipes of Pan"
Bentley, D.M.R. "Pan and the Confederation poets." CanL 81:59-71, 1979.

"The sower"
Jackel, David. "A rejoinder." Compass 7:73-4, 1979.

Mathews, Robin. "Charles G.D. Roberts reconsidered." Compass 7:69-72, 1979.

ROBERTS, Dorothy

The self of loss: new and selected poems
Brown, Allan. "3 Fiddlehead books." Brick 3:12-4, 1978.

Gibbs, Robert. Fiddlehead 113:138-42, 1977.

Hornyansky, Michael. UTQ 46:372-3, 1977.

Jones, Elizabeth. "The pleasures of innocence." CVII 3(4);3-5, 1978.

Mallinson, Jean. "Poetry miscellany." ECW 7/8:151-8, 1977.

Ware, Martin. DR 56:780-4, 1976-77.

ROBERTS, Kevin

Deep line
Lane, M. Travis. Fiddlehead 120:133-6, 1979.

West country
Almon, Bert. WCR 11(2):41, 1976.

Barbour, Douglas. "Canadian poetry chronicle: III." DR 56:560-73, 1976.

ROCHETTE, Pierre

Je t'attends au café Saint-Vincent
Le Bel, Michel. LAQ 1974:140-1.

ROGERS, Linda

Music for moondance
McCarthy, Dermot. Brick 1:29, 1977.

Thompson, Eric. "Plain and fantasy." CanL 65:101-4, 1975.

Some breath
Gasparini, Len. "Chips, nuts, and wafers." BiC 5(3):18, 1976.

Gotlieb, Phyllis. QQ 84:332, 1977.

Novak, Barbara. Quarry 25(3):74-5, 1976.

Rogers, Linda. "Life and claustrophobia." CanL 75:88-90, 1977.

ROSEBERG, Rose

Trips--without LSD
Cameron, Allen Barry. CF 50:311, 1970.

ROSENBERG, David

Leavin America
Rogers, Linda. "Medium or magician." CanL 62:121-4, 1974.

Stucky, David. Q&Q 39(4):10, 1973.

Paris & London
Gervais, C.H. Quarry 22(2):78, 1973.

A star in my hair
Coleman, Victor. "Jumbo's Victorian charm." Open letter 2d ser.,
1:63-5, 1971/72.

ROSENBLATT, Joe

General
Stenbaek-Lafon, Marianne and Norris, Ken. "An interview with Joe
Rosenblatt." CVII 4(1):32-7, 1979.

Blind photographer
Bradbury, Maureen. Q&Q 39(5):27, 1973.

ROSENBLATT, Joe

Bumblebee dithyramb
  Barbour, Douglas. "Petit four." BiC 1(11):19, 1972.

  Garnet, Eldon. Open letter 2d ser, 3:87-8, 1972.

  McNamara, Eugene. "The vatic upsurge." CanL 58:104-6, 1973.

  Rhind, P.E. Q&Q 38(11):11, 1972.

Dream craters
  Barbour, Douglas. "The poets and presses revisited: circa 1974." DR
  55:338-60, 1975.

  Dault, Gary Michael. "Garnet and other glows." BiC 4(2):24-5, 1975.

  Fletcher, Peggy. CA&B 50(4):26-7, 1975.

  Gutteridge, Don. Brick 1:20-1, 1977.

  Safarik, Allan. "Charting the sea of tranquility." CanR 2(1);33-4,
  1975.

  Thomas, Peter. "Contrasting virtues." CanL 70:106-7, 1976.

  Watt, F.W. "Why poetry? Eleven answers." CF 55(651):40-1, 1975.

Loosely tied hands: an experiment in punk
  Brown, Allan. "Black moss: six offerings." Waves 7(2):68-71, 1979.

  Norris, Ken. "Land eels and illogical ghazals." BiC 7(7):20-1, 1978.

  Pearson, Ian. Q&Q 44(10):12, 1978.

Top soil
  Amprimoz, Alexandre. "Dusted inside." CanL 82:99-101, 1979.

  Barbour, Douglas. "Poetry chronicle V." DR 58:149-69, 1978.

  Dault, Gary Michael. "Where the bee trucks, there trucks he." BiC
  6(6):16-7, 1977.

  Elson, Brigid. QQ 84:690-1, 1977.

  Fiamengo, Marya. "Canadian Aesop." CF 57(672):57, 1977.

  Hamilton, Jamie. Q&Q 43(1):31-2, 1977.

  Murray, Paul. Waves 5(2/3):124-5, 1977.

  Novak, Barbara. Quarry 26(3):85-6, 1977.

  Rapoport, Janis. "Metaphysics in concert." TamR 72:91-2, 1977.

  Sherman, Joe. Fiddlehead 117:139-40, 1978.

ROSENBLATT, Joe

Virgins & vampires
Barbour, Douglas. "Canadian poetry chronicle 2." DR 55:748-59, 1975-76.

Beardsley, Doug. "War and other measures." CVII 2(1):21, 1976.

David, Jack. Q&Q 41(10:19, 1975.

CanR 2(4):55, 1975.

Gasparini, Leonard. "Toading the line." BiC 4(11):22, 1975.

Gatenby, Greg. "On Virgins & vampires." TamR 70:88-91, 1977.

Greenglass, E.E. "I's and eyes." CanL 71:92-5, 1976.

Millage, Craig. Brick 2:23-5, 1978.

ROSENTHAL, Helene

Listen to the old mother
Barbour, Douglas. "Canadian poetry chronicle: III." DR 56:560-73, 1976.

Hamilton, Jamie. "Women." CanR 3(3):40, 1976.

Jewinski, Ed. Q&Q 42(1):26, 1976.

Marshall, Tom. "Dorothy's daughters: three more Emilys." CVII 2(2):29, 1976.

Rogers, Linda. "That old Carr smell." BiC 4(12):27-8, 1975.

Wayman, Tom. "Mothers, writers, instruments and fathers." UWR 11(2):110-6, 1976.

ROSS, Eustace

The surface and the terror: poetry of Eustace Ross (Eds. Raymond Souster and John Robert Colombo.)
Gerber, Philip L. FPt5:46-54, 1970.

ROSS, W.W.E.

    General
      Arnason, David. "Canadian poetry: the interregnum." CVII 1(1):28-32, 1975.

      Stevens, Peter. "W.W.E. Ross: plus qu'un poète imagiste." Ellipse 20:102-9, 1977. (Tr. George Maclaine Lang.)

      Sutherland, John. "An unpublished introduction to the poetry of W.W.E. Ross." Sutherland 1972:162-4.

ROTSTEIN, Nancy-Gay

    Through the eyes of a woman
      Lever, Bernice. Q&Q 41(10):19, 1975.

ROUSSEAU, Claude

    Les rats aussi ont de beaux yeux
      Dionne, René. "Sur les voies de notre poésie (1)." Relations 366:340-1, 1971.

      Lapointe, Gatien. LAQ 1971:156-7.

ROUTHIER, Adolphe-Basile

    General
      Auclair, Elie J. "L'Hymne national 'O Canada.'" Quebec-histoire 2(2):84-6, 1973.

    "O Canada"
      Auclair, Elie J. "L'Hymne national 'O Canada.'" Quebec-histoire 2(2):84-6, 1973.

ROUTIER, Simone

    General
      O'Donnell, Kathleen. "Dorothy Livesay and Simone Routier: a parallel study." HAB 23(4):28-37, 1972.

      Pageau, René. "Simone Routier poète de l'espérance." CC-R 4(3):53-8, 1976.

      Pageau, René. "La voix de Simone Routier." CC-R 6(3):63-75, 1978.

ROUTIER, Simone

Ceux qui seront aimés
  Pageau, René. "Simone Routier poète de l'espérance." CC-R 4(3):53-8, 1976.

ROWE, Terry

General
  Thompson, Valerie. "You've come long way, baby." Q&Q 41(3):4, 1975.

Terry Rowe's moods of love
  Novak, Barbara. Q&Q 43(1):31, 1977.

The warmth of Christmas
  David, Jack. Q&Q 39(12):12, 1973.

ROY, André

Corps qui suivent
  Bonenfant, Joseph. LAQ 1977:178-80.

  Nepveu, Pierre. "La jeune poésie, la critique peut-être..." Lettres qué 6:13-5, 1977.

D'un corps à l'autre
  Nepveu, Pierre. "André Roy: le cinéma en miettes." Lettres qué 4:16-8, 1976.

En image de ça
  Nepveu, Pierre. "André Roy: le cinéma en miettes." Lettres qué 4:16-8, 1976.

L'espace de voir
  Kushner, Éva. "Vers une poésie de la poésie?" LAQ 1974:115-8.

Les passions du samedi
  Corriveau, Hugues. LAQ 1979:161-3.

  Nepveu, Pierre. "Du corps et de quelques poètes." Lettres qué 16:21-3, 1979-80.

Le sentiment du lieu
  Beaudet, André. LAQ 1978:146-7.

Vers mauve
  Giguère, Richard. "Les Herbes rouges: une grande petite revue." LAQ 1975:118-21.

ROY, Jean-Louis

Terre féconde
 Racine, Gaëtan. LAQ 1979:163-4.

ROY, Jean-Yves

À plein corps
 Gallays, François. LAQ 1970:146.

ROYER, Jean

Les heures nues
 Roussan, Wanda de. LAQ 1979:164-5.

Nos corps habitables
 Arcand, Pierre-André. LAQ 1974:145-6.

La parole me vient de ton corps
 Arcand, Pierre-André. LAQ 1974:145-6.

ROYER, Louis

Poésie O
 Caron, Louis. LAQ 1970:149.

RUEBSAAT, Norbert

Cordillera
 Dempster, Barry. Q&Q 45(13):33, 1979.

RUTLAND, Enid Delgatty

The cranberry tree
 Hornyansky, Michael. UTQ 48:350, 1979.

SABELLA, Marcel

Le jour incendié
 Wyczynski, Paul. "Voix québécoises." LAQ 1974:136-8.

SABOURIN, Marcel

Chansons
Bergeron, Bertrand. LAQ 1979:165-6.

SAFARIK, Alan

Selected translations from the text of Okira
Barbour, Douglas. "Poetry chronicle V." DR 58:149-69, 1978.

Fiamengo, Marya. "From a Japanese garden." CVII (2):32-3, 1976.

Johnson, Jane. CA&B 52(1):28, 1976.

MacCulloch, Clare. "Th lly fadth & ltd & haikus to illuminate." BiC 4(11):19-22, 1975.

Novak, Barbara. Quarry 25(4):75-6, 1976.

Sarna, Lazar. "A southwesterner meandering while East meets West." ECW 108-9, 1976.

Stuewe, Paul. Q&Q 41(12):32, 1975.

ST. JACQUES, Elizabeth

Silver sigh & shadows blue
Fletcher, Peggy. "Humour and sadness." CA&B 54(1):36-7, 1978.

SAINT-GERMAIN, André

Chemin de desserte
Le Bel, Michel. LAQ 1973:124-5.

Triptyque
Le Bel, Michel. LAQ 1973:124-5.

SAINT-PIERRE, Madeleine

Emergence
Saint-Amour, Robert. LAQ 1971:165.

SAINT-YVES, Denuis

En débordement de quoi
Corriveau, Hugues. LAQ 1978:94-6.

Mourir s'attendre quelque part
Haeck, Philippe. LAQ 1979:167-8.

SANGSTER, Charles

General
Hamilton, Willis D. Charles Sangster. New York:Twayne, 1971.
(Twayne's world author series: Canada: TWAS 172.)

Stephens, Donald. "Charles Sangster: the end of an era." Woodcock
1974:54-61.

Tierney, Frank M. "The unpublished and revised poems of Charles
Sangster." SCL 2:108-16, 1977.

Hesperus and other poems
Spettigue, D.O. "Literature of Canada series." QQ 81:311-3, 1974.

Walker, Susan. Q&Q 39(4):11, 1973.

The St. Lawrence and the Saguenay and other poems
Spettigue, D.O. "Literature of Canada series." QQ 81:311-3, 1974.

Walker, Susan. Q&Q 39(4):11, 1973.

SARAH, Robyn

Shadowplay
Hornyansky, Michael. UTQ 48:351, 1979.

Stevenson, Warren. "Move over Musgrave." CanL 80:103-4, 1979.

Zonailo, Carolyn. Room of one's own 3(4):42, 1978.

SARNA, Lazar

Letters of state
Aubert, Rosemary. Q&Q 44(16):9, 1978.

Barbour, Douglas. "Canadian poetry chronicle: VII." DR 59:154-75,
1979.

SARNA, Lazar

Letters of state (cont'd.)
Bartlett, Brian. "Crumbs in a plastic bag." BiC 8(2):17, 1979.

Linder, Norma West. "Poetic states of mind." CA&B 54(2):34-5, 1979.

McNally, Paul. Fiddlehead 121:156-7, 1979.

SAVARD, Félix-Antoine

General
Savard, Félix-Antoine. Journal et souvenirs 1961-1964. Montréal: Fides, 1973-75.

Smith, Donald. "Félix-Antoine Savard répond aux questions de notre collaborateur." Lettres qué 3:35-8, 1976.

Smith, Donald. "Hommage à Mgr. Félix-Antoine Savard." RUL 9(1):115-8, 1976.

L'abatis
Blais, Jacques. "La poésie du pays: Félix-Antoine Savard et Rina Lasnier." Blais 1975:269-94.

Aux marges du silence
Pontbriand, Jean-Noel. LAQ 1975:109-10.

Le bouscueil
Lahalle, Bruno André. "Le bouscueil de Félix-Antoine Savard: entre la possession et l'inquiétude." PFr 5:60-6, 1972.

Marcotte, Gilles. EF 9;83, 1973.

Ricard, François. LAQ 1972:150-2.

Carnet du soir intérieur
Bouvier, Luc. LAQ 1979:170-2.

Symphonie du miserior
Drapeau, Jean-Claude. "Les mouvements musicaux dans la Symphonie du miserior de F.-A. Savard." Co-incidences 1(1):20-6, 1971.

SAVOIE, Paul

La maison sans murs
Bouvier, Luc. LAQ 1979:119.

Salamandre
Carpenter, Dave. CVII (1):12-3, 1975.

VieFr. 29:126-7, 1975.

SCHROEDER, Andreas

File of uncertainties.
Gibbs, Robert. Fiddlehead 90:112, 1971.

Purdy, Brian. "Andreas Schroeder at the Axle-Tree." PTor 15:n.p.,
1977.

Shucard, Alan R. WLWE 12(1):59-60, 1973.

The ozone minotaur
Barbour, Douglas. "The young poets and the little presses, 1969." DR
50:112-26, 1970.

Cogswell, Fred. Fiddlehead 83:76-7, 1970.

Shucard, Alan. "The O-Zone and other places." CanL 48:80-2, 1971.

Shaking it rough
Marken, Ronald. Brick 2:4-6, 1978.

SCHWARZ, Herbert T.

Tuktoyaktuk 2-3
Jewinski, Ed. Q&Q 42(1):26, 1976.

SCOBIE, Stephen

The birken tree
Abbey, Lloyd. "Anti-Epic and nostalgia." CanL 63:107-9, 1975.

In the silence of the year
Pivato, Joseph. "Mouth exhausted silence." CanL 52:106-8, 1972.

The rooms we are: poems 1970-1971
Barbour, Douglas. "The poets and presses revisited: circa 1974." DR
55:338-60, 1975.

Brown, Allan. "Two Sono Nis poets." Brick 3:35-6, 1978.

Ditsky, John. "Poetry chronicle." OntR 3:98-104, 1975-76.

Fraser, Keath. Q&Q 41(7):30, 1975.

Mackintosh, Mhari. NL 2:56-8, 1975.

Marshall, Tom. "The mythmakers." CanL 73:100-3, 1977.

Thomas, Peter. Fiddlehead 107:129-30, 1975.

292

SCOTT, Anne Lascelles

The climb: poems
Pyke, Linda Annesley. Q&Q 40(4):21, 1974.

The sun in winter
Novak, Barbara. Quarry 25(3):75, 1976.

Gotlieb, Phyllis. QQ 84:332-3, 1977.

Kishkan, Theresa. "Inside the common sitting room." CVII 2(3):46, 1976.

Smith, Raymond J. "Poetry chronicle." OntR 4:104-10, 1976.

SCOTT, Duncan Campbell

General
Brown, E.K. "Duncan Campbell Scott: a memoir." Brown 1977:112-44. (Originally published Selected poems of Duncan Campbell Scott with a memoir by E.K. Brown 1951:xi-xlii.)

Dagg, Melvin H. "Scott and the Indians." HAB 23(4):3-11, 1972.

Dragland, Stanley Louis, ed. Duncan Campbell Scott: a book of criticism. Ottawa: Tecumseh Press, 1974.

Dragland, Stanley Louis. Forms of imaginative perception in the poetry of Duncan Campbell Scott. Kingston, Ont.:Queen's Univ., 1971. (Ph.D. thesis.)

Geddes, Gary. "A piper of many tunes: Duncan Campbell Scott." Woodcock, 1974:148-60. (Originally published CanL 37:15-27, 1968.)

Kelly, Catherine. "In the listening world: the poetry of Duncan Campbell Scott." SCL 4(1):71-94, 1979.

Marshall, Tom. "Half-breeds: Duncan Campbell Scott." Marshall 1979:23-33.

Marshall, Tom. "The major Canadian poets: between two worlds: Duncan Campbell Scott." CF 57(672):20-4, 1977.

Mezei, Kathy. "D.C. Scott & Pelham Edgar." CN&Q 20:15-6, 1977.

Smith, A.J.M. "The poetry of Duncan Campbell Scott." Smith 1973:79-96.

Stich, K.P. ed. The Duncan Campbell Scott symposium. Ottawa: Univ. of Ottawa Press, 1980. (Re-appraisals: Canadian writers.)

Stow, Glenys. "The wound under the feathers. Woodcock 1974:161-77.

SCOTT, Duncan Campbell

"At Gull Lake: August 1810"
Slonim, Leon. "D.C. Scott's 'At Gull Lake: August 1810.'" CanL 81:142-3, 1979.

"The forsaken"
Beckmann, Susan. "A note on Duncan Campbell Scott's 'The forsaken.'" HAB 25:32-7, 1974.

"The Onondaga madonna"
Bentley, R.D.R. "'The Onondaga madonna': a sonnet of rare beauty." CVII 3(2):28-9, 1977.

"The piper of Arll"
Bentley, D.M.R. "Pan and the Confederation poets." CanL 81:59-71, 1979.

"Powassan's drum"
Cogswell, Fred. "No heavenly harmony: a reading of 'Powassan's Drum'." SCL 1(1976):233-7.

SCOTT, Francis Reginald

General
Brewster, Elizabeth. "The I of the observer: the poetry of F.R. Scott." CanL 79:23-30, 1978.

Dudek, Louis. "F.R. Scott and the modern poets." Dudek 1978:11-23. (Originally published Northern review 4(2):4-15, 1950-51.)

Higginson, M. Constance. "A thematic study of F.R. Scott's evolutionary poetry." JCP 1(1):37-48, 1978.

Marshall, Tom. "Major Canadian poets III: the modernists." CF 58(686):13-7, 1979.

Scobie, Stephen A.C. "The road back to Eden: the poetry of F.R. Scott." QQ 79:314-23, 1972.

Smith, A.J.M. "F.R. Scott and some of his poems." Smith 1973:115-24. (Also Woodcock 1974b: 14-25. Originally published CanL 31:25-35, 1967.)

The dance is one
Bennett, Donna A. "Reunion: contemporary Canadian poetry." LURev 6:236-9, 1973.

Hornyansky, Michael. UTQ 43:352-3, 1974.

Morley, Patricia. Quarry 22(3):77-9, 1973.

Muir, Ann. DR 53:781-3, 1973-74.

SCOTT, Francis Reginald

　　The dance is one (cont'd.)
　　　　Quill, Patricia.　Q&Q 39(6):13, 1973.

　　　　Pacey, Desmond.　Fiddlehead 99:94-6, 1973.

　　　　Purdy, Al.　"The age of F.R. Scott."　BiC 2(3):50-1, 1973.

　　　　Purdy, Al.　WascanaR 8(2):66-8, 1973.

　　　　Scobie, Stephen.　QQ 80:654-5, 1973.

　　　　Stevens, Peter.　"The perils of majority."　UWR 9(2):100-9, 1974.

　　The eye of the needle
　　　　Dudek, Louis.　"The eye of the needle--of no use to camels."　Dudek
　　　　1978:79-82.　(Originally published Delta 1:17-9, 1957.)

　　Selected poems
　　　　Gibson, Audrey.　"Poetic creditor."　BiC 1(10):26, 1972.

SCOTT, Francis Reginald, Tr.

　　Poems of French Canada
　　　　Stratford, Philip.　Q&Q 43(8):42, 1977.

SCRIVER, Stephen

　　Between the lines
　　　　Barbour, Douglas.　"Canadian poetry chronicle: VI."　DR 58:555-78,
　　　　1978.

　　　　Carpenter, David.　"Jock lyricism."　CVII 3(4):39, 1978.

SEMAJA

　　Light morning of the body; an even roll
　　　　Hamilton, Jamie.　Q&Q 41(10):18-9, 1975.

SENIOR, Nancy

　　I never wanted to be the holy ghost
　　　　Carpenter, David.　"Modesty in flight."　CVII 3(2):24-5, 1977.

SENIOR, Nancy

Poems
Barr, Arlee. Alive 39:7, 1974.

Lanczos, Elmar. WCR 9(3):50-1, 1975.

SERVICE, Robert W.

Bibliography
Roberts, F.X. "A bibliography of Robert William Service 1874-1958."
FDP 1:76-85, 1976.

General
Atherton, Stanley S. "The Klondike muse." CanL 47:67-72, 1971.
(Also published Woodcock 1974, 211-6.)

Hirsch, Edward. "A structural analysis of Robert Service's Yukon
ballads." SFQ 40:125-40, 1976.

Klinck, Carl F. Robert Service: a biography. Toronto: McGraw-Hill
Ryerson, 1976.

SHADBOLT, Jack

Mind's I
Klepec, Walter. Q&Q 40(2):11, 1974.

Livesay, Dorothy. "Painter into poet." CanL 60:114-6, 1974.

Olney, Gloria. WCR 8(3):43-5, 1974.

SHERMAN, Joseph

Chaim the slaughterer
Barbour, Douglas. "The poets and presses revisited: circa 1974." DR
55:338-60, 1975.

Dault, Gary Michael. "Garnet and other glows." BiC 4(2):24-5, 1975.

Dragland, Stan. Fiddlehead 104:115-7, 1975.

Thomas, Peter. "Contrasting virtues." CanL 70:106-7, 1976.

Watt, F.W. "Why poetry? Eleven answers." CF 55(651):40-1, 1975.

SHERMAN, Joseph

"The naming of names"
Sherman, Joseph. "From notes for a Jewish poem." Fiddlehead
88:84-93, 1971.

SHERMAN, Kenneth

Snake music
Fletcher, Peggy. "Vision and the personal dark." CA&B 54(4):26-7,
1979.

Daniel, Lorne. "From screen gems to animal acts." BiC 8(4):11-2,
1979.

Johnson, Sam. "The poet's space." Waves 7(2):60-3, 1979.

Sherman, Kenneth. Waves 7(3):75, 1979. (Re review by Johnson in
Waves 7(2):60-3, 1979.)

SHIELDS, Carol

Intersect
Bessai, Diane. "Poetry from Ottawa." CF 55(652):36-8, 1975.

Leigh, Simon. "Two minor talons and a tidal borealis." Fiddlehead
109:128-32, 1976.

Thompson, Eric. "Plain and fantasy." CanL 65:101-4, 1975.

Others
Levenson, Christopher. Quarry 22(4):75-6, 1973.

Zimmerman, Susan. "Musicales." BiC 2(4):27-30, 1973.

SHUMWAY, Mary

Headlands
Bradbury, Maureen. Q&Q 39(3):8, 1973.

SHUTE, Allan

Multimonster in paradise
Gasparini, Leonard. "Applaudeth one in three." BiC 4(11):16-8, 1975.

SICOTTE, Sylvie

Infrajour
Wyczynski, Paul. LAQ 1973:104-6.

Sur la pointe des dents
Savard, Michel. LAQ 1979:172-4.

SIEBRASSE, Glen

Jerusalem
Garnet, Eldon. Open letter 2d ser, 5:121-2, 1973.

Man: unman
Bowering, George. Quarry 19(3):63, 1970.

Thompson, Laurel. "Canadian poetry." UWR 6(1):86-90, 1970.

SKAPSKI, Mieszko Jan

In the meshes
Gibbs, Robert. Fiddlehead 90:113-4, 1971.

SKELTON, Robin

General
Sandler, Linda. "An interview with Robin Skelton." TamR 68:71-85, 1976.

Sandler, Linda. "Robin Skelton at the feast." BiC 4(4):5-6, 1975.

Because of love
Barbour, Douglas. "Poetry chronicle V." DR 58:149-69, 1978.

Coles, Don. "Eros wins but Mercury loses." BiC 6(7):28-9, 1977.

Hamilton, Jamie. Q&Q 43(7):45, 1977.

Jackel, David. "Private enthusiasms." CF 57(673):37-8, 1977.

Malcolm, Ian. Quarry 27(1):75-6, 1978.

SKELTON, Robin

Callsigns
Barbour, Douglas. "Canadian poetry chronicle: VII." DR 59:154-75, 1979.

Coles, Don. "Eros wins but Mercury loses." BiC 6(7):28-9, 1977.

Stuewe, Paul. Q&Q 43(1):31, 1977.

Georges Zuk: the underwear of the unicorn
Barbour, Douglas. "Canadian poetry chronicle:III." DR 56:560-73, 1976.

de Santana, Hubert. "Poetic torrents, erotic jewels." BiC 5(2):36-8, 1976.

Georges Zuk: selected poems
Yates, J. Michael. WascanaR 5(1):102-4, 1970.

The hunting dark
Garnet, Eldon. "Fading resonance." BiC 1(2):22, 1971.

Humes, Harry. Compass (KSC) 4:44-5, 1973.

Hutchinson, Alexander. "Waylaying the muse." CanL 51:78-80, 1972.

Noonan, Gerald. CF 51(612-3):81, 1972.

Musebook
Walker, Susan. Q&Q 39(2):12-3, 1973.

Private speech: messages 1962-70
Gibbs, Robert. Fiddlehead 90:117, 1971.

Hutchinson, Alexander. "Waylaying the muse." CanL 51:78-80, 1972.

Noonan, Gerald. CF 51(612-3):81, 1972.

Selected poems: 1947-1967
McCloskey, Mark. "The slattern muse." FPt 56:55-60, 1970.

Sergeant, Howard. "Poetry review." English 19:29-33, 1970.

Timelight
Abse, Dannie. "Travellings of the soul." TLS 3808:214, 1975.

Evans, J.A.S. Q&Q 41(3):24, 1975.

Hornyansky, Michael. UTQ 44:330-1, 1975.

MacCulloch, Clare. "'The onward journey' of Robin Skelton." AntigR 20:98-103, 1974.

SKELTON, Robin

Timelight (cont'd.)
Mathews, Robin. "Moonlighting in the soul." CF 55(650):64, 1975.

Ringrose, Christopher. "Assorted catch." CanL 71:102-4, 1976.

Sandler, Linda. "Robin Skelton at the feast." BiC 4(4):5-6, 1975.

SLABOTSKY, David

The mind of Genesis
de Santana, Hubert. "Poetic torrents, erotic jewels." BiC 5(2):36-8, 1976.

SLAVUTYCH, Yar

The conquerors of the prairies
Keywan, Zonia. "Ukrainian poetry." CanL 77:113-5, 1978.

SMART, Elizabeth

A bonus
Mallinson, Jean. "Smart's proverbs of hell." ECW 12:134-43, 1978.

SMEDMOR, Gloria

Out of my mind
Powell, Reid. Q&Q 39(2):13, 1973.

SMITH. A.J.M.

General
Darling, Michael. "An interview with A.J.M. Smith." ECW 9:55-61, 1977-78.

Djwa, Sandra. "A.J.M. Smith: métaphysique et squelettes blanchis." Ellipse 22:98-106, 1978. (Tr. Lucie Lemay.)

Djwa, Sandra A. "A.J.M. Smith: of metaphysics and dry bones." SCL 3:17-34, 1978.

Edel, Leon. "The worldly muse of A.J.M. Smith." UTQ 47:200-13, 1978.

Grady, Wayne. "Who is this man Smith?" BiC 7(9):8-11, 1978.

SMITH, A.J.M.

General (cont'd.)
Marshall, Tom. "Major Canadian poets III: the modernists." CF 58(686):13-7, 1979.

Ó Broin, Pádraig. "After strange gods." AntigR 1(1):70-80, 1970.

Rosenthal, M.L. "'Poor innocent': the poetry of A.J.M. Smith." MPS 8:1-13, 1977.

The classic shade: selected poems
Daniells, Roy. "Fringe benefit." CanL 79:74-6, 1978.

Darling, Michael. "Dean of Canadian poets." Waves 7(2):72-4, 1979.

David, Jack. Q&Q 44(7):44, 1978.

Fletcher, Peggy. "The printed page their classroom." CA&B 53(4):42-3, 1978.

Gatenby, Greg. "Poetry chronicle." TamR 77&78:77-94, 1979.

Hornyansky, Michael. UTQ 48:344-5, 1979.

Marshall, Tom. "Keeping up with the Smiths and the Joneses." BiC 7(4):16-7, 1978.

Mullins, Stanley G. UWR 14(1):71-3, 1978.

Collected poems
Dudek, Louis. "A load of new books: Smith, Webb, Miller/Souster, Purdy, Nowlan." Dudek 1978:168-74. (Originally published Delta 20:27-32, 1963.)

News of the phoenix
Brown, E.K. "A.J.M. Smith and the poetry of pride." Brown 1977:83-6. (Originally published Manitoba arts review 3:30-2, 1944.)

SMITH, Dorothy Cameron

Cameos
Salata, Estelle. CA&B 52(1):27, 1976.

Moments with...
Salata, Estelle. CA&B 52(3):41, 1977.

SMITH, Kay

At the bottom of the dark
  Booth, Luella Kerr. "Five book reviews." OV 8(3):n.p., 1972.

When a girl looks down
  Oliver, Michael Brian. "Tantramar- and Saint John and Fredericton-revisited." Fiddlehead 122:115-24, 1979.

SMITH, Steven

General
  Smith, Steven. "Poetics: exploring, exploring." PTor 41:n.p., 1979.

SNYDER, Richard

Mind pobie
  Delmaschio. WCR 9(3):48-9, 1975.

SOLWAY, David

Anacrusis
  Brown, Allan. "3 Fiddlehead books." Brick 3:12-4, 1978.

  Hornyansky, Michael. UTQ 46:371-2, 1977.

  Lane, M. Travis. "Cat and dog." Fiddlehead 111:139-42, 1976.

  Munton, Ann. DR 57:379-80, 1977.

The crystal theatre
  Barbour, Douglas. QQ 79:569-71, 1972.

  Hornyansky, Michael. UTQ 41:338, 1972.

Paximalia
  Barbour, Douglas. QQ 79:569-71, 1972.

  Tierney, Bill. AntigR 12:102-4, 1973.

The road to Arginos
  Barbour, Douglas. "Poetry chronicle V." DR 58:149-69, 1978.

  Bessai, Diane. "Unrepresentative." CF 57(677):50-1, 1977-8.

  Fletcher, Peggy. "One down, two to go." CA&B 52(4):43, 1977.

  Hornyansky, Michael. UTQ 47:355-6, 1978.

SOLWAY, David

The road to Arginos (cont'd.)
Malcolm, Ian. Quarry 26(2):61-3, 1977.

Newton, Stuart. "Poet's effort." CanL 76:113-4, 1978.

Stange, Ken. "Honey and light." CVII 3(3):5-7, 1978.

SOMMER, Richard

Blue sky notebook
Barbour, Douglas. "The poets and presses revisited: circa 1974." DR 55:338-60, 1975.

Lee, Dennis. "The new poets: fresh voices in the land." SatN 88(12):33-5, 1973.

Left hand mind
Barbour, Douglas. "Poetry chronicle V." DR 58:149-69, 1978.

Linder, Norma West. "Some better than others." CA&B 52(4):44, 1977.

Newton, Stuart. "Poet's effort." CanL 76:113-4, 1978.

Milarepa
Barbour, Douglas. "Poetry chronicle V." DR 58:149-69, 1978.

Linder, Norma West. "Some better than others." CA&B 52(4):44, 1977.

Newton, Stuart. "Poet's effort." CanL 76:113-4, 1978.

The other side of games
Linder, Norma West. "Tales well told." CA&B 54(1):34, 1978.

The other side of games
Miles, Ron. "Boxed set." CanL 81:138-9, 1979.

Rogers, Janet and Warland-Van Horne, Betsy. "Mandrake gestures hypnotically..." CVII 4(2):42-5, 1979.

SORESTAD, Glen A.

Pear seeds in my mouth
Barbour, Douglas. "Poetry chronicle V." DR 58:149-69, 1978.

Wind songs
Di Cicco, Pier Giorgio. Q&Q 42(4):25, 1976.

Ricou, Laurence. "Pub songs and wind songs." CVII 2(2):28, 1976.

SOUDEYNS, Maurice

L'orée de l'éternité
Henchiri, Sliman. LAQ 1972:157-8.

La trajectoire
Le Bel, Michel. LAQ 1974:126-7.

SOULE, Lawrence

The eye of the cedar
Ditsky, John. CF 50:405-6, 1971.

Fiamengo, Marya. "Careful and careless." CanL 53:104-5, 1972.

SOUSTER, Raymond

Bibliography
Wood, Karen Margaret. Raymond Souster: a stylistic analysis and a
chronology of poems. Montreal:Sir George Wiliams Univ., 1973. (M.A.
thesis.)

General
Cook, Hugh. "Development in the early poetry of Raymond Souster."
SCL 3:113-8, 1978.

Dudek, Louis. "A load of new books: Smith, Webb, Miller/Souster,
Purdy, Nowlan." Dudek 1978:168-74. (Originally published Delta
20:27-32, 1963.)

Dudek, Louis. "Un siffleux sous les étoiles: la poésie de Raymond
Souster." Ellipse 5:74-90. (Tr. Rodolphe Lacasse.)

Fournier-Ouellet, A. Emile Coderre, Raymond Souster: two poets, two
cultures: similarities and contrasts. Montreal: McGill Univ., 1973,
c1974. (M.A. thesis.)

Geddes, Gary. "A cursed and singular blessing." CanL 54:27-36, 1972.

Moisan, Clément. "Poésie de la résistance." Moisan 1979:129-66.

Nause, John and Heenan, J. Michael. "Interview." CVII 3(2):8-11,
1977.

Wood, Karen Margaret. Raymond Souster: a stylistic analysis and a
chronology of poems. Montreal: Sir George Williams Univ., 1973.
(M.A. thesis.)

SOUSTER, Raymond

A local pride
    Dudek, Louis. "A load of new books: Smith, Webb, Miller/Souster, Purdy, Nowlan." Dudek 1978:168-74. (Originally published Delta 20:27-32, 1963.)

As is
    Scott, Peter Dale. "A Canadian chronicle." Poetry 115:353-64, 1970.

Change-up: new poems
    Baxter, Marilyn. "Six first from Oberon." CF 55(657):48-51, 1975-6.

    Garebian, Keith. Quarry 24(3):72-4, 1975.

    Levenson, Christopher. "Origins and lemons." BiC 3(8):26-7, 1974.

    McWhirter, George. Fiddlehead 105:132, 1975.

    Powell, D. Reid. Q&Q 41(2):27, 1975.

    Safarik, Allan. "Souster's ballpark." CanR 2(2):41-2, 1975.

    Sandler, Linda. "Souster." TamR 65:88-90, 1975.

    Watt, F.W. "Why poetry? Eleven answers." CF 55(651):40-1, 1975.

The colour of the times: the collected poems
    Arnason, David. Q&Q 39(9):7, 1973.

    Dudek, Louis. "Groundhog among the stars: the poetry of Raymond Souster." Dudek 1978:193-208. (Originally published CanL 22:34-49, 1964. Republished George Woodcock, ed. A choice of critics. Toronto: OUP, 1966.)

Double-header
    Barbour, Douglas. "Canadian poetry chronicle 2." DR 55:748-59, 1975-76.

    Evans, J.A.S. "Undertows and Ovid tones." BiC 4(8):19, 1975.

    McFadgen, Lynn. Q&Q 41(7):30, 1975.

Extra innings
    Barbour, Douglas. "Poetry chronicle V." DR 58:149-69, 1978.

    Fulford, Robert. "A certain love for Toronto." SatN 92(6):75-9, 1977.

    Gervais, C.H. "Two reporters, one commentator." BiC 6(7):24, 1977.

    Jackel, David. "Private enthusiasms." CF 57(673):37-8, 1977.

    MacEwen, Gwendolyn. Q&Q 43(6):44, 1977.

SOUSTER, Raymond

    Extra innings (cont'd.)
      Scobie, Stephen. Quarry 27(1):71-3, 1978.

      Sherman, Joseph. Fiddlehead 117:137-8, 1978.

    Hanging in
      Hicks, Lorne. Q&Q 45(6):47, 1979.

      Nicoll, Sharon. Fiddlehead 123:106-8, 1979.

    Lost and found
      Zaiss, David. "Perfect circles." Poetry 116:51-7, 1970.

    Place of meeting
      Dudek, Louis. "A load of new books: Smith, Webb, Miller/Souster, Purdy, Nowlan." Dudek, 1978:168-74. (Originally published Delta 20:27-32, 1963.)

    Raincheck
      Barbour, Douglas. "Canadian poetry chronicle:III." DR 56:560-73, 1976.

      Garebian, Keith. Quarry 24(4):74-6, 1975.

      Gasparini, Len. "Let's hear it for an old pitch-hinter." BiC 5(2):40, 1976.

      Levenson, Christopher. "Early Souster." CanL 73:124-26, 1977.

    Selected poems
      Doyle, Mike. "Singing small." CanL 59:123-25, 1974.

      Fetherling, Doug. "The cities within." SatN 88(1):36-8, 1973.

      Oughton, John. Open letter 2d ser, 15:120-1, 1973.

    So far, so good
      Barbour, Douglas. DR 40:427-9, 1970.

      Doyle, Mike. "Made in Canada?" Poetry 119:356-62, 1972.

    Ten elephants on Yonge Street
      Arnason, David. Q&Q 39(9):7, 1973.

    The years: poems
      Gibbs, Robert. Fiddlehead 94:131-2, 1972.

      Jonas, George. "It is hard not to be affected by his spell." SatN 86(12);35-6, 1971.

      McNamara, Eugene. Quarry 21(2):61-3, 1972.

      Solecki, Z.S. QQ 79:274-5, 1972.

SPARSHOTT, Francis

A cardboard garage
Barbour, Douglas. DR 50:424-5, 1970.

Hornyansky, Michael. UTQ 39:337, 1970.

Jones, D.G. "Voices in the dark." CanL 45:68-74, 1970.

The naming of the beasts
Aubert, Rosemary. QQ 45(14):28, 1979.

SPEARS, Heather

Asylum poems and others
Mallinson, Jean. "Words for the unspeakable." CF 56(661):27-30,
1976.

The Danish portraits
Mallinson, Jean. "Words for the unspeakable." CF 56(661):27-30,
1976.

From the inside
Barbour, Douglas. Q&Q 39(3):8, 1973.

Mallinson, Jean. "Words for the unspeakable." CF 56(661):27-30,
1976.

STANGE, Ken

Revenging language
Barbour, Douglas. "Poetry chronicle V." DR 58:149-69, 1978.

Fraser, Wayne. "Made human by humour." CVII 3(1):40-1, 1977.

Gatenby, Greg. "Dots, stars and diapasons." BiC 5(12):28-9, 1976.

Wolf cycle
Gervais, C.H. "Staying true." CanL 76:104-7, 1978.

STANLEY, George

The stick
Barbour, Douglas. "The poets and presses revisited: circa 1974." DR
55:338-60, 1975.

You: poems 1957-67
Gasparini, Len. "Six poets who found a critic." BiC 3(7):20-2, 1974.

STEDINGH, R. Wayne

From a bell tower
    Gibbs, Robert. Fiddlehead 90:110-1, 1971.

STEPHEN, Sid

Beothuck poems
    Barbour, Douglas. "Poetry chronicle IV." DR 57:355-71, 1977.

    Cooley, Dennis. "Of that time, of this place." CVII 2(3):18-9, 1976.

    Jordan, Kimberley. Brick 2:17-8, 1978.

    Oliver, Michael Brian. "Raising Canada." Fiddlehead 114:141-5, 1977.

    Smith, Patricia Keeney. "Whisper our trespasses." BiC 5(9):36, 1976.

    Woodcock, George. "Playing with freezing fire." CanL 70:84-91, 1976.

STEVENS, Peter

And the dying sky like blood
    Barbour, Douglas. "The poets and presses revisited: circa 1974." DR
    55:338-60, 1975.

    Gasparini, Len. "Fluid gig for McNamara's band." BiC 4(3):24-6, 1975.

    Kerr, Don. "Singing the hero and misfit." CVII 2(1):34-5, 1976.

    Wallace, Bronwen. Quarry 24(4):59-60, 1975.

    Woodcock, George. "Purdy's prelude and other poems." CanL 64:92-8, 1975

The bogman Pavese tactics
    Barbour, Douglas. "Canadian poetry chronicle: VI." DR 58:555-78, 1978.

    Hamel, Guy. "Recent Fiddlehead poetry books." Fiddlehead 118:137-45,
    1978.

    Hornyansky, Michael. UTQ 47:354, 1978.

Breadcrusts and glass
    André, Michael. QQ 80:471, 1973.

    Estok, Michael. "All in the family: the metaphysics of domesticity."
    DR 52:653-67, 1973.

    Hornyansky, Michael. UTQ 42:371, 1973.

STEVENS, Peter

Family feelings and other poems
 Lever, Bernice. "Seven nearly alive books." Alive 40:18, 1974.

 McFadgen, Lynn. Q&Q 40(8):24, 1974.

 Marcellin, Phil. Alive 36:15, 1974.

 Rogers, Linda. "Handful of dust." CanL 65:119-20, 1975.

 Wallace, Bronwen. Quarry 24(2):57-9, 1975.

A few myths
 Gervais, C.H. Quarry 22(2):76-7, 1973.

 Gibbs, Robert. Fiddlehead 94:133, 1972.

 Gustafson, Ralph. "Circumventing dragons." CanL 55:105-8, 1973.

Nothing but spoons
 Barbour, Douglas. Quarry 13(2):63-4, 1970.

STEVENSON, Warren

Then and now
 Hamel, Guy. "Recent Fiddlehead poetry books." Fiddlehead 118:137-45, 1978.

 Jenoff, Marvyne. "Seven books from two small presses." CVII 3(4):40-5, 1978.

STRARAM, Patrick

En train d'être en vers où être, Québec...
 Gallays, François. LAQ 1971:166.

4 x 4
 Bourque, Paul-André. "Avatars de l''underground'(?)!" LAQ 1974:146-7.

Irish coffees au no name bar and vin rouge valley of the moon
 Cloutier, Guy. LAQ 1972:158-9.

STRUTHERS, Carolyn

Oh, it's hard not to be immortal
B., D.G. ApF 2:r22-3, 1975.

Gasparini, Len. "Six poets who found a critic." BiC 3(7):20-2, 1974.

Novak, Barbara. Quarry 23(4):71-2, 1974.

SUKNASKI, Andrew

General
David, Jack. "An elfin plotting: an interview with Andrew Suknaski."
CVII 3(1):10-2, 1977.

Melnyk, George. "Interview: the ghosts that haunt the poetic lays of
Andrew Suknaski, Westerner." BiC 6(4):31-2, 1977.

Melnyk, George. "Suknaski: multiculturalism in action." Q&Q
43(1):17, 19, 1977.

The ghosts call you poor
Brown, Doug. Quarry 28(1):71-5, 1979.

Daniel, Lorne. Q&Q 44(15):33, 1978.

Hornyansky, Michael. UTQ 48:349-50, 1979.

Moritz, A.F. "Lost glories, found clichés." BiC 8(1):14, 1979.

Precosky, Don. Fiddlehead 122:131-4, 1979.

Leaving
Gasparini, Len. "One plus three." CanL 63:92-5, 1975.

Octomi
Barbour, Douglas. "Suknaski's geography of blood." CVII 2(4):12-3,
1976.

Daniel, Lorne. Q&Q 42(15):38, 1976.

Fitzgerald, Judith. EngQ 9(4):124-5, 1976/77.

On first looking down from Lion's Gate Bridge
McCarthy, Dermot. "Mosquitoes and mundane heroism." ECW 5:75-9,
1976.

Melnyk, George. "Harnessing dream horses." BiC 5(7):14, 1976.

Woodcock, George. "Playing with freezing fire." CanL 70:84-91, 1976.

310

SUKNASKI, Andrew

Wood mountain poems
    Baglow, John. CanR 3(5):52, 1976.

    Barbour, Douglas. "Poetry chronicle IV." DR 57:355-71, 1977.

    Barbour, Douglas. "Suknaski's geography of blood." CVII 2(4):12-3, 1976.

    Daniel, Lorne. "Finely tuned." CF 56(667):61, 1976-7.

    Lee, Dennis. "The new poets: fresh voices in the land." SatN 88(12):33-5, 1973.

    Melnyk, George. "Harnessing dream horses." BiC 5(7):14, 1976.

    Stuewe, Paul. Q&Q 42(9):36-7, 1976.

    Woodcock, George. "Playing with freezing fire." CanL 70:84-91, 1976.

Writing on stone (poem-drawings 1966-76)
    Barbour, Douglas. "Suknaski's geography of blood." CVII 2(4):12-3, 1976.

SULLIVAN, D.H.

HE: a short biography of HIM
    Billings, R. Quarry 23(3):75-6, 1974.

    Liman, Claude. "Open sesame." CVII 3(4):25-8, 1978.

    Millage, Craig. Brick 1:25-7, 1977.

The Pandora sequence: Alice among the sister people
    Cavanagh, Dave. "Reports from the front." BiC 5(2):36, 1976.

    Currie, Sheldon. AntigR 23:87-8, 1975.

Wind sun stone and ice
    Currie, Sheldon. AntigR 39:105-6, 1979.

SUMMERFIELD, Edith

Patchwork portraits
    Lever, Bernice. "Seven nearly alive books." Alive 40:18, 1974.

    Marcellin, Phil. Alive 36:9, 1974.

SUTHERLAND, Fraser

In the wake of
Bradbury, Maureen. Q&Q 40(11):21, 1974.

Di Cicco, Pier Giorgio. Alive 36:9, 1974.

Johnston, Kevin. Quarry 23(4):80, 1974.

Rogers, Linda. "Handful of dust." CanL 65:119-20, 1975.

Madwomen
Bartlett, Brian. "Crumbs in a plastic bag." BiC 8(2):17, 1979.

David, Jack. Q&Q 45 (3):19, 1979.

Strange ironies
Barbour, Douglas. Q&Q 39(3):8, 1973.

Within the wound
Amprimoz, Alexandre. "Poetic journeys." CanL 79:92-4, 1978.

Farmiloe, Dorothy. Q&Q 43(1):32, 1977.

Hickmore, G.L. Quarry 26(4):65-6, 1977.

Morton, Colin. "Examining the individuals." CVII 3(1):42-3, 1977.

Oliver, Michael Brian. "Raising Canada." Fiddlehead 114:141-5, 1977.

Winter, Estelle. CA&B 52(3):42, 1977.

SUTHERLAND, John

John Sutherland: essays, controversies and poems
Morley, Patricia. "The still centre." CanL 60:103-5, 1974.

SWARD, Robert

Honey bear on Lasqueti Island B.C.
Browne, Colin. "Delight from Lasqueti." CVII 4(2):4-5, 1979.

Di Cicco, Pier Giorgio. "No man is an island, true, but there can be a circean catch to regionalism." BiC 8(1):21-2, 1979.

SWEDE, George

Tell-tale feathers
Di Cicco, Pier Giorgio. "No man is an island, true, but there can be a circean catch to regionalism." BiC 891):21-2, 1979.

SZUMIGALSKI, Anne

Woman reading in the bath: poems
Almon, Bert. WCR 9(2):53-5, 1974.

Blackhall, S.E. Quarry 23(3):77-8, 1974.

Downes, G.V. CVII 1(1):3, 1975.

Powell, D. Reid. Q&Q 40(5):19, 1974.

Rogers, Linda. "Jumping naked into the front." BiC 3(6):18, 20,
1974.

TÉTRAU, François

Cirque électrique
Kushner, Éva. "Vers une poésie de la poésie?" LAQ 1974:115-8.

THACKERY, Brian

The bent wire & other poems
Haidl, Herb. Q&Q 39(10):9, 1972.

THÉBERGE, Jean-Yves

De temps en temps
Gaulin, André. LAQ 1979:174-6.

Nepveu, Pierre. "Robert Mélançon. Gilles Cyr. Jean Charlebois.
Jean-Yves Théberge." Lettres qué 14:22-5, 1979.

Saison de feu
Le Grand, Éva. LAQ 1972:181.

THÉORET, France

Bloody Mary
Bonenfant, Joseph. LAQ 1977:157-60.

Vertiges
Corriveau, Hugues. "Poésie: des lèvres et des vertiges." NBdJ
81:87-90, 1979.

Giguère, Richard. LAQ 1979:105-6.

THÉRIAULT, Marie-Josée

    Lettera amorosa
      Audet, Noël. "Au sujet d'une lettre d'amour, en poésie--Marie José
      Thériault." V&I 4:542-3, 1979.

    Poèmes
      Siguret, Françoise. LAQ 1973:129.

THIBAUDEAU, Colleen

    Bibliography
      McKay, Jean. "A Colleen Thibaudeau checklist." Brick 5:71-8, 1979.

    General
      "Colleen Thibaudeau." Brick 5:1979. (Whole issue.)

    Colleen Thibaudeau
      Lacey, Edward. "Canadian bards and South American reviewers." Nj
      4:82-120, 1974.

    My granddaughters are combing out their long hair
      Bayard, Caroline. Q&Q 44(10):12, 1978.

    Ten letters
      Di Cicco, Pier Giorgio. Q&Q 42(4);25, 1976.

      Oughton, John. "Simple songs, tricky cycles." BiC 5(4):20-1, 1976.

THISDEL, Jacques

    Après-midi, j'ai dessiné un oiseau
      Giguère, Richard. "Trois tendances de la poésie québécoise." LAQ
      1976:114-6.

      Lefrançois, Alexis. Liberté 108:193-8, 1976.

THISTLE, Mel

    Touch me gently
      Cogswell, Fred. QQ 78:325-6, 1971.

THOMAS, Peter

Love without lies: the trailing cord
    Lane, M. Travis. Fiddlehead 99:105-8, 1973.

The wailing cord
    Hoekema, Henry. WCR 9(3):41-3, 1975.

THOMAS, Walter Keith

Bonding of bone
    Solecki, Sam. Fiddlehead 112:151-5, 1977.

THOMPSON, J.O.

Three
    Gervais, C.H. "Staying true." CanL 76:104-7, 1978.

    Klepac, Walter. Q&Q 39(12):12, 1973.

THOMPSON, John

At the edge of the chopping there are no secrets
    Bradbury, Maureen. Q&Q 40(4):20, 1974.

    Gibbs, Robert. "Almost without speech." Fiddlehead 104:134-7, 1975.

    Lee, Dennis. "The new poets: fresh voices in the land." SatN 88(12):33-5, 1973.

    Levenson, Christopher. QQ 86:718-20, 1979.

    Marshall, Tom. "A consciousness on the knife edge." ECW 12:204-9, 1978.

    Novak, Barbara. "Poetry chronicle." TamR 75:88-95, 1978.

    "The twain meet." CanR 1(4):27-8, 1974.

Stilt Jack
    Levenson, Christopher. QQ 86:718-20, 1979.

    Marshall, Tom. "A consciousness on the knife edge." ECW 12:204-9, 1978.

    Norris, Ken. "Land eels and illogical ghazals." BiC 7(7):20-1, 1978.

    Novak, Barbara. "Poetry chronicle." TamR 75:88-95, 1978.

    Oliver, Michael Brian. "Tantramar-and Saint John and Fredericton-revisited." Fiddlehead 122:115-24, 1979.

THOMPSON, Kent

Hard explanations
Lane, Patrick. New 12:40-1, 1970.

THORNTON, J.B.

Voir/see THORNTON MCLEOD, Joan B.

THORNTON MCLEOD, Joan B.

La Corriveau & the blond and other poems
Barbour, Douglas. "Poetry chronicle IV." DR 57:355-71, 1977.

Garebian, Keith. Q&Q 42(7):40, 1976.

Henderson, Brian. "Warning! on the death of the avant garde." ECW
5:103-5, 1976.

McFadgen, Lynn. "The way she says it." BiC 5(8):13-4, 1976.

TIDLER, Charles

Flight: the last American poem
Johnson, Sam F. Q&Q 43(3):12, 1977.

Straw things
Barbour, Douglas. Q&Q 39(2):13, 1973.

Whetstone almanac
Power, Nick. Q&Q 41(13):33-4, 1975.

TIERNEY, Frank M.

The way it stands
Dailey, Ross. "Four from Borealis." CanR 1(4);26-7, 1974.

Leigh, Simon. "Two minor talons and a tidal borealis." Fiddlehead
108:120-4, 1976.

TOMLINSON, Randy

Down under it all
Gibbs, Robert. Fiddlehead 90:114, 1971.

TOURANGEAU, Jean

Suite martriniquaise
Bourque, Paul-André. "Poètes et artistes du Québec." LAQ 1975:139-45.

TRACHUK, John

Whistling
Heenan, J.M.H. "Two from Borealis." CVII 3(4):15-7, 1978.

TRACY, Neil

Collected poems
Cogswell, Fred. "A good minor poet." CanL 73:109-10, 1977.

Hornyansky, Michael. UTQ 45:343, 1976.

Voice line
Bailey, Don. Quarry 20(3):52, 1971.

TREGEBOV, Michael

Changehouse
Popham, Beth. Quarry 27(2):87-8, 1978.

Powell, Craig. "Beginnings of formidable gifts." CVII 3(1):44-5, 1977.

TREMBLAY, Gaston

Souvenances
Moisan, Clément. LAQ 1979:92.

TREMBLAY, Gemma

General
Pageau, René. "Coup d'oeil sur l'oeuvre de Gemma Tremblay." ActN 60:86-96, 1970.

Les seins gorgés
Major, Jean-Louis. UTQ 39:429-30, 1970.

Souffles du midi
Bolduc, Yves. LAQ 1972:155-6.

TREY, Roger Ten

Broken wing
Gervais, C.H. "The west coast seen." Quarry 19(4):57-9, 1970.

TROTTIER, Pierre

Sainte-mémoire
Marcotte, Gilles. EF 9:78-80, 1973.

Renaud, André. LAQ 1972:156.

TROWER, Peter

General
Twigg, Alan. "Talking straight with Trower." Q&Q 44(11):25, 1978.

The alders and others
Barbour, Douglas. "Poetry chronicle V." DR 58:149-69, 1978.

Mathews, Robin. "Two B.C. harbingers." CVII 3(1):34-5, 1977.

Purdy, Al. "A flooding past." CanL 76:126-7, 1978.

Pyke, Linda. "A mari usque ad mare: four poetic landscapes." Q&Q
42(17):29, 1976.

Between the sky and the splinters
Hogan, Homer. Q&Q 40(12):26, 1974.

Safarik, Allan. "In the footsteps of service." CanR 2(2):43-4, 1975.

Moving through mystery
Barbour, Douglas. "The young poets and the little presses, 1969." DR
50:112-26, 1970.

Gervais, C.H. "The west coast seen." Quarry 19(4):57-9, 1970.

Ragged horizons
Barbour, Douglas. "Canadian poetry chronicle: VII." DR 59:154-75,
1979.

Bartlett, Brian. "Torn and tattered comparisons." CVII 4(3):42, 44,
1979.

Bell, John. Quarry 28(2):78-81, 1979.

Dempster, Barry. Q&Q 44(5):9, 1978.

Fletcher, Peggy. "The printed page their classroom." CA&B
53(4):42-3, 1978.

TROWER, Peter

Ragged horizons (cont'd.)
Gasparini, Len. "Urbanity and mean streets." BiC 7(6);19-20, 1978.

Hornyansky, Michael. UTQ 48:350-1, 1979.

Schoemperlen, Diane. Event 8(1):185, 1979.

Scobie, Stephen. "Exercises." CF 58(686):50, 1979.

Woodcock, George. "Workers in a landscape." ECW 12:210-5, 1978.

TURCOTTE, Jean Alexandre

Cloclophile
Jans, Adrien. "Jeune poète sherbrookois." PFr 3:174-5, 1971.

TURNER, Myron

The river and the window
Almon, Bert. WCR 11(2):41-2, 1976.

Barbour, Douglas. "The poets and presses revisited: circa 1974." DR 55:338-60, 1975.

Christy, Jim. "Inventing oracles." Alive 41:34, 1975.

TYNDALL, John

Howlcat fugues
Barbour, Douglas. "Canadian poetry chronicle: VI." DR 58:555-78, 1978.

UVUAY, Marie

L'outre-vie
Benoit, Monique. LAQ 1979:176-8.

Signe et rumeur
Nepveu, Pierre. "La jeune poésie, la critique peut-être..." Lettres qué 6:13-5, 1977.

UHER, Lorna

Crow's black joy
Di Cicco, Pier Giorgio. "No man is an island, true, but there can be a circean catch to regionalism." BiC 8(1):21-2, 1979.

No longer two people
Amprimoz, Alexandre L. Quarry 28(4):75-7, 1979.

Brown, Allan. "Playing parts: five from Turnstone Press." Waves 8(1):67-71, 1979.

ULRICH, W.D.

The tree in the room
Gibbs, Robert. Fiddlehead 90:114-5, 1971.

UPWARD, Ed

Seems valuable
McNamara, Eugene. "Ghetto long little dogie." BiC 6(8):16-7, 1977.

VAILLANCOURT, Marie Claire

Déjà son geste
Cotnoir, Louise. LAQ 1979:100-1.

VALGARDSON, W.D.

In the gutting shed
Cogswell, Fred. "Three Manitoba poets." Sphinx 7(v.2(3)):68-70, 1977.

Middleton, L.M. CA&B 52(3):41, 1977.

Oliver, Michael Brian. Fiddlehead 111:121-2, 1976.

Pyke, Linda. "A mari usque ad mare: four poetic landscapes." Q&Q 42(17):29, 1976.

Quickenden, Robert. "Some thoughts spinning skyward." CVII 2(3):44-5, 1976.

Scobie, Stephen. "Hill poems from the plain." BiC 6(3):41-2, 1977.

VANIER, Denis

General
Beausoleil, Claude. "Le texte vaniérien." Cul Q 8-9:27-51, 1976.

Bélanger, Claude. "Pour baiser Vanier." BdJ 38:63-79, 1973.

Comme le peau d'un rosaire
Hébert, François. "Lefrançois, Beaulieu, Nepveu, Vanier." Liberté 114:93-9, 1977.

Lesbiennes d'acid
Bolduc, Yves. LAQ 1972:160-1.

Charron, François. "Denis Vanier: violence, répercussions." Presqu'amérique 1(10):23-4, 1972.

L'odeur d'un athlète
Bourassa, André-G. "Entre l'espace et le temps: ou le lieu de rencontre de Pierre Morency, Jean-Aubert Loranger, Denis Vanier et Michel van Schendel." Lettres qué 14:18-21, 1979.

"La 303 suprême dont les balles ne tuent pas"
Bourassa, André-G. "Chaîne et trame. Rina Lasnier, Denis Vanier et Josée Yvon." Lettres qué 5:11-3, 1977.

VAN SCHENDEL, Michel

Veiller ne plus veiller
Bourassa, André-G. "Entre l'espace et le temps: ou le lieu de rencontre de Pierre Morency, Jean-Aubert Loranger, Denis Vanier et Michel Van Schendel." Lettres qué 14:18-21, 1979.

VAN TOORN, Peter

In Guildenstern county
Currie, Sheldon. AntigR 16:111-3, 1974.

Lee, Dennis. "The new poets: fresh voices in the land." SatN 88(12):33-5, 1973.

Leeway grass
Barbour, Douglas. DR 51:137, 1971.

Cogswell, Fred. Fiddlehead 88:105, 1971.

Tierney, Bill. AntigR 1(4):110, 1971.

VARNEY, Edwin

Human nature
Morrissey, Stephen. "Extending the limit." CVII 3(2):62, 1977.

Newton, Stuart. "Review." Event 7(1):139-42, 1978.

VERNON, Lorraine

No. 3, Frank Street
Hamel, Guy. "Recent Fiddlehead poetry books." Fiddlehead 118:137-45, 1978.

VÉZINA, France

Slingshot
Dupré, Louise. LAQ 1979:178-9.

VIETS, Roger

"Annapolis Royal, 1788."
Vincent, Thomas B. "Viets' 'Annapolis Royal, 1788.'" CN&Q 13:13, 1974.

VIGNEAULT, Gilles

Bibliography
Gagné, Marc. Gilles Vigneault: Bibliographie descriptive et critique, discographie, filmographie, iconographie, chronologie. Quebec: Presses de l'Univ. Laval, 1977.

General
Barbry, François-Régis. François-Régis Barbry interroge Gilles Vigneault: passer l'hiver. Paris: Centurion, 1978. (Les interviews.)

"Un barde québécois: Gilles Vigneault... sur le vif!" Forces 30:40-8, 1975.

Bourassa, André-G. "Les poètes de la musique." Lettres qué 11:32-7, 1978.

"Entretien avec Gilles Vigneault." Esprit, 425:1275-85, 1973.

Gagné, Marc. "Essai sur la thématique de Gilles Vignault[sic]." Culture 3:3-23, 1970.

Gagné, Marc. Propos de Gilles Vigneault. Montréal: Nouvelles éd. de l'ARC, 1974. (Itinéraires, 1.)

322

VIGNEAULT, Gilles

General (cont'd.)
Kandalaft, Cécile G. "Deux ou trois choses qu'il sait de lui-même." Châtelaine 14:36-7;60-2, 1973.

"A Québec bard: Gilles Vigneault... live! An interview with Forces." Forces 30:58-61, 1975. (Tr. Geneviève Cabana.)

Ce que je dis c'est en passant
Saint-Amour, Robert. LAQ 1970:142.

Les gens de mon pays
Saint-Amour, Robert. VIP 4:53-81.

Les neuf couplets
Gagné, Marc. "Gilles Vigneault: Les neuf couplets." LAQ 1973:120-1.

Silences
Bouvier, Luc. LAQ 1978:150-2.

VILLEMAIRE, Yolande

Machine-t-elle
Giguère, Richard. "Les Herbes rouges: une grande 'petite revue.'" LAQ 1975:118-21.

VIRGO, Sean

Deathwatch on Skidegate
Aubert, Rosemary. Q&Q 45(11):11, 1979.

Kleinzahler, August. "Hemlock and better." BiC 8(8):16-7, 1979.

Narrows and other poems
Aubert, Rosemary. Q&Q 45(11):11, 1979.

Kleinzahler, August. "Hemlock and better." BiC 8(8):16-7, 1979.

VUJOVIC, Slobodan

Minute après minuit
Demers, Jeanne. LAQ 1973:126-7.

WADDINGTON, Miriam

Bibliography
  Ricou, L.R. "Miriam Waddington: a checklist 1936-1975." ECW
  12:162-91, 1978.

General
  Ricou, L.R. "Into my green world: the poetry of Miriam Waddington."
  ECW 12:144-61, 1978.

  Wachtel, Eleanor. "Miriam Waddington in Vancouver." Room of one's
  own 3(1):2-7, 1977.

Dream telescope
  Compass (KSC) 4:42-3, 1973.

Driving home: poems new and selected
  Almon, Bert. "Triumphs of the sun: 3 seasoned poets--Dorothy Livesay,
  Miriam Waddington & Phyllis Webb." New 24:106-8, 1974.

  Compass (KSC) 4:42-3, 1973.

  Estok, Michael. "All in the family: the metaphysics of domesticity."
  DR 52:653-67, 1973.

  Hobsbaum, Hannah. Outposts 105:35-6, 1975.

  Hornyansky, Michael. UTQ 42:374-5, 1973.

  Levenson, Christopher. QQ 80:469-70, 1973.

  MacCulloch, Clare. "To be the landscape." Fiddlehead 103:96-101,
  1974.

  Mountford, C. Q&Q 38(12):8, 1972.

  Mulhallen, Karen. CF 52(626):48-9, 1973.

  Nynych, Stephanie J. "At home with the world." BiC 1(12):10, 12,
  1972.

  Potts, Maureen. WLWE 12(2);243-6, 1973.

  Wayman, Tom. "Miriam Waddington's new talent." CanL 56:85-9, 1973.

Mister never
  Aubert, Rosemary. Q&Q 44(11):39-40, 1978.

  Barbour, Douglas. "Canadian poetry chronicle: VI." DR 58:555-78,
  1978.

  Bartlett, Brian. "We dipped and we flipped." BiC 7(8):16, 1978.

  Brown, Allan. "Playing parts: five from Turnstone Press." Waves
  8(1):67-71, 1979.

WADDINGTON, Miriam

The price of gold
Barbour, Douglas.   "Poetry chronicle IV."   DR 57:355-71, 1977.

Challis, John.   Laomedon 3(1):74-5, 1977.

Chamberlin, J.E.   "Poetry chronicle."   HudR 30:108-24, 1977.

Fletcher, Peggy.   CA&B 52(1):26, 1976.

Gatenby, Greg.   Q&Q 42(12):13, 1976.

Levenson, Christopher.   Quarry 26(4):77-80, 1977.

Lever, Bernice.   Waves 5(213):122-3, 1977.

Livesay, Dorothy.   "Gazing into the clouds of whimsy."   CVII 3(1):15, 1977.

MacCulloch, Clare.   "Her ninth symphony."   BiC 5(10): 28, 1976.

Oliver, Michael Brian.   "Miscellanies, metamorphosis, & myth."   CanL 74:95-101, 1977.

Sherman, Joseph.   Fiddlehead 117:135-7, 1978.

Watt, F. W.   "Games and grownups."   CF 57(671):40-1, 1977.

Say yes
Jones, D. G.   "Voices in the dark."   CanL 45:68-74, 1970.

Pacey, Desmond.   "A Canadian Quintet."   Fiddlehead 83: 79-86, 1970.

Reeves, F. D.   "Faces at the bottom."   Poetry 118: 234-8, 1971.

Zitner, S. P.   CF 49:299, 1970.

WAH, Fred

General

Bowering, George.   "The poems of Fred Wah."   Cp 12(2): 3-13, 1979.

Among
Barbour, Douglas.   "Three west coast poets and one from the east."   LURev 6:240-5, 1973.

Bowering, George.   "Lines on the grid."   Open letter 2d series, 8:94-5, 1974.

MacKenzie, Brenda.   Q&Q 39(4):10, 1973.

WAH, Fred

Pictograms from the interior of B.C.
Barbour, Douglas. "Canadian poetry chronicle: III." DR 56:560-73, 1976.

Cowan, Doris. "Theodo lights." BiC 5(8):8,9, 1976.

Fuhrman, Michael. Q&Q 42(9):36, 1976.

McCaffery, Steve. "Anti-phonics." Open letter 3d ser, 5:87-92, 1976.

Nichol, bp "A conversation with Fred Wah: T.R.G. report one: translation (part 3)." Open letter 3d ser, 9:34-52, 1978.

Scobie, Stephen. "Shades of precision." CanL 79:89-90, 1978.

WAINWRIGHT, J.A.

Moving outward
Fetherling, Doug. "As good as Cohen on his good days." SatN 86(3):28, 1971.

Pollack, Claudette. Quarry 20(1):40-2, 1971.

Stevens, Peter. QQ 78: 326-7, 1971.

The requiem journal
Friedman, Jack. "On tangled sheets'n things." ECW 4:96-9, 1977.

WALKER, Jeremy

Apocalypse with figures
Cameron, A.A. Brick 1:45-6, 1977.

Hornyansky, Michael. UTQ 44:332-3, 1975.

WALLACE, Jim

Blowing dust off the lens
Popham, Beth. Quarry 27(2):84-5, 1978.

326

WALLACE, Joe

General
   Acorn, Milton. "In wry memoriam: Joe Wallace." CanD 12(4&5):38-43, 1977.

   Safarik, Allan and Livesay, Dorothy. "How I began--selections from an inteview with Joe Wallace..." CVII 1(1):35-42, 1975.

WALMSLEY, Tom

Lexington hero
   Daniel, Lorne, Q&Q 43(1):31, 1977.

   Madoff, Mark. "Colloquy with death." CF 57(677):51-2, 1977-8.

   Scherzer, David. "Wa-did-diddy-Tommy do?" CVII 3(2):54, 1977.

Rabies
   Powell, D. Reid. Q&Q 42(1):26, 1976.

WARMAN, Cy

General
   Cole, Wayne. "The railroad in Canadian literature." CanL 77:124-30, 1978.

WARR, Bertram

Acknowledgement to life. The collected poems
   Cogswell, Fred. QQ 78:325-6, 1971.

   Fetherling, Doug. "Poetic journal." TamR 57:80-4, 1971.

   Hornyansky, Michael. UTQ 40:372-3, 1971.

WARRIOR, M.C.

Quilting time
   Barbour, Douglas. "Canadian poetry chronicle:VII." DR 59:154-75, 1979.

WATSON, Wilfred

The sorrowful Canadians & other poems
   Barbour, Douglas. Open letter 2d ser, 5:115-8, 1973.

WAYMAN, Tom

General

Malcolm, Ian. "Tom Wayman: the essential voice." Quarry 27(2):71-6, 1978.

Mundwiler, Leslie. "After realism: McFadden and Wayman." CVII 3(2):36-40, 1977.

Pearce, Jon. "The lives behind things: an interview with Tom Wayman." Quarry 28(4):57-70, 1979.

Walker, Susan. "Wayman: poetry of the working world." Q&Q 40(12):15, 1974.

For and against the moon: blues, yells and chuckles

Anderson, Marlowe D. "Way out with Wayman: the engaged voice." CVII 2(1):38-42, 1976.

Barbour, Douglas. Q&Q 40(8):23, 1974.

Mackskimming, Roy. "A quatrain of contenders." BiC 3(7):5-6, 9, 1974.

Marshall, Tom. "Five poets from five countries." OntR 2:86-94, 1975.

Mundwiler, Leslie. "Layton and Wayman: poets and the history of Joe Blow." CanD 10(7):60-2, 1975.

Solecki, Sam. "Political poetry." CF 54(647):46-7, 1975.

Weis, Lyle. "A war is going on: Wayman's poems." Sphinx 6(v.2(2)):59-61, 1976.

Free time: industrial poems

Barbour, Douglas. "Poetry chronicle V." DR 58:149-69, 1978.

David, Jack. Q&Q 43(5):43, 1977.

Marshall, Tom. "The way of this world." BiC 6(5):21, 1977.

McNamara, Eugene. Fiddlehead 115:140-2, 1977.

Moritz, A.F. EngQ 10(3):83-5, 1977.

Rosenblatt, Joe. "Of plebians and proletariats." TamR 72:88-90, 1977.

WAYMAN, Tom

Money and rain: Tom Wayman live!
Barbour, Douglas. "Canadian poetry chronicle: III." DR 56:560-73, 1976.

Cameron, Barry. "Poetic historians." CanL 75:106-7, 1977.

Di Cicco, Pier Giorgio. "From Chile con amor." BiC 4(12):28-9, 1975.

Lane, M. Travis. Fiddlehead 109:119-22, 1976.

Lent, John. "A whole voice." CF 56(662):55-6, 1976.

McFadgen, Lynn. Q&Q 41(13):32, 1975.

Solecki, Sam. "The country of everyday." CVII 2(2):36-7, 1976.

Weis, Lyle. "A war is going on: Wayman's poems." Sphinx 6(v.2(2)):59-61, 1976.

Waiting for Wayman
Anderson, Marlowe D. "Way out with Wayman: the engaged voice." CVII 2(1):38-42, 1976.

Barbour, Douglas. Q&Q 39(5):27, 1973.

Bennett, Donna A. "Reunion: contemporary Canadian poetry." LURev 6:236-9, 1973.

Bowering, George. "A singular voice." CanL 60:112-4, 1974.

Cameron, Allen Barry. CF 53(631):33-4, 1973.

Lee, Dennis. "The new poets: fresh voices in the land." SatN 88(12):33-5, 1973.

Sherman, Joseph. Fiddlehead 99:103-5, 1973.

Safarik, Allan. "Marty and Wayman." TamR 62:86-9, 1974.

Stevens, Peter. QQ 80:657-8, 1973.

Wagner, Linda W. "Four young poets." OntR 1:89-97, 1974.

Weaver, Robert. "The arrival of Tom Wayman." SatN 88(7):41, 1973.

Whittaker, Ted. "Hammer and songs." BiC 2(2):42-3, 1973.

WEBB, Phyllis

General
Mays, John Bentley. "Phyllis Webb." Open letter 2d ser, 6:8-33, 1973.

WEBB, Phyllis

    General (cont'd.)
     Webb, Phyllis. "Polishing up the view." CVII 2(4):14-5, 1976.

    The sea is also a garden
     Dudek, Louis. "A load of new books: Smith, Webb, Miller/Souster,
     Purdy, Nowlan." Dudek 1978:168-74.

    Selected poems, 1954-1965
     Almon, Bert. "Triumphs of the sun: 3 seasoned poets--Dorothy Livesay,
     Miriam Waddington & Phyllis Webb." New 24:106-8, 1974.

     Barbour, Douglas. Quarry 21(1):61-3, 1972.

     Fox, Gail. CF 52(616):70-1, 1972.

     Lane, M. Travis. "Rare mountain air." Fiddlehead 92:110-4, 1972.

     MacFarlane, Julian. CapR 1:53-8, 1972.

     Ronan, Tom. Tuatara 8/9:107-8, 1972.

     Stevens, Peter. "Shaking the alphabet." CanL 52:82-4, 1972.

     Weaver, Robert. "A puritan Dudek; an inefficient Webb." SatN
     86(11):50-2, 1971.

     Zitner, S.P. "Peeling off." BiC 1(4):21-2, 1971.

WEERASINGHE, Asoka

    Poems for Jeannie
     Boland, Viga. CA&B 52(3):42, 1977.

WELCH, Liliane

    Winter songs
     Bouraoui, H.A. "Crystalline vision." Waves 6(3):69, 1978.

WEST, Ann J.

    The water book
     Stevenson, Warren. "Move over Musgrave." CanL 80:103-4, 1979.

     Zonailo, Carolyn. Room of one's own 3(4):41-2, 1978.

WEST, David S.

    Black and white the horses
      Hamel, Guy. "Reading West." Fiddlehead 120:123-6, 1979.

    Franklin and McClintock
      Barbour, Douglas. "Canadian poetry chronicle: VII." DR 59:154-75, 1979.

      Farley, Tom. JCP 2(1):99-100, 1979.

      Fernstrom, Ken. Q&Q 44(14):45, 1978.

      Hall, Phil. "Franklin and McClintock--it leaves me cold." UWR 14(2):110-1, 1979.

      Hamel, Guy. "Reading West." Fiddlehead 120:123-6, 1979.

    Poems and elegies: 1972-1977
      Hamel, Guy. "Reading West." Fiddlehead 120:123-6, 1979.

WHITEHOUSE, Ian

    Negotiations with the universe
      Gibbs, Robert. Fiddlehead 90:116, 1971.

WHITEN, Clifton

    Putting the birthdate into perspective
      Barbour, Douglas. DR 50:424, 1970.

      Jones, D.G. "Voices in the dark." CanL 45:68-74, 1970.

WHYTE, Jon

    General
      Q&Q 39(5):11, 1973.

    Three
      Gervais, C.H. "Staying true." CanL 76:104-7, 1978.

      Klepac, Walter. Q&Q 39(12);12, 1973.

WILDEMAN, Marlene

    Barn clothes
      Isaacs, Fran. Room of one's own 3(4):44, 1978.

WILKINSON, Anne

    General
      Lecker, Robert. "Better quick than dead: Anne Wilkinson's poetry."
      SCL 3:35-46, 1978.

      Smith, A.J.M. "A reading of Anne Wilkinson." Smith 1973: 134-41.
      (Originally published The collected poems of Anne Wilkinson and a
      prose memoir. Toronto: Macmillan Co. of Canada, 1968:xiii-xxi.)

WILKINSON, Marjorie

    Lamp in the northern wind
      Fletcher, Peggy. "No two alike." CA&B 53(2):43-4, 1978.

WILLIS, Mary

    The rhythm of the dark
      Monk, Patricia. Quarry 24(2):54-5, 1975.

WILSON, Bruce

    Kojivo
      Fitzgerald, Judith. EngQ 9(4):124-5, 1976/77.

WINTER, Jack

    The island
      Lanczos, Elmar. "Three from fiddlehead." WCR 10(2):49-50, 1975.

WISEMAN, Christopher

    The barbarian file
      Barbour, Douglas. "The poets and presses revisited: circa 1974." DR
      55:338-60, 1975.

      Gasparini, Leonard. "Flat, muddled and egotistical." BiC 4(10):27,
      29, 1975.

      Thompson, Eric. "Plain and fantasy." CanL 65:101-4, 1975.

    Waiting for the barbarians
      NcNeal, David S. CF 51(620):39, 1972.

WOLD, Bert

    Poems, a collection
      Harper, A.J.W. OV 10(2):n.p., 1975.

WOODCOCK, George

    General
      Hughes, Peter. George Woodcock. Toronto: McClelland & Stewart, 1974. (Canadian writers, 13.)

      Woodcock, George. "Fragments from a tenth-hour journal." Nj 3:26-39, 1973.

      Woodcock, George. "Intermittences of place and poetry." CVII 2(4):18-20, 1976.

    Anima, or, Swann grown old: a cycle of poems
      Brown, Allan. "Black Moss: six offerings." Waves 7(2):68-71, 1979.

      Duffy, Dennis. "George Woodcock." ECW 16:126-9, 1979-80.

      Gasparini, Len. "Urbanity and mean streets." BiC 7(6):19-20, 1978.

    Notes on visitations: poems, 1936-1975
      Barbour, Douglas. "Canadian poetry chronicle:III." DR 56:560-73, 1976.

      Gustafson, Ralph. "Worthwhile visitations." CanL 71:89-92, 1976.

      Hornyansky, Michael. UTQ 46:373-4, 1977.

      Long, Tanya. Q&Q 42(4);24, 1976.

      Quickenden, Robert. "A veteran over youth's hot coals." CVII 2(2):30-1, 1976.

      Such, Peter. "Three grand old parties." BiC 5(2):9-11, 1976.

WRIGHT, Charles

    The dream animal
      Carlile, Henry. "Three poets." NwR 10(3):124-8, 1970.

    The grave of the right hand
      Pollack, Claudette. Quarry 20(1):44-5, 1971.

WYNAND, Derk

Snowscapes
Barbour, Douglas. "Canadian poetry chronicle 2." DR 55:748-59, 1975-76.

Beardsley, Doug. "A trial of immortality: recent Canadian poetry." Nj 6:118-27, 1976.

Browne, Colin. "Exercises in the desert." CVII 2(1):30-1, 1976.

Ditsky, John. "Poetry chronicle." OntR 3:98-104, 1975-76.

Draper, Gary. Brick 1:40-1, 1977.

Lillard, Charles. NL 3:52-5, 1976.

Smith, Patricia Keeney. "Ice and fire." CanL 74:107-10, 1977.

Thomas, Peter. Fiddlehead 107:130-2, 1975.

YATES, J. Michael

General
Yates, J. Michael. Colombo 1971:106-16.

Breath of the snow leopard
Barbour, Douglas. "Canadian poetry chronicle 2." DR 55:748-59, 1975-76.

Candelaria, Frederick. WCR 10(2):75-7, 1975.

Fox, Gail. Quarry 25(3):72, 1976.

Lane, M. Travis. "Be bold, be bold, be not too bold: the subject in poetry." Fiddlehead 106:121-7, 1975.

Quickenden, Robert. NL 3:42-7, 1976.

Stevens, Peter. "Zeroing in on zero." CanL 79:94-6, 1978.

Esox nobilior non esox lucius
Amprimoz, Alexandre L. Quarry 27(3):74-8, 1978.

Labrie, Ross. "Pike's peak." CanL 80:94, 96, 1979.

Lillard, Charles. MHRev 46:153-5, 1978.

334

YATES, J. Michael

The Great Bear Lake meditations
Aide, William. Quarry 20(2):55-6, 1971.

Atherton, Stan. Fiddlehead 89:94-5, 1971.

Barbour, Douglas. DR 51:143, 1971.

Fetherling, Doug. "Poetic journal." TamR 57:80-4, 1971.

Hornyansky, Michael. UTQ 40:375-6, 1971.

Purdy, Al. WascanaR 5(2):60-1, 1970.

Reid, John. "The paper north." CanL 51:95-7, 1972.

Skelton, Robin. MHRev 17:131-2, 1971.

Turner, Gordon P. "The breath of Arctic men: the Eskimo north in poetry from within and without." QQ 83:13-35, 1976.

Nothing speaks for the blue moraines: new and selected poems
Amabile, George. DR 54:363-5, 1974.

Arnason, David. Q&Q 40(5):18-9, 1974.

Bringhurst, Robert. "Clints & grikes." CanL 65:112-4, 1975.

Douglas, Charles. "Poetry: presence and presentation." LURev 7(2)/8(1&2):74-85 1976.

Henderson, Brian. "Negative capabilities." ECW 2:65-7, 1975.

Lillard, Charles. WCR 9(1):47-8, 1974.

Reed, John R. "Instructive alchemies." OntR 1:78-88, 1974.

Parallax
Gibbs, Robert. Fiddlehead 90:116-7, 1971.

The Qualicum physics
Biguenet, John. "Yates the obscure." WCR 11(2):36-7, 1976.

Stevens, Peter. "Zeroing in on Zero." CanL 79:94-6, 1978.

Stuewe, Paul. Q&Q 42(4):25, 1976.

YELIN, Shulamis

Seeded in Sinai
Ravel, Aviva. "Directions: two poets." ECW 4:80-5, 1976.

YEO, Marg

The custodian of chaos
Barbour, Douglas. "Canadian poetry chronicle 2." DR 55:748-59, 1975-76.

Mulhallen, Karen. "Woeman of the guard." BiC 5(4):19-20, 1976.

Ravel, Aviva. "Directions: two poets." ECW 4:80-5, 1976.

Evolutions
Lanczos, Elmar. "Three from fiddlehead." WCR 10(2):49-50, 1975.

Game for shut-ins
Weppler, Torry L. CF 52(618-9):46-7, 1972.

YOUNG, Ian

General
"Just an English-speaking person." CVII 4(3):45-8, 1979.

Common or garden gods
Bayard, Caroline. Q&Q 42(9):35-6, 1976.

Di Cicco, Pier Giorgio. "Gay in not so jocund company." BiC 5(5):15-6, 1976.

Friedman, Jack. "On tangled sheets'n things." ECW 6:96-9, 1977.

Millard, Peter. "Taking off the disguise." CVII 2(2):35, 1976.

Smith, Patricia Keeney. "A variety of voices." CanL 78:91-4, 1978.

Year of the quiet sun
Barbour, Douglas. "The young poets and the little presses, 1969." DR 50:112-26, 1970.

Garnet, Eldon. "For the poets, the landscape is the great Canadian myth." SatN 85(2):31-3, 1970.

YOUNG, Mark

Brother Ignatius of Mary
Marcellin, Philip. Alive 34:8, 1974.

YVON, Josée

"Pour une autopsie de la mort brutale sans éviction du jour au
lendemain"
    Bourassa, André-G. "Chaîne et trame. Rina Lasnier, Denis Vanier et
    Josée Yvon." Lettres qué 5:11-3, 1977.

ZABORSKA, Marta

Seeing stone
    Brown, Allan. "Black Moss: six offerings." Waves 7(2):68-71, 1979.

ZANES, John

Uncle John's frigate
    Barbour, Douglas. Q&Q 39(3):8, 1973.

    Hornyansky, Michael. UTQ 42:373, 1973.

ZEND, Robert

From zero to one
    Barbour, Douglas. "Canadian poetry chronicle: VI." DR 58:555-78,
    1978.

    Douglas, Charles. 'Poetry: presence and presentation." LURev
    7(2)/8(1&2):74-85 1976.

    Levenson, Christopher. "Tragedy viewed from a distance." SatN
    89(2):33-4, 1974.

    MacLulich, T.D. "All trad not bad." ECW 2:62-4, 1975.

    Wynand, Derk. MHRev 31:168-9, 1974.

OAB
    Douglas, Charles. "Poetry: presence and presentation." LURev
    7(2)/8(1&2):74-85, 1976.

ZIEROTH, Dale

Clearing: poems from a journey
Hicks, Lorne. CF 54(640-1):20-1, 1974.

Lee, Dennis. "The new poets: fresh voices in the land." SatN 88(12):33-5, 1973.

Sarna, Lazar. "Its own headstart." ECW 1:62-3, 1974.

Stevens, Peter. "An honest voice." CanL 61:118-9, 1974.

Woodcock, George. Q&Q 40(1):13, 1974.

ZIMMERMAN, Adam

The ebony box
Hamilton, Jamie. Alive 41:34-5, 1975.

ZONAILO, Carolyn

Auto-da-fé
Mallinson, Jean. "Linked fictions, nerve-ends, and faith in language." CVII 4(3):25-8, 1979.